DRYDEN AND POPE
IN THE EARLY NINETEENTH
CENTURY

It is a mistake to suppose that the eighteenth century ended with the year 1800. It lasted in the upper currents of opinion till at least 1832. Leslie Stephen

DRYDEN AND POPE
IN THE
EARLY NINETEENTH CENTURY

A study of changing literary taste
1800–1830

BY THE LATE
UPALI AMARASINGHE

CAMBRIDGE
AT THE UNIVERSITY PRESS
1962

PUBLISHED BY

THE SYNDICS OF THE CAMBRIDGE UNIVERSITY PRESS

Bentley House, 200 Euston Road, London, N.W.1

American Branch : 32 East 57th Street, New York 22, N.Y.

West African Office: P.O. Box 33, Ibadan, Nigeria

©

CAMBRIDGE UNIVERSITY PRESS

1962

Printed by

ADLARD AND SON, LIMITED

London and Dorking

CONTENTS

Foreword   *page* vii

Preface   xi

Introduction   1

PART I. EDITIONS OF THE AUGUSTAN POETS

Chapter **I.** Editions of Dryden   9

     II. Editions of Pope   35

PART II. PERIODICAL LITERATURE

III. The *Edinburgh Review*   63

IV. The *Quarterly Review*   93

V. *Blackwood's Edinburgh Magazine*   117

VI. The 'Pope Controversy' and the Minor
      Reviews   130

PART III. OTHER CONTEMPORARY SOURCES

VII. Anti-Augustan Criticism   137

VIII. Pro-Augustan Criticism   177

IX. Conclusion   209

Appendix **I.** Editions of Johnson   217

     II. Bibliography of the 'Pope Controversy',
       1806–26   222

Bibliography   225

Index   231

FOREWORD

It is hard for anyone who knew Upali Amarasinghe at all well, as I had the privilege of doing, to feel reconciled to his early death. Though, therefore, I am more than glad to have the opportunity of paying tribute to his memory, I cannot avoid a dark thought about a world which could wither him so suddenly from apparently splendid health, and make those whom he loved and who loved him in return so heartrendingly sad and lonely. One does not, of course, enter a protest at such things with any hope that they will not recur for others. The only general consolation is that they are not more frequent than they are.

Upali had not long begun a very promising career as a University Lecturer in English. He had served for two years as Assistant Lecturer in the University of Ceylon, and had recently been promoted to a University Lectureship in the University of Malaya. Then, about Christmas time in 1959, he was suddenly struck down by a kidney disease, and died shortly after. He had only been able to enjoy a few years of marriage and he had only had time to do a small part of what he might have done in English studies.

I first came to know Upali in 1953, when the Faculty of English at Cambridge appointed me to supervise his research for the Ph.D. Degree. In discussion his brain worked rapidly and easily. He had considerable intellectual curiosity, and a cheerful determination to face hard problems at close quarters and try to find satisfying solutions to them. His reactions to literature were bright, sensitive and supple, and at the same time wholesome. He thought about poetry and criticism clearly, perceptively and comprehensively. Still more important, he had a nature without any trace of meanness in it. He was a force for good, all the more so because there was nothing priggish or self-righteous or even, apparently, deliberately moral about him. He was just thoroughly decent by nature.

From 1953 until 1956, when Upali successfully submitted his dissertation for the Cambridge Ph.D. I saw a good deal of him, and he often visited my mother and myself in our home. He was a great favourite with both of us, and with good reason. We were both delighted when he came to marry, and hoped for him and his wife long years of happiness.

I was abroad in the winter of 1959 when he died, and did not hear of his death till a mutual friend told me of it some time afterwards. It was shocking news. Upali had been back in Cambridge that summer for a visit, and we had had a number of interesting talks and several keenly contested games of tennis. He had seemed in excellent health and full of life. He was deeply happy in his marriage, and in his work.

The present book is the most substantial piece of work Upali has left behind, and I am very glad it is being published. The book seems to me a model in its avoidance of any ostentatious splashing of superficial learning or irresponsible generalizations, and its steady refusal to be satisfied with anything less than the truth about a well-circumscribed (though vitally important) period in the history of English literary taste and criticism. Upali fixed his lively and searching mind intently on the task of giving a really adequate account of the complex and changing attitudes towards Augustan poetry during the first thirty years of the nineteenth century. In the course of his book he brings us close to the ambivalences and contradictions and shifts of reaction which form part of the very life of literary taste and criticism. It is only after presenting the reader with the complicated facts that Upali offers some broad conclusions, and even then he does not offer them as substitutes for an intimate sense of the facts themselves. These he presents in his typically clear, readable and easily forward-moving style. The fact that the book is so readable, indeed, makes me hope that it will become as well known as it deserves to be, and that it may stimulate others to write studies as honest and as unshowily perceptive on carefully bounded but important topics in the history of literary taste and criticism.

THEODORE REDPATH

Trinity College,
Cambridge
March 1962

PREFACE

This book is a detailed study of the attitudes towards Augustan poetry current in the years between 1800 and 1830. 'Augustan poetry' has been taken here to mean the tradition of English poetry represented by the work of Dryden, Pope, and Johnson. New currents of taste were particularly active in the period in question, as is well known, and it was at that time that the reputations of the Augustan poets passed through their most important transitional phase. The attempt to answer the question 'What were the various complex forces which affected the critical reputations of Dryden, Pope, and Johnson during the earlier nineteenth century?' has formed the central theme of the following pages. No scholar has, as far as I know, yet attempted a comprehensive exploration of this subject, and it is therefore hoped that the following inquiry will throw some original light upon this interesting though hitherto neglected aspect of early nineteenth-century criticism and taste.

Throughout the period during which I have worked on this inquiry, I have had the benefit of the help of Dr R. T. H. Redpath, Director of English Studies at Trinity College, Cambridge. It is a particular pleasure for me to place on record here my sincere thanks to him. The frequent stimulating discussions we have had together on almost every aspect of the inquiry have been of inestimable help. To Dr F. R. Leavis, Director of English Studies at Downing College, I am equally indebted for help, for many rewarding hints and suggestions, and for the unfailing kindliness with which he has followed the progress of my inquiries.

U. A.

INTRODUCTION

The early nineteenth century is commonly described in literary surveys and histories as the Age of Wordsworth. Yet, as Newman Ivey White pointed out in *The Unextinguished Hearth*, the truth was that the majority of readers in the early nineteenth century were 'as stubbornly unaware that theirs was the Romantic age as the ancients were that they were ancients'. The year 1798 is indeed conventionally taken to mark the beginning of the Romantic age, though the appearance of the anonymous *Lyrical Ballads*, produced by Cottle the publisher in Bristol for two young friends, caused no great sensation among the majority of readers. As Wordsworth observed, it was necessary for him to *create* the taste by which he was to be judged and appreciated, and this is sufficient caution against any easy assumptions about the nature of literary taste in the early nineteenth century.

The attempt to determine the tastes of an earlier age is a matter in which we must proceed warily. But in studying attitudes towards Augustan poetry in the early nineteenth century we are fortunate at the outset in having an account of literary taste in England at the beginning of the decade in which the *Lyrical Ballads* appeared. I refer to the words written by Francis Jeffrey in 1816:

When we were at our studies some twenty-five years ago, we can perfectly remember that every young man was set to read Pope, Swift, and Addison, as regularly as Virgil, Cicero, and Horace. All who had any tincture of letters were familiar with their writings and their history; allusions to them abounded in all popular discourses and ambitious conversation; and they and their contemporaries were universally acknowledged as our great models of excellence, and placed without challenge at the head of our national literature. New books, even when allowed to have merit, were never thought of as fit to be placed in the same class, but were generally read and forgotten, and passed away like the transitory meteors of a lower sky; while *they* remained in their brightness, and were supposed to shine with a fixed and unalterable glory.[1]

The English Augustan poets, then, were at the zenith of their reputation and fame at the beginning of the decade in which the *Lyrical Ballads* first appeared. The standards set by the Augustan poets so dominated the literary taste of the age that the first edition of five hundred copies of the poems of Wordsworth and Coleridge attracted so few purchasers, that Cottle with considerable reluctance was compelled to dispose of them to a London bookseller at a loss to himself. The wheel had of course swung full circle by later Victorian times; not only was the poetical genius of Wordsworth and Coleridge almost universally recognised by then, but the status of the Augustans had altered so completely that Arnold was able to pronounce in 1880, in a tone of comparative confidence, his celebrated opinion of the two principal poets of the Augustan age, 'Dryden and Pope are not classics of our poetry, they are classics of our prose'.

This great revolution in taste is often assumed to have taken place in the early nineteenth century. Mark Pattison's account, for example, of the 'dethronement' of the school of Pope when judged by the new standards introduced into English criticism by Wordsworth and Coleridge, may be taken as a representative account of this change:

The ascendancy of this doctrine, which made imagination the test of poetry, had an immediate influence upon the estimation in which Pope was held by his countrymen. The poetical dynasty which went by his name was dethroned. For nearly a century this school had occupied the field without rival . . . But all this was now at an end. Tried by the new test, the whole of English poetry from the Restoration down to Mason and Hayley was pronounced a mistake. It was declared to be mere versification; the name of poetry was denied it. It wanted soul. It wanted nature. It did not touch the heart. It had no trumpet call. Its rhythm was 'sing-song'.[2]

But the truth about critical reactions to the Augustan tradition in

---

[1] *Edinburgh Review* (September 1816), p. 1.

[2] 'Pope and his Editors', *British Quarterly Review*, 1872; reprinted in Mark Pattison's *Essays*, ed. Nettleship (1889), II, 355.

the early nineteenth century was not as simple as this account suggests. No immediate and final rejection of the kind described by Pattison actually took place; and the revaluation of Augustan poetry to which he draws attention, though important and influential, was only one of the numerous literary tendencies of the age. His view that a simple 'dethronement' of the school of Pope occurred at this time can only be sustained through an almost total disregard of the great variety and diversity of critical opinion characteristic of the time.

For 'it is a mistake to suppose', as Leslie Stephen pointed out long ago, 'that the eighteenth century ended with the year 1800. It lasted in the upper currents of opinion till at least 1832.' Indeed, the literary standards which, according to Francis Jeffrey, dominated literary taste in the 1790s, survived vigorously into the nineteenth century, though now increasingly open to modification. The *Edinburgh Review*, for example, informs us in January 1808 that, among contemporary readers, Pope, Swift, and Johnson enjoyed the 'fullest sunshine of reputation'. Even Arnold, in relegating the Augustans to the status of 'classics of our prose', agreed that 'all through the eighteenth century and down even to our own times, the stereotyped phrase of approbation for good verse found in our early poetry has been, that it even approached the verse of Dryden, Addison, Pope, and Johnson'. The revolution in taste which was effected most decisively by Arnold's own criticism, then, was far from being an accomplished fact earlier in the century. Arnold supplies evidence that it was more typically a late-Victorian than a Regency phenomenon.

Nevertheless, during the early nineteenth century the reputation of the Augustan poets, under the impact of the new Romantic tendencies, underwent a serious crisis. Although one of the major tendencies of the age was towards what may be described as the Victorian assessment of the tradition, it is a sign of the transitional complexity of the age that anti-Augustan and pro-Augustan criticism, of varying degrees of intensity, for a time existed side by side. And it is an over-simplification

3

to classify the critics and readers of the time in terms of simple antagonism and sympathy, for unexpected ambivalences of attitude were not uncommon. Poets who were openly hostile to the Augustan tradition were sometimes indebted at crucial points in their own development to the influence of the poets they despised. And it is a paradox typical of the age that even genuine admirers of the Augustans were able to absorb some of the unmistakably 'Romantic' impulses of their own time, without any diminution of respect for the older tradition. A completely unambiguous critical faith was especially rare in the early nineteenth century, and the explicit and implicit attitudes of most critics towards the Augustans contained both hostile and sympathetic tendencies.

For this reason no facile generalisations about the nature of early nineteenth-century literary taste can be long sustained. There is no substitute for a close study of the actual criticism of the poetry of Dryd_n, Pope, and Johnson made during this period.

This will make it plain that a proper understanding of early nineteenth-century reactions to the Augustan poets can only be possible through a study of tendencies already evident in the previous century. We find that the origins of the celebrated 'Pope Controversy' of the early nineteenth century are to be found in the mid-eighteenth century, and also that the 'unnatural civil war between the Drydenists and the Popists' which Isaac D'Israeli noticed in the early 1820s may itself be traced back to the same period. For this reason the work of eighteenth-century pioneers of the Romantic movement has been included in this inquiry. The anti-Augustan and pro-Augustan tendencies of the eighteenth century both underwent modification in the early nineteenth century, under the influence of distinctively new currents of taste; and one concern of this book has been to define the nature and significance of these modifications.

Investigation also shows that the persistence of Augustan standards in the early nineteenth century—most commonly seen in adverse criticism of the rising generation of Romantic poets—was not confined to criticism. Augustan influence is also seen in the poetry of the age. Simple generalisations are again difficult here, because the great variety of poetical interests at that time caused the work of the Augustans to be associated with strikingly different tendencies in early nineteenth-century poetry. It was not only the poets who were interested in producing 'imitations' of the Augustan manner who benefited from the Augustan tradition.

A comprehensive study of the reputations of Dryden, Pope, and Johnson during this period must take into account not only the views of those who were professionally interested in literature, but also the views of the common reader of the day. Which particular poems of the Augustan age, it is natural to ask, were in the early nineteenth century most widely read and most highly admired? What were the relative statuses of Dryden and Pope in the opinion of most readers in the early nineteenth century? In what ways did a reading of Wordsworth or Coleridge, or of other poets, influence the average reader's appreciation of the work of the Augustans? Decisive answers to such questions are not always easy to arrive at. But the information which may be gleaned from contemporary journals, memoirs, diaries, and letters, together with the views about the opinions of the reading public at large which may be found particularly in the work of publishers, editors, and reviewers, has helped materially towards finding provisional answers.

PART I
EDITIONS OF THE AUGUSTAN POETS

EDITIONS OF DRYDEN

I. SCOTT'S DRYDEN (1808)

The editor and the public

Scott's popular reputation as a writer of Romantic fiction and poetry—during the Regency he commanded a reading public equalled only by Byron—has been largely responsible for the undeserved neglect of his substantial achievements as an editor. Scott was self-critical enough to realise that the patience and industry which he devoted to his critical tasks was in sharp contrast to the more slapdash enthusiasm of his own creative work, and when Anna Seward chid him for sacrificing his own poetry in order to edit Dryden ('Mr White has recently told me that you had published a voluminous edition of Dryden. ... I almost grieve that you ... should employ your golden hours in removing the leaden incrustations of former editors'[1]) Scott replied with characteristic modesty, not only depreciating the value of his own work, but unhesitatingly preferring the poetry of Dryden's age to that of his own. 'As for poetry,' he said, 'it is very little labour to me, indeed, 'twere pity of my life should I spend much time on the light and loose sort of poetry which alone I can pretend to write.' Comparing Dryden's age with his own, Scott continued, '... but my dear Miss Seward, "in these days were giants in the land" and we are but dwarfs beside them'.[2]

Those who regard Scott as a conventional early nineteenth-century 'Romantic' may be surprised that the work of the Augustan poets was one of his principal interests as an editor. Impressive evidence of the diligence with which he conducted

[1] Letter to Scott, 29 January 1807. *The Letters of Sir Walter Scott*, ed. H. J. C. Grierson, I, 353 n.

[2] *Ibid.* I, 353–4.

9

his editorial inquiries may be found in his letters to George Ellis, Wordsworth, Southey, James Ballantyne, Lady Abercorn, Edward Forster, Dr Leyden, and Anna Seward;[1] and it is plain that he regarded his edition of Dryden, in Dr F. R. Leavis's phrase, as 'a work of piety'. In a letter to Dr Leyden, in the summer of 1806, Scott described it as his 'grand opus'.

Scott's respect for Johnson as poet and critic is better known. He prepared a two-volume edition of the *Rambler*, to which he prefixed a new Life of the author, and provided signed notes to John Wilson Croker's edition of Johnson's *Tour to the Hebrides*, which appeared in 1831. According to James Ballantyne, Johnson was Scott's favourite poet. Nor were the other Augustan poets neglected. Many years of careful preparation went into the production of Scott's nineteen-volume edition of the complete works of Swift; and Lockhart says that Scott long cherished an ambition to produce an edition of the complete works of Pope (on the lines of his Dryden and Swift), although, probably through the failure of his edition of Shakespeare for Constable in 1826, which completely disrupted his editorial plans, this scheme was never realised.[2]

Although George Ellis, Lockhart and several others had hoped that Scott's edition of Dryden would lead to a revival of interest in Dryden's poetry among the general reading public of the time, it is unlikely that this was Scott's own primary intention. For him it was rather a work of affectionate piety, an experience rewarding for its own sake. Nonetheless, Scott's

---

[1] In 1805 Scott told George Ellis that he was engaged in reading several hundred pamphlets in order to deepen his understanding and knowledge of the background of Restoration literature, and, in 1806, confessed that Dryden remained his 'principal companion'. Scott made a special visit to London in the spring of 1807 where, through Lady Abercorn's help, he was able to reach sources of information not available to him in Scotland. 'I am bent on rendering the edition of Dryden', he informed her, 'as perfect as I can.' His correspondence with Wordsworth probably influenced some of his criticism of Dryden's *Tales*.

[2] The financial crisis of 1826 which overwhelmed both Scott and Constable completely ruined Scott's edition of Shakespeare. 'Ultimately, I have been told', Thomas Constable informs us, '*the sheets were sold in London as waste paper!*' (*Archibald Constable and his Literary Correspondents*, III, 241.) It is not surprising that Scott's edition of Pope, which was to follow, was abandoned.

letters and editorial notes are of special interest to us; first because they throw some light on the effect which Scott felt some of Dryden's poetry would have upon contemporary readers, and secondly for the information he gives us about the fluctuations in the reputations of Dryden and Pope in the latter half of the eighteenth century.

The progress of Scott's editorial work on Dryden in the years between 1805 and 1807 can be followed in his letters. We learn that among his initial difficulties was the moral problem of bringing out a complete edition of Dryden at that time.[1] There were passages in Dryden which Scott felt were likely to offend, and he was deeply disturbed by the problem of whether or not he should act as *censor morum*.[2] George Ellis, who was probably unaware of the seriousness with which Scott felt the impiety of tampering with Dryden's text, advised him at first to follow the same 'principle as the castrated edition of Cowley'. Ellis was probably unprepared for the intensity of Scott's rejoinder, as violent as it was eloquent: 'I will not castrate John Dryden. I would as soon castrate my own father, as I believe Jupiter did of yore . . .' Yet Scott was too closely in touch with his reading public not to realise that an unexpurgated edition of Dryden would cause offence, and a letter to Ellis, written some months later and much less confident in tone, illustrates the pressure which the reading public could wield upon an editor against his own critical instincts: 'After all, there are some passages in his translations from Ovid and Juvenal that will hardly bear reprinting, unless I would have the Bishop of London and the whole corps of Methodists about my ears.'[3]

[1] Most editions of Dryden since Warton's (edited by H. J. Todd and first published in 1811) left out passages in his text—particularly from the Translations —liable to cause offence. Even relatively innocuous passages were disapproved of, and Warton's comment on the opening paragraph of *Absalom and Achitophel*—'very abominable and filthy lines'—indicates the direction in which taste was moving. (Dryden, ed. Todd, 1, 210 n.)

[2] See, for example, the series of letters exchanged by Scott and George Ellis on this subject from 26 October 1805 to 13 May 1806.

[3] The passages which particularly disturbed Scott were in the fourth book of Lucretius and in Ovid's Instructions to his Mistress. See his letter to Ellis, 7 April 1806. (*Scott's Letters*, ed. Grierson, 1, 284.)

11

In his anxiety over the probable reception of this edition, Scott showed himself aware of the moral climate of an age soon to produce the Reverend Thomas Bowdler's family edition of Shakespeare, and of the effect which this change was having upon the reading of Augustan poetry.[1] Moral disapproval of the poetry of the Augustans, and of their personal lives, becomes increasingly common in the early nineteenth century, and is a tendency to be reckoned with in any history of their reputations. Scott's edition of Dryden, though ultimately unexpurgated, caused no outcry from the Methodists or the Bishop of London, but Scott found it politic on the very opening page of his 'Advertisement' to defend Dryden from moral censure:

In collecting the pieces of one of our most eminent English classics— one who may claim at least the third place in that honoured list, and who has given greater proofs of versatility of talent than either Shakespeare or Milton, though justly plainly inferior to them in their own peculiar provinces—the Editor did not feel himself entitled to reject any part of his writings: even of those which reflect little honour on the age, by whose taste they were dictated. Had a selection been permitted, he would have excluded several of the Comedies, and some part of the Translations: but this is a liberty which has not lately been indulged to editors of classical poetry. Literary history is an important step in that of man himself; and the unseductive coarseness of Dryden is rather a beacon than a temptation.[2]

In the account which Scott gives us of the fluctuating reputations of Dryden and Pope among poets and readers in the latter half of the eighteenth century, it is worth noting that he

[1] Noting the growing 'prudishness' with which Regency society had come to regard the eighteenth-century novel, Scott commented '. . . but Colonel Jack and Moll Flanders will not bear introduction into modern society'. (Letter to Messrs Hurst, Robinson and Co., Booksellers, 25 February 1822. *Archibald Constable and his Literary Correspondents*, 1873, III, 199.) Scott's own standards were far from priggish, and what he objected to most (like Byron) was moral hypocrisy and cant. Commenting on the charges of 'indecency' levelled against the Augustans, Scott observed to Ellis: 'Are not the pages of Swift, and even of Pope, larded with indecency, and often of the most disgusting kind? and do we not see them upon all shelves and dressing-tables, and in all boudoirs?' (Letter to Ellis, October–November 1805, *Scott's Letters*, ed. Grierson, I, 265.)
[2] Scott's Dryden, 1808, Vol. I, 'Advertisement', pp. i–ii.

is careful to distinguish between the poetry of Dryden and Pope and the work of those influenced by them. This is important because the distinction was not always made at the time. One can easily forget that the most damaging criticism by writers like Wordsworth and Coleridge was aimed not so much at Dryden and Pope as at their imitators. In his account of the reputations of Dryden and Pope, Scott himself seems to be more preoccupied with the influence which they exerted upon the work of poets than with their popularity among average readers. We learn from the periodical literature of the age, for example, that although Pope became less congenial as an object of imitation for many poets, he still remained a firm favourite of the common reader. One contemporary observer estimated that where one person read Dryden in the early nineteenth century at least ten read Pope, and that where one line of poetry was recited from Dryden a hundred were repeated from the works of Pope.[1] Until the middle of the eighteenth century, according to Scott, Dryden, who was commonly acknowledged the founder of the school of 'reformed English poetry', had shared with Pope the true 'sovreignty of Parnassus'. Greater discrimination in the appreciation of their work—perhaps through Johnson's influence—became more widespread later:

As the eighteenth century advanced, the difference between the styles of these celebrated authors became yet more manifest. It was then obvious, that though Pope's felicity of expression, his beautiful polish of sentiment, and the occasional brilliancy of his wit, were not easily imitated, yet many authors, by dint of a good ear, and a fluent expression, learned to command the unaltered sweetness of his melody, which, like a favourite tune, when descended to hawkers and ballad-singers, became disgusting as it became common. The admirers of poetry then reverted to the brave negligence of Dryden's versification, as, to use Johnson's simile, the eye, fatigued with the uniformity of a lawn, seeks variety in the uncultivated glade or swelling mountain. The preference for which Dennis, asserting the cause of Dryden, had raved and thundered in vain, began, by de-

[1] See Chapter II, Roscoe's Pope.

grees, to be assigned to the elder bard; and many a poet sheltered his harsh verse and inequalities under an assertion that he belonged to the school of Dryden.[1]

In his reference to the 'unaltered sweetness' of Pope's melody Scott overlooks the wide range and flexibility of Pope's style, which readily accommodated all the varied tones of the speaking voice; and he insists that its greatest disadvantage was the ease with which it lent itself to undistinguished imitation. It is a point which Hazlitt made with great force in 'Mr Northcote's Conversations' and elsewhere.[2] It is plain that Scott felt himself temperamentally more in sympathy with Dryden than with Pope,[3] yet unlike many other critics he refrained from praise of one at the expense of the other. His own poetry, like that of Keats and other Romantics, was not unaffected by the revived interest in the 'brave negligence' of Dryden, and Lockhart among others considered this influence of crucial importance.[4] Nonetheless, Scott was anxious to preserve Dryden's poetry from the excesses it sometimes encouraged among his imitators, and was critical of the weaknesses inherent in the 'Dryden revival'.[5]

[1] Scott's Dryden, I, 478–9. Cowper, whom Scott does not mention, was influential in the revival of interest in Dryden. See below, Chapter VII. The relative merits of Dryden and Pope were the subject of a controversy between Anna Seward and Joseph Weston in 1789.

[2] Hazlitt, *Collected Works*, ed. Waller and Glover, VII, 105.

[3] Nonetheless, rebuking in 1812 a 'minor author of the tenth grade' who had condemned Pope, Scott remarked to R. P. Gillies—'We must not limit poetical merit to the class of composition which exactly suits our own particular tastes.' (R. P. Gillies, 'Recollections of Scott', *Fraser's*, September 1835, XII, 253.)

[4] J. G. Lockhart, *Memoirs of the Life of Sir Walter Scott* (1837–8), II, 7–8. George Ellis also regarded Dryden as an important influence upon Scott's poetry. For Dryden's influence upon Keats, see Chapter VII, § 2.

[5] 'Churchill—

Who, born for the universe, narrowed his mind,
And to party gave up what was meant for mankind—

'Churchill was the first to seek in *Mac-Flecknoe*, the *Absalom* and *The Hind and the Panther*, authority for bitter and personal sarcasm, couched in masculine, though irregular versification, dashed from the pen without revision, and admitting occasional rude and flat passages, to afford the author a spring to comparative elevation. But imitation always approaches to caricature; and the powers of Churchill have been unable to protect him from the oblivion into which his poems are daily sinking, owing to the ephemeral interest of political subjects and his indolent negligence of severe study and regularity. To imitate Dryden, it were well to study

Although Scott himself was unaffected by the reception of his conscientious and scholarly edition of Dryden—Saintsbury, in an admiring tribute in the Preface to his own edition, based largely on Scott's, described it as 'one of the best-edited books on a large scale' in English—many of Scott's friends were seriously disappointed. Their reactions were most fully expressed by Scott's son-in-law and biographer, Lockhart:

I wish I could believe that Scott's labours had been sufficient to recall Dryden to his rightful station, not in the opinions of those who make literature the business or chief solace of their lives—for with them he has never forfeited it—but in the general favour of the intelligent public. That such has been the case, however, the not rapid sale of two editions, aided as they were by the greatest of living names, can be no proof; nor have I observed among the numberless recent reprints of the English booksellers a single re-print of even those tales, satires, and critical essays, not to be familiar with which would, in the last age have been considered disgraceful to anyone making the least pretension to letters.[1]

Lockhart's comments, which were made in the mid-1830s, while deploring the change which had taken place in Dryden's reputation, partly confirm Leslie Stephen's opinion that Augustan prestige remained high among the literary *élite* until the third decade of the nineteenth century. Nevertheless, Lockhart's charge that Dryden was entirely neglected by the English booksellers of his day is far from accurate.[2] Scott's own publisher, Constable, who was necessarily interested in profits, like all members of his trade, felt that there was a considerable demand for Dryden among the contemporary public, and, informing Scott about the printing of a further 1000 copies of his Dryden, wrote: 'It would not only answer my purpose,

---

his merits, without venturing to adopt the negligencies and harshness, which the hurry of his composition and the comparative rudeness of his age rendered in him excusable. At least, those who venture to sink as low, should be confident of the power of soaring as high; for surely it is a rash attempt to dive, unless in one conscious of ability to swim.' (Scott's Dryden, I, 479–80.)

[1] Lockhart, *Life of Scott*, II, 161.

[2] Lockhart possibly intended a contrast with the greater interest displayed by Scottish booksellers. For the interest shown by English booksellers in Dryden in the early nineteenth century see M. Van Doren, *The Poetry of John Dryden* (New York, 1920), p. 253.

but be received by the public with kindness, at least such are my feelings.' Scott himself had no great respect for the literary standards of booksellers and publishers, yet he praised the adroitness with which they kept a business-like finger upon the taste of the reading public. The sales of the new edition of Scott's *The Works of John Dryden* (1821) confirmed Constable's judgement.[1]

Lockhart probably had extravagant expectations and so was over-pessimistic in his account of the reception accorded to the edition. He surmised, upon the basis of a 'not rapid sale of two editions', that a widespread decline of interest in Dryden had taken place among the 'intelligent public'. This does not seem entirely justified in the light of information from other sources. Hallam, for example, in a largely favourable notice of the edition in the *Edinburgh Review* of October 1808, said that it would have had a much wider sale were it not for its price, and censured the publishing trade (eternal misunderstanding) for producing books accessible only to the 'wealthy amateur', and not the 'whole class of readers'. Inevitably an expensively produced eighteen-volume edition of Dryden was not designed for the common reader, and was far beyond his means.[2]

Hallam's review may be taken as representative of the 'intelligent public's' reaction to Scott's Dryden. His criticism was not partisan, for Scott had stopped writing for the *Edinburgh*, and was now a leading spirit in the Tory group which ran its newly founded rival, the *Quarterly Review*. This partly explains Hallam's occasionally ambiguous tone, though, as Lockhart pointed out in the second volume of his *Life of Scott*, it is plain that Hallam shared Scott's high admiration for Dryden.

[1] 'You will have heard,' Constable wrote to Scott on 22 February 1822, 'that the new edition of Dryden moves very fairly.'

[2] For Scott's own criticism of the costliness of books during the Regency, see his letter to Anna Seward, dated 13 January 1807: 'Indeed the price of new Books in general is an increasing evil . . . But Books are no longer solely respected for their insides since they have been honourd with admission into the drawing room . . . The great genius who invented the gilded inlaid or Japan bookstands for boudoirs and drawing rooms did a great service to the print engraver and bookseller, but I question whether literature in general has not suffered from the invention.' (*Scott's Letters*, ed. Grierson, I, 346.)

Hallam found Scott's defence of Dryden's morality over-ingenious; though, unlike Wordsworth, he censured Dryden not so much for pruriency as for the amorality of his underlying attitude. Hallam's distinction is important, and it is interesting that in supporting his view that Dryden's 'ignorance of virtuous emotions . . . is the cardinal defect of his poetry', it was in the refined strength of Pope's moral sensibility that Hallam found his most forceful contrast.[1] Nonetheless, though aware of Pope's moral superiority, Hallam shared the growing tendency among his contemporaries to regard with suspicion Pope's proneness to 'studied' epigrammatic wit. Like Scott, Hallam preferred Dryden's flexible and abundant intellectual energy—'his thoughts, his language, his versification, have all a certain animation and elasticity, which no one else has equally pos-sessed'—to the more deliberate discipline of Pope's intelligence. As for the views of the reading public at large, Hallam noted that Dryden's prose was universally admired—'it would be superfluous to echo the praise of Dryden's prose style, which is in everyone's mouth'—and confirmed Scott's opinion that Dryden's lyrics, particularly *Alexander's Feast*, were still widely popular.

Finally, Hallam touched upon an aspect of Dryden's work which Scott does not mention, but which was of great import-ance in the reading of Dryden's poetry in the nineteenth century: his subject-matter. Hallam felt that the materials out of which Dryden commonly wrought his poetry were not specially suitable for poetry—an allegation made against Augustan poetry as a whole—yet Hallam, unlike many of his contemporaries, saw in this not a cause for censure of Dryden, but for praise of his confident ingenuity:

The pleasure which we receive from Dryden's poetry is more

---

[1] '. . . with what dignified feelings must he [Pope] have been invested for the moment, when he wrote the epistle to Lord Oxford! This tone was quite unknown to Dryden; it was a strain of a higher mood: and he could as easily have reached the pathos of *Eloisa* as the moral sublime of this epistle.' (*Edinburgh Review*, October 1808, p. 131.) Hallam's use of the terms 'sublime' and 'pathetic'—often used as criteria to disparage Pope in the early nineteenth century (see Chapter II, §§ 1 and 2)—in order to define Pope's range and refinement, is particularly striking.

exclusively due to him, because he was seldom much assisted by his subject. In varied and interesting narratives, in tragedies which excite emotion by their incidents, it is a matter of curious and difficult analysis, to separate the merit of the artist from the richness of the materials. But Dryden wrought commonly without much selection, and felt a confidence that any subject would become poetical under his hand.[1]

Critical standards

The loose term 'Romantic', when applied to a writer like Scott, tends to give a misleading idea of his critical position. For Scott, unlike some of his contemporaries, was among those who assimilated the newer Romantic tendencies of the age without any serious diminution of his interest in and enjoyment of Augustan poetry.[2] His literary taste, though sympathetic towards the new tendencies, always remained firmly traditional: reading his critical work we never have the impression (which we have unmistakably in reading Wordsworth or Coleridge), that Scott regarded himself as a pioneer in a new epoch of creative literature and criticism. Greatly as he admired the genius of Wordsworth, Coleridge, and Southey, we learn from Lockhart that it was Byron (whom he once spoke of as the only poet of transcendent talent that England had produced since Dryden) whom Scott regarded as the great poetical genius of his time. As for contemporary fiction, Scott's admiration for Jane Austen (whose Augustan affinities are plain to any reader of her novels) has been recorded in his review of *Emma* for the *Quarterly Review*. Indeed, Scott's traditional loyalties were so strong that he often remarked that he derived more pleasure from the Augustan strength of Johnson's verse than from the

[1] *Edinburgh Review*, xiii (1808), 132.

[2] 'Important as Scott's poetry was in the English Romantic revival, as a critic he can hardly be counted among the Romanticists. His attitude, nevertheless, differed radically from that of the school represented by Jeffrey and Gifford.' (Margaret Ball, *Sir Walter Scott as a Critic of Literature*, New York, 1907, p. 134.) Miss Ball's summing up of Scott's critical position as being fundamentally 'Augustan', though 'Romantic' in special cases is, on the whole, fair. She shows herself less aware of many aspects of Jeffrey's criticism, however, when in contrasting him with Scott she describes him as a kind of die-hard Augustan, unable to break away from the 'dictation of his predecessors'. See Chapter III.

more Romantic appeal of contemporary poetry. James Ballantyne, for example, told Lockhart:

But, in fact, he had often said to me that neither his own nor any modern popular style of composition was that from which he derived most pleasure. I asked him what it was. He answered— Johnson's; and that he had more pleasure in reading *London*, and *The Vanity of Human Wishes*, than any other poetical composition he could mention; and I think I never saw his countenance more indicative of high admiration than while reciting aloud from those productions.[1]

Although a study of Scott's reviews, essays, letters, and even of his novels,[2] helps us to a fuller understanding of his appreciation of Augustan poetry in general, his most comprehensive discussion of Dryden's poetry is to be found in the first volume of his edition. Here Scott prefaced his critical observations with a short account of his own theory of poetry, which is particularly interesting for the light it throws on the basic differences between Scott's assumptions about poetry and those of some of his Romantic contemporaries. It soon becomes plain that the essence of poetry did not lie for Scott—as it did for Wordsworth or Coleridge or Shelley—in any emotional or subjective transmutation of experience. The eighteenth-century tradition which Scott inherited is apparent in his belief that it lay rather in the extension of the powers of 'reason':

The distinguishing characteristic of Dryden's genius seems to have been, the power of reasoning, and of expressing the result in appropriate language. This may seem slender praise; yet these were the talents that led Bacon into the recesses of philosophy, and conducted Newton to the cabinet of nature ... This power of ratiocination, of investigating, discovering, and appreciating that which is really excellent ... is the most interesting quality which can be possessed by a poet. It must indeed have a share in the composition of everything that is truly estimable in the fine arts, as well as in philosophy.[3]

Scott himself was aware of the limitations of 'reason', yet his

---

[1] Lockhart, *Life of Scott*, II, 132.

[2] For an attractive picture of 'Glorious John', see *The Pirate*, Chapter XIV. In *Old Mortality*, Dryden is referred to as 'the great High Priest of all the Nine'.

[3] Scott's *Dryden*, I, 481–2.

belief that creative genius in other fields of knowledge, especially science and philosophy, was animated by the same 'vivifying spirit' that moved the poet is particularly interesting at a time when it was Thomas Love Peacock's main charge that not only was poetry tending less and less to be concerned with the 'real business of life', but that the best contemporary intelligence had ceased to be interested in poetry ('intellectual power and intellectual acquisitions have turned themselves into other and better channels'[1]). Scott was, of course, more tolerant of the Romantic tendencies of the age, and made no such charges himself; yet it is equally true that among the features in the contemporary situation which caused Peacock most alarm was the disappearance of basic assumptions about the nature and function of poetry which Scott had tended to take for granted. Nevertheless, 'reason' or the 'power of intellect', which seemed to Scott to be the 'distinguishing characteristic of Dryden's genius', also seemed to him, paradoxically enough, the source of Dryden's limitations as a poet as well. Relating this criticism to Dryden's formative years as a dramatic poet, Scott remarked:

The early habits of Dryden's education and poetical studies gave his researches somewhat too much of a metaphysical character; and it was a consequence of his mental acuteness, that his dramatic personages often philosophised or reasoned, when they ought only to have felt.

It is interesting to see the substance of Dryden's criticism of Donne's love-poetry applied here by Scott to Dryden's own verse. Dryden's interest in the creative power of reason (a source of strength in his best work), led him at weaker moments to show less than sufficient interest in the milder and more

1 Noting the want of intellectual strength in contemporary verse, Peacock complained, '. . . it is a lamentable spectacle to see minds, capable of better things, running to seed in the specious indolence of these empty aimless mockeries of intellectual exertion.' (*The Four Ages of Poetry*, ed. H. F. Brett-Smith, 1921, p. 17.) For an analysis of the radical abeyance of the critical intelligence in poetry in the early nineteenth century, see Matthew Arnold's *The Function of Criticism at the Present Time*. For a discussion of this aspect of early nineteenth-century poetry, see Chapter VIII.

tender passions ('the finer and more imperceptible operations of love, in its sentimental modifications'). This lack of interest in the 'pathetic'—a deficiency felt by Wordsworth, Hazlitt, Francis Jeffrey and several other early nineteenth-century critics—was partly compensated, in Scott's opinion, by Dryden's occasional mastery of the 'sublime' ('the more lofty, the fiercer, the more ambitious . . . feelings of the heart, in all its dark or violent workings ').

In considering Dryden's claim to be regarded as a truly Augustan poet, however, it was upon the range and power of his use of language that Scott laid greatest stress. In this respect, Scott felt Dryden had not been equalled either by Pope[1] or by Milton and Shakespeare. This seemingly extravagant claim was advanced with due care and deliberation:

With this power (of expressing what he felt and conceived) Dryden's poetry was gifted in a degree, surpassing in modulated harmony that of all who had preceded him, and inferior to none that has since written English verse. He first shewed that the English language was capable of uniting smoothness and strength . . . What was said of Rome adorned by Augustus, has been, by Johnson, applied to English poetry improved by Dryden; that he found it of brick and left it of marble. This reformation was not merely the effect of an excellent ear, and a superlative command of gratifying it by sounding language; it was, we have seen, the effect of close, accurate, and continued study of the power of the English tongue.[2]

Scott's observations are partly derived no doubt from Johnson's well-known tribute to Dryden's 'modulated harmony'—'he knew how to choose the flowing and sonorous words; to vary the pause and adjust the accents; to diversify the cadence, and yet preserve the smoothness of the metre'.[3] Yet, while Johnson was here primarily interested in Dryden's skill as a musician in verse, Scott goes much further. In his recognition of the

---

[1] Scott characterised Dryden's satirical temper as largely 'Juvenalian', and implied that Pope's was typically 'Horatian'. The extraordinary range of Dryden's style was evident in its ability to compass not only the scourging vehemence of Juvenal, but at the same time all the 'nicer and more delicate touches of satire' typical of Horace. Scott therefore described his satirical temper as 'Juvenalian' not to indicate a limitation, but to draw attention to his inclinations.

[2] Scott's Dryden, I, 485.

[3] 'Johnson's Life of Dryden', Lives of the English Poets, ed. G. Birkbeck Hill, I, 466.

effect of Dryden's verse upon the organic life of the English language, the extension in the possibilities of communication which his poetry implied, Scott partly anticipates Hopkins's awareness of the tough, sinewy strength and living rhythmic power of Dryden's English.[1]

In substantiating his claim that Dryden's range as a poet had not been equalled even by Shakespeare and Milton, it is to Dryden's use of language that Scott most often refers. It is also worth noting that in his criticism of the various *genres* used by Dryden, Scott showed himself free of some of the prejudices about their relative value which became widely accepted in the later nineteenth century. It is well known, for example, that satirical poetry had come to be regarded with appreciably less favour by several early nineteenth-century critics, but this movement in taste—which may be traced back to Joseph Warton, and before him to William Ayres and Robert Shiels, in the previous century—does not appear to have affected Scott's criticism of Dryden's work in this mode. Indeed, it is evident that Scott derived as much pleasure from Dryden's satires as he did from his lyrics, and he seems to have been unaffected by (or unaware of) the view, currently being advanced by William Lisle Bowles and others, that satire should be relegated to an inferior order of poetry.[2]

[1] 'What is there in Dryden? Much, but above all this: he is the most masculine of our poets; his style and his rhythms lay the strongest stress of all our literature on the naked thew and sinew of the English language.' (G. M. Hopkins, Letter to Robert Bridges, 6 November 1887. In *The Letters of Gerard Manley Hopkins to Robert Bridges*, ed. C. C. Abbott, 1935, pp. 267-8.)

[2] See Chapter II. Scott's shrewd appreciation of Dryden's satirical technique—especially his control of tone—is well illustrated by his analysis of the portrait of 'Zimri': 'While other court poets endeavoured to turn the obnoxious statesman—[Shaftesbury]—into ridicule on account of his personal infirmities and extravagancies, Dryden boldly confers upon him all the praise for talent and for genius that his friends could have claimed, and trusts to the force of his satirical expression for working up even these admirable attributes with such a mixture of evil propensities and dangerous qualities that the whole character shall appear dreadful, and even hateful, but not contemptible.' (Scott's Dryden, I, 493.)

Scott's analysis may be compared with T. S. Eliot's summing up of the essential technique of Dryden's 'portraits': 'Dryden continually enhances: he makes his object great in a way contrary to expectation; and the total effect is due to the transformation of the ridiculous into poetry.' (*Homage to John Dryden*, 1924, p. 15.)

The great early nineteenth-century revival of interest in the lyric, among the most influential developments in the taste of the age, produced Scott's best lyric, 'Proud Maisie', and some of the most distinctive triumphs of the 'great' Romantics. For this reason Scott's belief that Dryden's supremacy in this *genre* remained unchallenged—'in lyrical poetry, Dryden must be allowed to have no equal'—has a special interest. In choosing *Alexander's Feast*—which he admired for its power in presenting 'lofty and striking ideas' in language which had the naked forcefulness of 'the most humble prose'—as Dryden's best lyric, Scott was well within the traditions of popular eighteenth-century taste.[1]

It was Dryden's narrative poems, however, written in the final years of his life, that were most popular in the early nineteenth century, and Scott was happy to concur with the common reader of the day in his appreciation of them. Even the more radically Romantic members of the new generation of poets and critics were drawn towards them, and Wordsworth, for example, once declared that he considered Dryden's *Fables* the 'most poetical of his works'.[2]

For the most part Scott felt that Dryden, in recreating, in terms of Restoration language and sensibility, the tales of Chaucer and Boccaccio, had equalled or surpassed his originals. For example, he considered Dryden's 'spirited and animated version' of Chaucer's *The Knight's Tale*, which Dryden himself

[1] According to Van Doren, *Alexander's Feast* appeared more often in eighteenth-century anthologies and miscellanies than any other of Dryden's poems. Hallam noted of its popularity in the early nineteenth century, 'Everyone places this ode among the first of its class, and many allow it no rival'. (*Edinburgh Review*, XIII, 1808, 132.)

[2] Yet, despite his admiration of the *Fables*, Wordsworth strongly disproved of the morality of Dryden's *Sigismonda and Guiscardo*. It is possible that he directly influenced Scott's criticism here. The origin of Scott's comment, 'A worse fault occurs in the whole colouring of Sigismonda's passion, to which Dryden has given a coarse and indelicate character, which he did not derive from Boccaccio' (Scott's *Dryden*, I, 498), was very probably a letter which Wordsworth wrote to him as early as 1805—'I think Dryden has much injured the story by the marriage, and degraded Sigismunda's character by it. He has also ... degraded her character still more by making her love absolute sensuality and appetite (Dryden has no other notion of passion)'. (*The Early Letters of William and Dorothy Wordsworth*, ed. E. De Selincourt, 1935, p. 542.)

had reckoned 'not much inferior to the *Iliad* or the *Aeneid*', as 'one of the best pieces of composition in our language'. But it was in his criticism of the *Fables* that Scott's more Romantic tendencies found decisive expression. Dryden's *Palamon and Arcite* he found inferior to its original; defining the inadequacies of the more modern version, Scott declared: 'Some points, also, of sublimity, have escaped the more modern poet . . . while he falls something short of him [Chaucer] . . . in pathetic effect.' The frequency with which the terms 'sublime' and 'pathetic' were invoked in early nineteenth-century criticism of Augustan poetry is one of the more revealing symptoms of the taste of the age,[1] and it is therefore of special interest to have Scott give us an example of Chaucerian 'sublimity', which he felt Dryden had failed to preserve. It was the effect of this couplet taken from Chaucer's description of the statue of Mars:

> A wolf ther stood biforn him at his feet
> With eyen rede, and of a man he eet.

It is evident from the tinglings of terror that these lines were meant to excite, that the 'sublime' for Scott meant something more than merely the 'exalted' and 'lofty' emotions in poetry: it had obvious connections with the eighteenth-century taste for the 'awe-inspiring' and the 'terrible': not so much the 'sublime' of Milton as the 'sublime' of Burke.[2] A delight in such 'beauties of a terrific order' also partly helps to explain the fascination with which early nineteenth-century readers read Dryden's *Fables*, and it is indeed passages of this kind which Scott describes as being most popular among all classes of readers in his own time:

To select instances would be endless: but every reader of poetry has by heart the description of Iphigenia asleep, nor are the lines in *Theodore and Honoria*, which describe the approach of the apparition,

---

[1] Warton first employed these terms to discuss Augustan poetry in his *Essay on Pope*. See Chapter II, § 1.

[2] For a detailed and interesting study of the various meanings of this term, see Samuel H. Monk, *The Sublime. A study of Critical Theories in XVIIIth Century England* (New York, 1935).

and its effects upon animated and inanimated nature, even before it becomes visible, less eminent for beauties of the terrific order.[1]

Scott's ability to absorb these 'Romantic' tendencies of his age, without any essential loss to his sense of the more characteristic virtues of the Augustan tradition as a whole, and the poetry of Dryden in particular, makes him specially interesting as a representative and influential literary figure of the early nineteenth century. It suggests the transitional complexity of the taste of his age, and confirms that an interest in the newer 'Romantic' impulsions characteristic of the time did not necessarily imply a neglect of the Augustan achievement.

2. THE 'WARTON' DRYDEN (1811)

The editor and the public

Soon after Scott had begun collecting material for his edition of Dryden, he was informed by George Ellis that others were busy with the same editorial work. Ellis was anxious lest this news should affect Scott's plans.[2] But he need not have feared, for it was typical of Scott that he regarded other editors of Dryden as 'collaborators' rather than as 'competitors'. He was seriously disappointed when the Reverend Edward Forster, who had partly prepared an edition of Dryden, abandoned the venture; and, when Forster could not be persuaded to change

---

[1] Scott's Dryden, I, 496–7. Hallam confirmed the wide popularity of this passage from *Theodore and Honoria* in the *Edinburgh Review*, XIII, 1808. Warton, too, singled out this passage for special comment in the notes to his own edition of Dryden. It is striking that Hunt chose the *identical* passages referred to by Scott to illustrate the variety of Dryden's versification (when contrasted with Pope's) in his essay *What is Poetry?*: 'Compare with this [a passage from *The Rape of the Lock*] the description of Iphigenia in one of Dryden's stories from Boccaccio:

It happened—on a summer's holiday
That to the greenwood shade . . . etc.

For a further variety take, from the same author's *Theodore and Honoria*, a passage in which the couplets are run one into the other, and all of it modulated, like the former, according to the feeling demanded by the occasion:

Whilst listening to the murmuring leaves he stood—
More than a mile immersed within the wood, etc.'

(*English Critical Essays: The 19th Century*, ed. E. D. Jones (1916), pp. 339–40.)
[2] See Ellis, Letter to Scott, 26 October 1805 (*Scott's Letters*, I, 266 n.).

his mind, Scott contented himself with urging him to produce, instead, 'a handsome and complete edition' of an earlier English poet with Augustan affinities, Ben Jonson, adding the interesting comment: 'he is one of our neglected classics'.[1]

The most interesting early nineteenth-century edition of Dryden, after Scott's, was the edition of *The Poetical Works* brought out by H. J. Todd in 1811. This was printed in uniform size with Malone's edition of *The Prose Works*, to which it was intended as the companion volume, and together they covered the same ground as Scott's edition. As a matter of fact, most of Todd's editorial work had already been done for him. His text was based largely on Derrick's edition, published by Tonson in 1760, while most of the critical notes which appear in the edition had been prepared by Joseph Warton.[2] Indeed, Warton's share in the 1811 edition is so important that it would perhaps be fairer to refer to it as the 'Warton' edition of Dryden.

Joseph Warton's plans for bringing out an edition of Dryden (on the lines of his edition of Pope, which made its belated appearance in 1797) were never realised in his lifetime. Todd, in his 'Advertisement', offers no explanation, but merely records in passing that the 1811 edition had been 'many years in contemplation'. The true explanation may be found perhaps in the attitude towards Dryden's poetry which was current among a majority of readers in Warton's time. Warton's limiting criticism of Augustan poetry had already 'raised a sort of literary outcry against him' among his contemporaries, and it was very probably a lack of sympathy in the reading public which accounts for Warton's failure to publish his edition of Dryden. It was not until over a decade after Warton's death in 1800 that Todd utilised his textual and critical notes for his Regency edition of *The Poetical Works*. The appearance of the edition after this delay suggests that important changes in the attitude of the reading public towards Augustan poetry were

---

[1] Scott, Letter to Forster, 27 October 1805 (*Scott's Letters*, 1, 267).
[2] Some critical notes in the edition were the work of Warton's son, John Warton.

taking place at about this time, and that what had once been judged likely to be ill-received could now be published.

Closer study of the 1811 edition reveals that the critical standards behind it were strangely diverse even inconsistent. Indeed, Todd's standards were far from purely Wartonian. He prefaced the edition with Johnson's *Life*, quoting with approval in his 'Advertisement' Malone's high praise of Johnson's criticism and especially his assessment of Dryden's poetry: 'a more beautiful and judicious piece of criticism perhaps has not appeared since the days of Aristotle'. This praise of Johnson's standards becomes rather incongruous when a study of Warton's notes reveals that many of them were conscious and uncompromising disagreements with many of Johnson's particular judgements, and were based on strikingly dissimilar critical pre-occupations. It is this very puzzling inconsistency that gives the 1811 edition of Dryden its great interest as a representative document: it reflects well the transitional uncertainties in the attitude to Augustan poetry typical of the reading public of its time.

Critical standards

Warton's most interesting disagreements with Johnson may be found in his critical notes to three of Dryden's poems: *Absalom and Achitophel*, *MacFlecknoe*, and the *Ode to the Memory of Mrs Anne Killigrew*. Other disagreements are not difficult to find, but these illustrate most clearly their conflicting critical attitudes. Underlying most of Warton's criticism may be discerned two major objections to Dryden's poetry: first, that Dryden's subjects—being too often primarily concerned with 'occasional' situations and social or political interests—were of their very nature unsuitable for poetry, and had failed to transcend their immediate context; and, secondly, that the emotional responses evoked by Dryden's poems—even of those highly praised by Johnson—were unrelated to what Warton considered the essentially 'poetic' emotions. These objections are well illustrated in Warton's terse summing-up comment on Johnson's criticism of *Absalom and Achitophel,* which he quotes in his notes in order to register his own disagreement:

> If this be considered, says Dr Johnson, as a poem political and controversial, it will be found to comprise all the excellencies of which the subject is susceptible; acrimony of censure, elegance of praise, artful delineations of characters, variety and vigour of sentiment, happy turns of language, and pleasing harmony of numbers; and all these raised to such a height, as can scarcely be found in any other English composition. On this exaggerated panegyric I will only beg leave to observe, that if this poem is of a nature purely and merely political and controversial, it does not partake of the essence of real poetry.[1]

The matter-of-factness of Warton's dismissal contrasts strongly with Johnson's praise. That Warton himself felt *Absalom and Achitophel* to be a poem 'merely political and controversial' is plain in his subsequent notes; what is more, he regarded this defect of the poem as a failure representative of Augustan poetry in general. In a general observation which followed, he linked the failure of *Absalom and Achitophel* to transcend its immediate context with the fate of all 'personal and occasional satire', exemplified for him by the changing attitude of the reading public to Pope's *Dunciad*:

> It is an undoubted fact, though it may appear a strange assertion that this poem [*Absalom and Achitophel*], once so famous, is in the present age but little read. I have met with many well-informed literary persons, who have frankly owned they never went through it, and knew little of it but from the report of its former celebrity. So short-lived and transitory is personal and occasional satire. *The Dunciad* of Pope begins to be neglected.[2]

Though Warton noted that it was still a 'strange assertion' to suggest that Dryden's poetry in the final decades of the eighteenth century was not as widely read as people supposed, his comments indicate the nature of the critical phase through which it was then passing. Personal and topical interest must surely have added an edge to the pleasure with which Dryden's poems had been read earlier in the century, and the diminishing

---

[1] Todd's Dryden, I, 266 n.
[2] *Ibid.* I, 272 n.

of this immediacy of interest implied for Warton that they had 'dated' badly, and would become increasingly unintelligible with time. He felt that the results of this defect in the subject-matter of Augustan poetry were particularly evident in the growing obscurity of the fourth book of *The Dunciad*, despite Johnson's praise of the richness and diversity of its satire:

It is difficult to understand fully the meaning of Pope in the fourth book of *The Dunciad* ... To make the poem tolerably intelligible, which every day renders more and more necessary, it has become unavoidable to print it with those many and long notes given to him by his friends, Swift, Arbuthnot, Cleland, Savage, Warburton, and others, without which the names, families, abodes, and employments of the contemptible scribblers must have remained totally unknown.[1]

That an enjoyment of the rich satirical variety of the poetry of *The Dunciad* did not require an intimate knowledge of 'the names, families, abodes, and employments' of its insignificant satirical victims, was plainly not a view seriously entertained by Warton. For him, the elaborate apparatus of notes seemed an essential accompaniment, a necessary evil. It probably never occurred to him that the kind of detective-interest satisfied by such notes might conceivably hinder rather than help the reader, distracting his attention from appreciation of the poetry.[2]

As for Warton's criticism of the emotional response evoked by Dryden's poetry, it will be seen that he employs the critical

[1] *Ibid.* II, 170–1.

[2] Some remarks of Dr F. R. Leavis seem particularly relevant to Warton's criticism of the fourth book of *The Dunciad*: ' "The art," says Professor Sutherland, "which Pope lavished upon this poem (*The Dunciad*) has too often been obscured by an unnecessary concern for his victims." Yes; and more generally, by an unnecessary concern *with* his victims—a concern of a kind that notes, especially obtrusive ones, inevitably encourage. "The fading of its personalities", remarked by Professor Sutherland as something that appreciation of *The Dunciad* suffers from, is really an advantage, and one we ought not to refuse. For eighteenth-century readers it must have been hard not to start away continually from the poetry to thinking of the particular historical victim and the grounds of Pope's animus against him; for modern readers it should be much easier to appreciate the poetry as poetry—to realise that Pope has created something the essential interest of which lies within itself, in what it is.' (*The Common Pursuit*, pp. 88–9.)

touchstones associated with his *Essay on Pope*.[1] Anticipating Scott and other early nineteenth-century critics, Warton praised Dryden's command of the 'sublime' but found his lack of interest in the 'pathetic' a major weakness. Not all Warton's criticism of Dryden was merely unsympathetic, but the qualities in Dryden which chimed in with his own special interests generally received the greatest stress. The odes and elegies were especially pleasing to Warton; he shared Johnson's delight in Dryden as a musician in verse; he calls the lines *To the Memory of Mr John Oldham* 'the most harmonious in its numbers of all that this great master of harmony has produced'.[2] Even more interesting was his criticism of the *Ode on St Cecilia's Day*, which he regarded as Dryden's finest poem; here Warton contrasted the 'sublimity' of the opening stanza—its 'awful' and 'august' associations—with the unfortunately 'epigrammatic turn' of its conclusion:

If Dryden had never written anything but this Ode, his name would have been immortal, as would that of Gray, if he had never written anything but his *Bard*. It is difficult to find new terms to express our admiration of the variety, richness, and melody of its numbers; the force, beauty, and distinctness of its images; the succession of so many different passions and feelings; and the matchless perspicuity of its diction. The scene opens, in the first stanza, in an awful and august manner ... No particle of it can be wished away, but the epigrammatic turn of the four concluding lines.[3]

These tendencies are also apparent in Warton's criticism of the *Fables*, in which he anticipated, recognisably, early nineteenth-century interests. Curiously enough, in illustrating Dryden's improvements upon Chaucer and Boccaccio, Warton selected the very passage from *Theodore and Honoria* which both Scott and Hallam chose as being universally popular among contemporary readers of all classes:

> Whilst listening to the murmuring leaves he stood
> More than a mile immersed within the wood,

[1] See Chapter II, § 1.
[2] Todd's Dryden, II, 257.
[3] *Ibid.* II, 345–6.

At once the wind was laid; the whispering sound
Was dumb; a rising earthquake rocked the ground,
With deeper brown the grove was overspread,
A sudden horror seiz'd his dizzy head . . .

The heightened solemn tone of these lines 'which so strongly
paint the sensations of a man upon the sudden approach of some
strange, mysterious and supernatural danger', their undefined
yet terrifying undertones, all suggest that they had for Warton
those qualities of the 'sublime' which he admired so highly.[1]
Nevertheless, Warton's response to Dryden's poetry was not a
simple one, and his criticism of the conclusion of the *Ode on
St Cecilia's Day* and *Absalom and Achitophel* must not be taken
to imply an inflexible prejudice against all epigrammatic or
satirical verse. Just as moralistic prejudices often interfered
with a proper appreciation of Byron's wit in the Regency,
Warton's inhibitions sometimes prevented him from responding
sensitively to the essentially Restoration temper of Dryden's
best satirical verse. For example, Warton's excessive disapproval of the opening of *Absalom and Achitophel* was the result
of his inability to see the negligent daring of the wit with which
Dryden, without offending the king himself and in a poem
defending the monarchy, could refer to Charles's 'promiscuous
use of concubine and bride'.[2] Yet a good deal of Warton's

[1] Spenser's account of the 'sensations of a man upon the sudden approach of
some . . . supernatural danger'—the Red Crosse Knight's entry into the House of
Morpheus—may be forcibly contrasted with Dryden's:
'And more, to lulle him in his slumber soft,
A trickling streame from high rocke tumbling downe . . .
Mixt with a murmuring winde, much like the sowne
Of swarming Bees, did cast him in a swowne . . .'
(*The Faerie Queene*, 1, 41.)
Not only is Dryden's passage more melodramatic, but his typically eighteenth-
century evocation of the 'august', the 'awful' and the 'sublime' are quite absent
in Spenser's incantatory sensuousness. Dryden is also obviously influenced by the
school of landscape painting inaugurated by the great French seventeenth-century
masters, and their somewhat stereotyped scenes. The 'deeper brown' is directly
borrowed from them (old varnish?).

[2] Warton noted of the opening of *Absalom and Achitophel*: 'How gross and indelicate must the taste of that age have been, when St *Evremont* could quote these
very filthy and abominable lines in a letter addressed to the celebrated Dutchess
of Mazarine!' (Todd's Dryden, 1, 210 n.)

criticism of satirical verse is free from such prejudice. It is not often noted, for example, that part of his purpose in adversely criticising *The Dunciad* was to draw attention to the contrasting merits of *MacFlecknoe*, which he considered as possibly the best satire in any language:

Will it be thought an extravagant and exaggerated encomium to say, that in point of pleasantry, various sorts of wit, humour, satire, both oblique and direct, contempt and indignation, clear diction, and melodious versification, this poem is perhaps the best of its kind in any language. Boileau, who spent his life, exhausted his talents, and soured his temper, in proscribing bad poets, has nothing equal to it. It is precisely in the style and manner mentioned by Horace—

> modo tristi, saepe jocoso,
> Defendente vicem modo Rhetoris atque Poetae,
> Interdum urbani, parcentis viribus atque
> Extenuantis eas consulto.[1]

Warton was familiar with the work of the Roman Augustans at first hand, and was not (unlike some of the early nineteenth-century critics he influenced) insensitive to the Augustan dignity and strength of Dryden's verse. Elsewhere too, in his criticism of the *Epistles*, Warton admired Dryden's 'Horatian' temper, singling out especially his 'ease', 'propriety' and his reflective wisdom.[2]

Finally, in considering the conflict of Johnson's and Warton's ideas in Todd's Dryden, it is worth noting that the work of the Augustans was sometimes contrasted with that of other poets who were felt to have transcended the limitations of Augustan taste. This may be seen, for example, in Warton's uncompromising disagreement with Johnson upon the merits of the *Ode to the Pious Memory of the Accomplisht Young Lady, Mrs Anne Killigrew*:

At length we are arrived at the *Ode on the Death of Mrs Anne Killigrew*, which Dr Johnson, by an unaccountable perversity of judgement . . . has pronounced to be undoubtedly the noblest Ode that our

---

[1] Todd's Dryden, II, 170 n.

[2] See the notes to Epistle 13: *To my honoured kinsman, John Dryden.* (Todd's Dryden, II, 236.) Warton described this poem of Dryden's as 'one of the most truly Horatian epistles in our language'.

language ever has produced ... But such a paradoxical judgement cannot be wondered at in a critic, that despised the *Lycidas* of Milton, and the *Bard* of Gray.[1]

Here we are at the heart of the matter. In unequivocally preferring the poetry of the 'minor' Milton and Gray to that of Dryden, Warton was giving expression to a movement in taste that was directly to influence attitudes towards Augustan poetry. Thomas Warton, for example, whose Preface to his edition of Milton's *Poems upon Several Occasions* (1785) is an extraordinarily interesting document, believed that the taste for the kind of emotional response evoked by Milton's early poems (which Arnold later described as 'simple, sensuous, and passionate') had been lost during the Augustan age, but was being re-discovered in his own day.[2] Noting that Milton's early poems had, for a variety of reasons, been neglected from the 'infancy of their circulation', Thomas Warton claimed that a notable revival of interest in them had occurred in his time:

It was late in the present century, before they attained their just measure of esteem and popularity. Wit and rhyme, sentiment and satire, polished numbers, sparkling couplets, and pointed periods, having so long kept undisturbed possession in our poetry, would not easily give way to fiction and fancy, to picturesque description, and romantic imagery.[3]

[1] *Ibid.* II, 259–60 n.

[2] Miltonic influence and 'imitation' may be found throughout the eighteenth century, though it offered no serious challenge to Augustan standards in poetry until late in the century. But it is found in those works of Pope which remained fashionable (*Windsor Forest, Eloisa to Abelard* and so on) and is dominant in Gray and Collins. There was an association with Spenser implied in such descriptions as the 'faery way of writing', but the vocabulary was mainly derived from Milton.

[3] Preface to Milton's *Poems upon Several Occasions*, 2nd ed. 1791, v. Some remarks of De Maar in his *History of Modern English Romanticism* (1924), seem relevant here: 'By 1763 *Paradise Lost* had been reprinted at least 46 times ... Measured by the criterion of the frequency of editions, Milton's reputation may well be said to have been continuous. It may also be accepted that, considering the 18th Century as a whole, the demand for his poems was greater than the demand for the works of Dryden and Pope.' (Chapter II, 28.) Two points arise out of this. First De Maar's estimate of the relative popularity of Milton and the Augustan poets is based upon a purely statistical criterion (the frequency of editions) which does not appear to be very reliable, partly because it is contradicted by the evidence of eighteenth-century critics themselves; and secondly, Thomas Warton's account of a late eighteenth-century 'revival' of Milton referred principally to his early poems rather than to the *Paradise Lost*, which as De Maar observed found many

The Romantic revaluation which Thomas Warton refers to here was far from complete. Yet, the rediscovery of the 'simple, sensuous, and passionate' appeal of Milton's early work, and other pre-Restoration poetry, had for the Wartons and some of their contemporaries a liberating effect: it seemed to enable them to go beyond the frontiers of Augustan poetry.

Todd's edition of Dryden, then, is a valuable document throwing light on changing attitudes towards Augustan poetry. The conflict of Johnson's and Warton's evaluations of Dryden's poetry, and the critical inconsistencies which it engendered, is itself a typical product of that transitional age, the early nineteenth century.[1] General critical opinion was still relatively amorphous, and the Augustan standards could survive side by side with the newer impulses in taste.

publishers in the eighteenth century, though Warton seems to have overlooked the fact that the *Poems upon Several Occasions* were included in several complete editions of Milton during the eighteenth century.

[1] In Warton's time, of course, his views still expressed very much the minority voice. One of the incidental interests of Todd's 1811 edition of Dryden is the information which it gives us regarding the personal relationship between Johnson and Joseph Warton. Warton, who had himself been a member of Johnson's immediate circle, was a little overwhelmed by Johnson's dominating personality. Regarding the differences which they were known to have had, Warton informs us: 'I have been censured, I am informed, for contradicting some of Johnson's critical opinions. As I knew him well, I ever respected his talents, and more so his integrity; but a love of paradox and contradiction, at the bottom of which was vanity, gave an unpleasant tincture to his manners, and made his conversation boisterous and offensive. I often used to tell the mild and sensible Sir Joshua Reynolds that he and his friends had contributed to spoil Johnson, by constantly and cowardly assenting to all he advanced on any subject. Mr Burke only kept him in order, as did Mr Beauclerc also, sometimes by his playful wit.' (Notes to *Ode to the Memory of Mrs Anne Killigrew*, Todd's Dryden, II, 260 n.)

CHAPTER II

EDITIONS OF POPE

According to the *Quarterly Review* of October 1825, a reassuring confirmation of a lively contemporary interest in Augustan poetry was the appearance of 'three voluminous editions of Pope within the present century'. These editions were: Joseph Warton's edition, which, after its belated appearance in 1797, was reprinted in 1803 (9 vols, Basle), and again in 1822 (9 vols, London); secondly, the Reverend William Lisle Bowles's edition, which was first published in 1806, and reprinted, with considerable modifications, in 1812; and, finally, William Roscoe's edition (8 vols, 1824), which was reprinted in 1847.

The interesting feature about these three editions of Pope is the manner in which they are interrelated. Bowles believed that Warton had been inhibited from speaking out in his own time by a public sympathetic to Augustan poetry, and he therefore regarded his own edition of Pope as embodying Warton's critical principles carried to their logical conclusion. The critical introduction and notes to Warton's edition (1797) were based largely upon his *Essay on the Genius and Writings of Pope*, which had first appeared in 1756; and Bowles informs us of the effect which it had upon contemporary readers:

The *Essay on the Life and Genius of Pope*, by the late editor, Dr. Warton, raised a sort of literary outcry against him, as if he meant to deny to Pope his fair and just pretensions to the name of poet. He seems particularly to have been misunderstood by Johnson. I have endeavoured to state the grounds of this difference, upon principles which I think will be easily recognised; and ... venture to state my own ideas of the general poetic character of Pope.[1]

The reader who cares to make the relevant comparisons will be immediately struck by the extent to which Bowles's estimate of

[1] 'Concluding Observations', Bowles's Pope (1806), x, 362.

Pope's poetry corresponds with Warton's.[1] A closer glance may reveal differences, too, but the nature of the descent from Warton may be observed by comparing the following quotations, which establish the central elements in the tradition:

When we speak of the poetical character derived from passions of *general Nature*, two obvious distinctions must occur, without regard to Aristotle; those which, derived from the passions, may be called *pathetic*, and those which, derived from the same source, may be called *sublime*.[2]

Although Bowles's sense may not be entirely clear in this passage, it was for the absence of the two poetical qualities he refers to here—the 'sublime' and the 'pathetic'—that he censured Pope most severely. The source of these key-terms which Bowles employed in criticising Pope may be found in Warton's *Essay on Pope*, in which he had declared exactly fifty years before Bowles's edition appeared:

The sublime and the pathetic are the two chief nerves of all genuine poesy. What is there transcendently Sublime or Pathetic in Pope?[3]

Bowles's edition of Pope soon provoked a storm of controversy which was more prolonged, though perhaps less one-sided, than the 'literary outcry' that had followed the publication of the first part of Warton's *Essay on Pope* in 1756. The conflicting attitudes towards Augustan poetry, which, in the case of Dryden's poetry, we have already observed in the contradictions and inconsistencies within Todd's 1811 edition, manifested themselves in Pope's case in a more dramatically explicit form: a series of critical exchanges extending over a period of

---

[1] Bowles was, in fact, more than merely Joseph Warton's editorial successor; he was almost a conscious disciple. Joseph Warton was Headmaster of Winchester College; Bowles was educated there, and he was later influenced by Warton's brother, Thomas, who was Professor of Poetry at Oxford. Peter Cunningham described Bowles, in a note in the second edition of Campbell's *Specimens*, as 'one of Joseph Warton's Winchester wonders', and noted that 'the taste he imbibed there for the school of Romantic poetry was strengthened and confirmed by his removal to Trinity College, Oxford, when Tom Warton was Master there'.

[2] Bowles's *Pope*, x (1806), 369.

[3] Warton's *Essay on Pope*, i: 'Dedication to Young', p. x (1772), 3rd edn.

more than twenty years.[1] This controversy, which was intimately related to the editions of Pope which appeared in the early nineteenth century was one of the many ways in which protest at the relegation of Pope to the rank of a secondary poet found concrete expression. In the Preface to his edition, Roscoe claimed that one of his principal motives in publishing it was the wish to preserve Pope's poetry from what he felt to be the excessively limiting criticism of both Warton and Bowles.

I. JOSEPH WARTON'S POPE (1797)

The editor and the public

Dr Johnson noted, shortly after the publication of the first volume of Warton's *Essay*, that Warton was 'a little disappointed in not being able to persuade his readers to be of his opinions as to Pope', and it was clearly this unsympathetic reception of his first volume which led him to postpone the publication of his second volume for twenty-six years.[2] Warton himself was perfectly well aware that, in his own time, his views commanded little support in the reading public. Edith J. Morley, in her study, 'Joseph Warton: a comparison of his Essay on the Genius and Writings of Pope with his Edition of Pope's Works' (1924), demonstrated that some of Warton's

---

[1] The reviews, letters, essays, and pamphlets which go to make up the controversy provide a considerable body of documentary evidence, in which we may partially discern, among other things, the fluctuating taste for Augustan poetry in the years between 1806 and 1826. A study of the controversy will be found in Chapter VI.

[2] Edmund Gosse wrote: 'His *Essay on Pope*, though written with such studied moderation that we may, in a hasty reading, regard it almost as a eulogy, was so shocking to the prejudices of the hour that it was received with universal disfavour, and twenty-six years passed before the author had the moral courage to pursue it to a conclusion.' ('Two Pioneers of Romanticism: Joseph and Thomas Warton', *Proceedings of the British Academy*, VII, 1915, 157.)

views on Pope underwent modification during his lifetime.[1] Whether these changes resulted from the pressure of contemporary opinion or from modifications in his own taste (or from a combination of both) is not easy to determine. Whatever the cause, Warton's later criticism of Pope became increasingly tactful and persuasive. A trace of bitterness and impatience, however, may sometimes be observed in Warton's response to the intractability of the reading public. 'For one person who can adequately relish, and enjoy a work of the imagination,' he exclaimed in his *Essay*, 'twenty are to be found who can taste and judge of observations on familiar life, and the manners of the age.' Nevertheless Warton's criticism—in strong contrast to that of Pope's Grub-street contemporaries—was always moderately expressed, and he made his attitude to Pope explicit early in his *Essay*:

I revere the memory of Pope, I respect and honour his abilities; but I do not think him at the head of his profession. In other words, in that species of poetry wherein Pope excelled he is superior to all mankind: and I only say, that this species of poetry is not the most excellent one of the art.[2]

Critical standards

A useful way of distinguishing between the temper of Warton's anti-Augustan criticism and that of many critics who were influenced by him, is to note that his celebrated—or notorious—question, 'What is there transcendently sublime or pathetic in Pope?' was not originally intended merely as a means of defining Pope's limitations. This question, posed at the very

---

[1] Confirmation of Edith Morley's claim may be found in W. D. MacClintock's study *Joseph Warton's Essay on Pope* (1933). MacClintock provides an interesting history of the five editions of Warton's *Essay* which appeared in his lifetime, and records the modifications which he made in it from time to time. Volume One of Warton's *Essay* appeared in 1756, 1762, 1764, 1782 (together with Volume Two), and in 1786. Warton died in 1800, but in 1806, the year in which Bowles's edition of Pope first appeared, there was also published a further two-volume edition of Warton's *Essay*. According to MacClintock, Warton had already completed 200 pages of his second volume by 1762. That he refrained from publishing it for two decades is a further confirmation that it was the unpopularity of Warton's views in his own time, rather than his indolence, which held up publication for so long.

[2] Warton, *Essay on Pope*, I, 'Dedication', p. iv.

beginning of the first volume of Warton's *Essay*, was for him primarily a point of departure in his inquiry into the validity of Pope's claim to be regarded as a great poet. There was not a great deal in Pope's poetry to satisfy Warton's special demands, but it is worth insisting that he did not himself regard his search for the 'sublime' and the 'pathetic' in Pope's poetry as wholly unsuccessful.

Warton's predilection among Pope's poems for those with 'Romantic' affinities (at the expense of those which relied more on the operation of the 'wits' rather than the workings of 'Fancy'), anticipated a tendency that was to influence—more than half a century later—an increasing number of readers. Warton's bold prophecy (made as early as 1756) about the kind of interest which posterity would bring to a reading of Pope's poems is therefore specially interesting in the light of developments in taste in the early nineteenth century:

I think one may venture to remark, that the reputation of Pope, as a Poet, among posterity, will be principally owing to his *Windsor Forest*, his *Rape of the Lock*, and his *Eloisa to Abelard*; whilst the facts and characters alluded to and exposed, in his later writings, will be forgotten and unknown and their poignancy and propriety little relished. For WIT and SATIRE are transitory and perishable, but NATURE and PASSION are eternal.[1]

It is a tribute to Warton's extraordinary powers of anticipation that the poems which he singled out in the mid-eighteenth century were, in fact, among those which were specially popular in the early nineteenth century. Yet Warton's explanation of the tendencies which would result in a partial withdrawal of interest from Pope's later writings demands closer scrutiny. Indeed, the view he advances here, that 'satire' and 'wit' were of their very nature 'transitory and perishable', appears strange in a critic who had elsewhere demonstrated his appreciation of the Roman Augustan satirists. Furthermore, the delight which many derive, even today, from a reading of Pope's later satires (despite the even more complete fading in

[1] *Ibid.* I, 344, 1772 edn.

39

the public memory of 'the facts and characters attended to and exposed' there), suggests that this was not a primary cause of their neglect in the early nineteenth century.[1]

However, the poems which Warton singled out as being most likely to be read by posterity are also important in quite a different way: they are intimately related to Warton's search for the highest poetical qualities in Pope. These qualities Warton believed to be principally three in number: command over the 'sublime' and the 'pathetic' emotions in poetry, and the force of a 'creative and glowing Imagination'—it was these qualities, and these alone, Warton felt, that could 'stamp a writer with the exalted and uncommon character' of a true poet, 'which so few possess, and of which so few can properly judge'.[2]

Examining Pope's poetry on the basis of these requirements, Warton felt that one of the *genres* in which Pope's peculiar genius appeared to little advantage was the lyric. Warton's main objection here was to what he felt was the intrusion of 'wit' in Pope's lyrics; for, according to Warton, 'wit' was of its very nature 'flagrantly unsuitable to the dignity, and foreign to the nature, of the lyric'.[3] The proper function of the lyric, according to Warton, was the communication of simple yet intense emotions which, when successful, could astonish and transport the sensitive reader by their poignancy. The intrusion of anything like 'wit'—even the 'tough reasonableness' which T. S. Eliot admired 'beneath the slight lyric grace' of Marvell's verse—would have been regarded as a violation of the solemn (rather than serious) decorum which Warton deemed essential in the lyric. The extent to which Warton's notion of the lyric corresponds with the assumptions underlying the great revival of lyrical poetry in the early nineteenth century, culminating in

---

[1] That this indifference to Pope's later writings could have been caused as much by limitations in the sensibility of readers as by alleged deficiencies in the nature of the poetry ('"WIT" and "SATIRE" are transitory and perishable'), was an explanation which evidently did not strike Warton.

[2] Warton's *Essay on Pope*, I, p. v.

[3] *Ibid.* I, 61.

Tennyson's specialised triumphs in this mode, needs hardly to be mentioned.

The *genre* against which Warton directed his most stringent criticism, however, was didactic verse.[1] Satirical verse was also coming to be regarded with some suspicion, though it is not true that Warton himself considered it a necessarily inferior kind of verse. The skill and delicacy with which Pope handled his ethical themes raised them, in Warton's eyes, above the level of versified morality, and he regarded Pope's best satirical poetry as being nearer in spirit to epic than to didactic verse:

If the moderns have excelled the ancients in any species of writing, it seems to be in satire; and particularly in that kind of satire which is conveyed in the form of the epopee, a pleasing vehicle of satire, seldom, if ever, used by the ancients . . . As the poet disappears in this way of writing, and does not deliver the intended censure in his own proper person, the satire becomes more delicate, becomes more oblique. Add to this, that a tale or story more strongly engages and interests the reader, than a series of precepts or reproofs, or even of characters themselves, however lively or natural.[2]

What Warton praises here is, of course, mock-epic satire, but it soon becomes clear that it was Pope's early satires, especially those he wrote while still in 'Fancy's Maze', rather than the mock-epic *Dunciad*, that appealed most to Warton. It was the satirical *The Rape of the Lock*, in fact, that Warton chose as Pope's finest poem, displaying the highest reach of a 'glowing and creative Imagination':

It is in this composition, Pope principally appears as a POET; in which he has displayed more imagination than in all his other works taken together.[3]

Curiously enough, Pope's preoccupation with contemporary life (which elsewhere Warton disparaged as a concern with

---

[1] 'For Didactic poetry being, from its very nature, inferior to Lyric, Tragic, and Epic poetry, we should confound and invert all literary rank and order if we compared and preferred the *Georgics* of Virgil to the *Aeneid*, the *Epistle to the Pisos* to the *Qualem Ministrum* of Horace, and Boileau's *Art of Poetry* to the *Iphigénie* of Racine.' (Warton's Pope, I, 173.)

[2] *Ibid.* I, 279.

[3] Warton's *Essay on Pope*, I, 254.

'modern manners', 'present life', 'transitory and perishable'),
did not affect Warton's praise of the poem:

> Upon the whole, I hope it will not be thought an exaggerated pane-
> gyric to say, that *The Rape of the Lock* is the best satire extant; that
> it contains the truest and liveliest picture of modern life; and that
> the subject is of a more elegant nature, as well as more artfully
> conducted, than that of any other heroi-comic poem.[1]

Pope's fanciful recreation of everyday fashionable life—
particularly manifested in his deft management of the machinery of the Rosicrucian Sylphs—was especially attractive to
Warton; and he preferred the 'delicacy', 'liveliness' and
'humour' of the poem to the best things in even Shakespeare's
A Midsummer Night's Dream. This is an important collocation,
for that play is obviously one of the sources of the 'faery' kind
of writing. Pope is being praised for having a foot in the other
tradition.

Warton's delight in the gay and vivacious appeal of Pope's
early satires was associated, however, with a corresponding lack
of sympathy with the later and more serious satires. Admittedly,
Warton fully approved of the wide contemporary popularity
of Pope's 'happy and judicious *Imitations* from Horace',[2] but
for the most substantial satirical achievement of Pope's later
years, *The Dunciad*, Warton had hardly a word of praise. He
could see no poetical merit at all in the fourth book of *The
Dunciad*, and readily agreed with Shenstone that it was best
regarded as a product of 'Mr Pope's dotage'.[3] *The Rape of the
Lock* remained for Warton a triumph of the 'glowing and
creative Imagination' which Pope never surpassed.

Warton's quest for the 'sublime' and the 'pathetic' in Pope's

---

[1] Warton's Pope, I, 252.

[2] 'Not less than four of his *Imitations* of Horace appeared 1737, which, by the
artful accommodations of modern sentiments to ancient, by judicious applications
of similar characters, and happy parallels, are become some of the most pleasing
and popular of all his Works, especially to readers of years and experience.'
(Warton's Pope, I, p. lvi.)

[3] Elaborating on Shenstone's remark, Warton informs us that he found the
poetry of the fourth book of *The Dunciad*: ' . . . flat in the whole, and including, with
several tolerable lines, a number of weak, obscure, *and even punning* ones' (my
italics). (Warton's Pope, I, p. lxii n.)

poetry did not go unrewarded. He was greatly moved by the poignancy of the *Eloisa to Abelard*, and was even more deeply appreciative of the *Elegy to the Memory of an Unfortunate Lady*. The exalted pathos and tenderness of this poem seemed doubly welcome to him in an age which tended to produce men of 'dry, distinct heads and cool imaginations': '. . . as it came from the heart, it is very tender and pathetic; more so, I think, than any other copy of verses of our author'. Among the other instances of the 'pathetic' which Warton found in Pope's work were the lines upon the death of his mother, which Pope included at the end of his *Epistle to Dr Arbuthnot*.

Evidence of the 'sublime', too, Warton informs us, could be found in Pope's poetry, and a passage which he specially admired was Pope's Prologue to Addison's *Tragedy of Cato*. Contrasting this Prologue with many of Dryden's which tended to be 'satyrical and facetious', Warton praised it for the 'solemn and sublime' elevation of its style. The 'sublime' implied very much more than merely 'elevation' to Warton, as it did to Scott, and this is clearly seen in Warton's criticism of the well-known description of the convent in *Eloisa to Abelard*, which he felt to be the finest evocation of sublimity in all Pope's poetry:

No part of this poem, or indeed of any of Pope's productions is so truly poetical, and contains such strong painting, as the passage to which we are now arrived;—the description of the convent, where Pope's religion certainly aided his fancy. It is impossible to read it without being struck with a pensive pleasure, and a sacred awe, at the solemnity of the scene, so picturesque are the epithets:

> In these *lone* walls, (their days eternal bound),
> These *moss-grown* domes with *spiry* turrets crown'd,
> Where *awful* arches make the noon-day night
> And the *dim* windows shed a *solemn* light
> Thy eyes diffused a reconciling ray . . .[1]

The tone, atmosphere and vocabulary of this passage are very clearly derived from Milton's *Il Penseroso*;[2] we remember the

[1] Warton's *Essay on Pope*, I, 328.
[2] See Warton's Pope, II, 36 n.

enthusiastic interest in Milton's early poems which Warton shared with his father and his brother Thomas. It was an interest which Gray, Collins, and Cowper, among his contemporaries, also found congenial, and the same 'romantic' effects, and this characteristic vocabulary, can be found in their verse.

Warton, then, was not merely a denigrator of Pope. Though there was not a great deal in Pope to satisfy his special critical demands, Warton was very far from believing that he was devoid of those qualities which he associated with the highest poetical excellence. Warton's main complaint, in fact, was that Pope had wasted his natural talents, and had failed to exploit the full potentialities of his genius. In a careful appraisal of Pope's actual achievement as a poet, Warton attempted to analyse the forces which had led Pope to suppress what Warton felt had been his true 'poetical enthusiasm':

There is nothing in so sublime a style as *The Bard* of Gray. This is a matter of *fact*, not of *reasoning*; and means to point out, what Pope *has actually done*, not what, if he had put out his full strength, he was *capable* of *doing*. No man can possibly think, or can hint, that the Author of *The Rape of the Lock*, and the *Eloisa*, wanted *imagination*, or *sensibility*, or *pathetic*; but he certainly did not so often indulge and exert those talents; nor give so many proofs of them, as he did of strong sense and judgement. This turn of mind led him to admire French models; he studied *Boileau* attentively; formed himself upon *him*, as Milton formed himself upon the Grecian and Italian Sons of *Fancy*. He stuck to describing *modern manners*; but these *manners*, because they are *familiar, uniform, artificial, and polished*, are, for these four reasons, in their very nature *unfit* for any lofty effort of the Muse ... Whatever poetical enthusiasm he actually possessed, he with-held and suppressed. The perusal of him ... affects not our minds with such strong emotions as we feel from *Homer* or *Milton* so that no man, of a true poetical spirit, is master of himself while he reads them. Hence he is a writer fit for universal perusal, and of general utility; adapted to all ages and all stations; for the old and for the young; the man of business and the scholar. He who would think, and there are many such, the *Faerie Queene, Palamon and Arcite, The Tempest*, or *Comus*, childish and romantic, may relish Pope. Surely it is no narrow, nor individious, nor niggardly encomium to say, he is the great Poet of Reason; the *First* of *Ethical* Authors in Verse; which he was by choice, not necessity.[1]

This passage manages to sum up with extraordinary economy the major themes of Warton's criticism of Pope, and some of these require additional comment. For example, Warton's attempt here to distinguish between Milton and Pope, by describing Milton as having formed himself upon the 'Grecian and Italian sons of Fancy' and Pope upon 'French models', anticipates a tendency that was to become commonplace of early nineteenth-century criticism of Augustan poetry. This distinction commonly implied limitations in the poetry of both Dryden and Pope, and was used to suggest the 'artificiality' of their subjects, and to support the view (often seriously maintained) that Augustan poetry was more 'French' than 'English' in its essential spirit. Jeffrey, for example, claimed that 'French taste' clipped and trimmed 'the wings of our English muse' during the Restoration; and Coleridge described the Augustans as primarily a 'school of French poetry, condensed and invigorated by English understanding'.

Another interesting feature in this passage is that Warton's crucial test, by which Pope's poetry is found wanting, is an application of the Longinian 'transport': a condition in which the emotions gained such an ascendancy over the controlling judgement, that 'no man of true poetical spirit is master of himself while he reads'. It need hardly be said that this was not the manner in which the Augustans would have wished to be read. For, although Pope had maintained, in his *Essay on Criticism*, that poetry could at moments transcend both Reason and Judgement,[2] any simple abandonment of them in the kind of overwhelming 'transport' described by Warton would have seemed to him, if practised as the rule and not the exception, a

---

[1] Warton's Pope, I, pp. lxviii–lxxi. It is interesting to compare Warton's account of Pope as the 'great Poet of Reason' with Voltaire's account of Boileau as 'le Poète de la Raison': 'Incapable peut-être du sublime qui élève l'âme, et du sentiment qui l'attendrit, mais fait pour éclairer ceux à qui la nature accorde l'un et l'autre, laborieux, sévère, précis, pur, harmonieux, il devint, enfin, le poète de la Raison.' (See Warton's *Essay on Pope*, I, p. xi.)

[2] Pope's *Essay on Criticism*, lines 140–55.

dangerous violation of emotional balance and decorum.
Francis Jeffrey, for example, commented on the disequilibrium
caused by the excessively 'Longinian' raptures of some early
nineteenth-century poets: 'There must be a "qu'il mourût"
and "Let there be light" in every line; and all their characters
must be in agonies and ecstacies, from their entrance to their
exit.'[1]

Finally, this passage brings out well Warton's attitude
towards ethical poetry. Byron, for example, who exclaimed
in a letter to John Murray from Ravenna—'In my mind the
highest order of poetry is ethical poetry'—would have been
delighted with Warton's account of Pope as the 'First of Ethical
Authors in Verse'. For, although Warton believed that ethical
interests could not by themselves produce the highest kinds of
poetry, he never undervalued the importance of a discriminating moral sensibility. However, it is with regard to his views
on this subject—probably through a confusion of his standards
with those of the early nineteenth-century critics he influenced
—that he has most often been misunderstood, for example by
Edmund Gosse.[2] Warton himself was within the best eighteenth-

---

[1] 'Let there be light' was one of the most frequently quoted examples of the
'sublime' given by Longinus: 'Thus too the lawgiver of the Jews, no common man,
when he had duly conceived the power of the Deity, showed it forth as duly. At
the very beginning of the Laws, "God said", he writes—What?, "Let there be
light, and there was light, let there be earth, and there was earth".' (*A Treatise
of the Sublime*, Chapter IX.)

[2] It is hard to explain Gosse's comment on the kind of pleasure which Warton
derived from reading Pope's *Eloisa to Abelard*: 'The absence of ethical reservation,
the licence, in short, was highly attractive to him.' ('Two Pioneers of Romanticism', *Proceedings of the British Academy*, VII, p. 158.) It is quite plain from Warton's
notes that 'absence of ethical reservation' and 'licence' were among the qualities
he disliked most actively in poetry. Warton's criticism also makes it plain that his
interest in *Eloisa* was related more to his delight in its pathos and awe-inspiring
Gothick solemnities than to anything else. Nor is Gosse very fair to Warton
(probably through confusing him with those whom he had influenced) in ascribing
to him a desire for the amoral indulgence of an 'excessive sensibility': 'He designed
or pretended to design, to emigrate to the backwoods of America, to live
　　With simple Indian swains, that I may hunt
　　The boar and tiger through savannahs wild
　　Through fragrant deserts and through citron groves
indulging, without the slightest admixture of any active moral principle in social
life, all the ecstacies, all the ravishing emotions, of an abandonment to excessive

century tradition in his high regard for moral decorum and discipline.

2. W. L. BOWLES'S POPE (1806)

The editor and the public

The second of the three major editions of Pope's *Complete Works* to appear between 1800 and 1830, was brought out in 1806 by the Reverend William Lisle Bowles. The nature of the interrelation between Bowles's edition of Pope and that of Joseph Warton has been briefly referred to already; yet, although Bowles regarded himself as a conscious disciple of Warton and fully endorsed his unfavourable ranking of Pope,[1] it is necessary at this stage to examine more closely the differences between the critical principles implicit in Bowles's edition of Pope and those implied in Warton's edition and more comprehensively discussed in his *Essay on the Genius and Writings of Pope*. This is particularly relevant to our inquiries, because the modification which Warton's critical principles underwent in Bowles's application of them is a representative early nineteenth-century development of essentially eighteenth-century anti-Augustan trends.

Though the substance of Bowles's criticism may appear at first glance to be little more than an elaboration of Warton's ideas, it is also immediately notable that the characteristic tone of his criticism of Pope (an aspect not unimportant in an inquiry into the history of taste) is strikingly different. While Warton's

---

sensibility.' ('Two Pioneers of Romanticism', p. 153.) Warton did play with the idea of emigrating to the backwoods—thus foreshadowing the proposed Coleridgean pantisocracy, and the sort of interests represented by Campbell's *Gertrude of Wyoming*. But Gosse has so coloured and heightened Warton's plan that it seems to have more in common with the feelings of the early Keats of 'Oh, for a life of sensations', than with the customary dignity and restraint of Joseph Warton.

[1] Replying to Isaac D'Israeli's unfavourable criticism of his work in the *Quarterly Review* (July 1820), Bowles commented: 'Dr Warton had declared, or, according to the *Quarterly* reviewer, had the merit of first declaring, of Pope, that he did not think him at the head of his profession, and that his species of poetry was not the most excellent one of his art. This is Warton's opinion, and this is mine'. ('An answer to the *Quarterly Review*', *Pamphleteer*, XL, 1822, 562.)

severest criticism was invariably courteously disciplined and moderate, Bowles's strictures are remarkable for their aggressive and uninhibited confidence. This contrast may be explained partly as a difference in temperament (Bowles's ferocities were probably beyond Warton), and partly too as a difference in social and literary background (Warton's essentially eighteenth-century propriety and restraint had evidently not communicated itself to his disciple).

A more complete explanation would also have to take into account changes that were taking place in the taste of the reading public at large. While Warton's seemingly iconoclastic *Essay* had aroused a 'literary outcry' against him in 1756, the headway which Wartonian principles had made in the intervening half-century made it possible for Bowles, in 1806, to appeal confidently to 'principles which I think will be easily recognised'. Bowles felt that these changes in the general taste of the age were working to his advantage, and that whereas Warton had been inhibited from speaking out by public sympathy towards Augustan poetry, he himself could with popular support and approval carry to a logical conclusion the Wartonian, as opposed to the Johnsonian, evaluation of Pope's poetry, in his own edition.

Events proved that Bowles's confident expectation of the support and approval of the majority of early nineteenth-century reviewers and critics was not justified. It is unlikely that Bowles himself anticipated the long-drawn-out controversy which his edition of Pope directly provoked, and the violence with which he had to defend his strictures on Augustan poetry testifies to the weight of opinion ranged against him even in the 1830s.[1] It is noteworthy, too, that although Bowles showed himself quite capable of dealing with a multitude of critics, he had few supporters among the active controversialists. In his own time it is quite plain that Bowles had little justification for regarding himself as the spokesman of the reading public

---

[1] For a more detailed study of the 'Pope Controversy' incited by Bowles's Pope, see Chapter VI.

at large. Later nineteenth-century commentators, though not often enthusiastic about his polemical methods, usually found themselves in agreement with his evaluation of Pope.

Critical standards

The difference between Bowles's estimate of Pope and that of Joseph Warton was more substantial than the difference of tone already noted. Although his criticism was based largely on Warton's principles, Pope's stature as a poet was considerably diminished in Bowles's appraisal. While Warton principally regarded Pope as a great poet who had not fully exploited the potentialities of his genius, he appeared to Bowles as a poet who, through inherent deficiencies of sensibility, belonged irrevocably to the second order of poets, and could never have risen above it.[1]

Having noted that Pope's 'predominant character' was illustrative of an inferior poetic spirit, Bowles hastened to add: 'When I say that this is his *predominant* character, I must be insensible to everything exquisite in Poetry, if I did not except, *instanter*, the *Epistle of Eloisa*.'[2] Bowles's admiration for this poem is easily explained. It appeared to him to evoke some of the essentially 'poetical' emotions described by Warton, and his criticism of it is representatively 'Romantic' in its appreciation:

Of the Pathetic, no one (considering the *Epistle of Eloisa* alone) has touched the chords so tenderly, so pathetically, and so melodiously. As far as this goes, Pope, therefore, in poetical and musical expression, has *no competitor*.[3]

Bowles made a point of stressing, however, that Pope's success in the *Eloisa* was not typical of his genius, and that the Romantic interests which engaged him while he dallied in 'Fancy's

---

[1] 'The author begs leave to add, that he flatters himself,' Warton declared, 'that no observations in this work can be so perversely misinterpreted and tortured, as to make him insinuate, contrary to his opinion and inclination, that POPE was not a *great* poet: he only says and thinks, he was not the greatest.' (*Essay on Pope*, II (1782), 'Advertisement', p. i.)

[2] Bowles's Pope, x, 365.

[3] *Ibid*. x, 369–70.

maze' soon disappeared from his verse, and were replaced by the 'thorns and briars of ineffectual satire and bitterness'.[1]

Among the various means employed by Bowles to discredit Pope's claims to be regarded as a great poet, his use of the four-fold classication of the English poets, devised by Warton in 1765, was perhaps the most insidious. Here is the relevant passage, from the beginning of the *Essay on Pope*:

Our English poets may, I think, be disposed in four different classes and degrees. In the first class I would place, our only three sublime and pathetic poets: SPENSER, SHAKESPEARE, MILTON. In the second class should be ranked, such as possessed the true poetical genius, in a more moderate degree, but who had noble talents for moral, ethical, and panegyrical poesy. At the head of these are Dryden, Prior, Addison, Cowley, Waller, Garth, Fenton, Gay, Denham, Parnell. In the third class may be placed men of wit, elegant taste and lively fancy in describing familiar life tho' not the higher scenes of poetry. Here may be numbered Butler, Swift, Rochester, Donne, Dorset, Oldham. In the fourth class, the mere versifiers, however smooth and mellifluous some of them may be thought should be disposed. Such as Pitt, Sandys, Fairfax, Broome, Buckingham, Lansdown. This enumeration is not intended as a complete catalogue of writers, and in their proper order, but only to mark out briefly the different species of our celebrated authors.[2]

Warton himself regarded his classification as a gradually ascending scale, in which the poets of each class were closely related to those higher up on the scale. For example, in giving Pope his proper rank at the end of the second volume of his *Essay on Pope*, Warton finally decided 'to assign him a place, next to Milton' (who belonged to the first order of poets), 'and just above Dryden' (who belonged to the second).

The principal modification which Bowles introduced into Warton's classification was that he radically altered the status

---

[1] *Ibid.* x, 369.

[2] *Essay on Pope*, I, p. xi, 'Dedication to Young'. The *Essay* was written in 1756; it is noteworthy that the name of Johnson is omitted. The reason is not clear; but it is possible that the omission was intended, and was connected with the well-known critical disagreements between Warton and Johnson.

of the second order of poets.[1] While Warton, partly because of his classical training, had a high regard for ethical poetry, and characterised the poets of the second order as those who possessed 'the true poetical genius, in a more moderate degree, but who had noble talents for moral, ethical, and panegyrical poesy', it is plain that Bowles, who scarcely bothered to disguise his disdain for it, always regarded ethical poetry as an inferior and pedestrian branch of the art. Upon this matter Bowles's views were strong enough for him to venture openly to criticise his master Warton for his critical 'injudiciousness' in seeking to compare mere 'satires and epistles' with pieces of 'genuine poetry'.[2]

The most striking difference between Bowles's views and those of Warton may be found in their disagreement over the merit of Pope's *The Rape of the Lock*. While Warton had regarded it as Pope's finest and most imaginative poem (the work in which he 'principally appears as a POET'), Bowles considered it, because of its subject-matter and its *genre*, a poem which belonged to an intrinsically inferior order. Bowles granted that Pope had undoubtedly managed his Sylphs with propriety and elegance, and had performed feats of dazzling ingenuity in his description of the game of Ombre, yet he firmly placed these as triumphs in a secondary order of poetry. Discrediting the imaginative skill which Warton had praised in Pope's use of his Rosicrucian Sylphs, Bowles achieved his most forceful contrast by invoking the 'aerial beings' of Shakespeare— Titania, Bottom, and the Fairies in *A Midsummer Night's Dream*:

Nothing can be more appropriate and elegant, than the lines which describe the employment assigned to the Sylphs in this Poem. But

---

[1] Bowles's emphatic claim that Pope was successful only in limited and inferior *genres* of poetry represents the culmination of a trend which has been traced back not only to Joseph Warton, but to William Ayres and Robert Shiels before him. For a fuller account of Warton's predecessors in this line of criticism, see Paul Leedy, 'Genre Criticism and Warton's *Essay on Pope*', *Journal of English and Germanic Philology*, No. 45 (1946), pp. 140–6.

[2] Bowles's Pope, x, 366–7.

how can Warton think, that in fancy they equal *anything of the kind*?
But there is no comparison between beings who

> —pluck the wings from painted butterflies
> To fan the moon beams

and those

> —who invention bestow
> To change a flounce.[1]

Bowles's strongest criticism of Pope and the Augustans was that
their poetry was principally concerned only with 'local manners' and 'artificial life', and that these preoccupations were
reflected in their unpoetical choice of imagery from the commonplace realities of fashionable life. His views here were again
different from Warton's, and are related to more strikingly
nineteenth-century interests. Warton noted that Pope's interest
in *The Rape of the Lock* was in the sophisticated surface of social
life, and that his imagery was consequently derived from
associated sources. Yet in maintaining that it was the use which
a poet made of his imagery, rather than its source, that mat-
tered, Warton felt he was supported by the best Roman
Augustan practice. 'If Virgil has merited such perpetual
commendation for exalting his bees, by the majesty and magnificence of his diction,' he asked, 'does not Pope deserve equal
praises, for the pomp and lustre of his language, on so trivial
a subject?'[2] And again: 'It is doubtless, as hard to make a
coffee-pot shine in poetry as a plough: yet Pope has succeeded
in giving elegance to so familiar an object, as well as Virgil.'[3]
For Bowles on the other hand, the presence in a poem of what

[1] Bowles's use here of the more 'romantic' passages in Shakespeare to show up
limitations in the quality of the Augustan sensibility, may be found in Warton too.
In *The Enthusiast: or The Lover of Nature* (1744) he contrasted Addison's mannered
sophistication ('coldly correct') with Shakespeare's spontaneous simplicity
('Shakespeare's warblings wild'). Warton's 'romantic' idea of Shakespeare in this
poem obviously owed a great deal to Milton's *L'Allegro*, and suggests the spirit
in which Shakespeare was sometimes revived in the late eighteenth century.
Professor Beers has noted of Bowles's interest in Shakespeare, for example: 'His
lines on Shakespeare recall Collins in their insistence upon the "elvish things" in
the plays.' (*A History of Romanticism in the 19th Century*, 1902, p. 62.) For Bowles's
contrast of Shakespeare and Pope, see Bowles's Pope, I, 317–20.

[2] Warton, *Essay on Pope*, I, 237.

[3] *Ibid.* I, 239.

Mr George Rylands has described as 'consecrated images' derived from the world of external nature, constituted a kind of guarantee of its excellence. 'Poetry' itself, he believed, resided in the subject-matter and imagery of a poem; the poet's 'execution' was a kind of embellishment.[1] This oversimple faith in the poetry inherent in the world of external nature, represented a not uncommon tendency of the time. It was strong enough for Coleridge to find it necessary explicitly to dissociate himself from it in the *Biographia Literaria*.

A final distinction between the criticism of Bowles and that of Warton remains to be made. Many contemporary readers, Bowles observed, regarded the heroic couplet as the most harmonious metrical form yet devised, and he attributed its popularity largely to the influence of Johnson. The return to favour of pre-Restoration poets is evident in Bowles's criticism of Johnson:

Johnson seems to have depreciated, or to have been ignorant of, the metrical powers of some Writers prior to Pope. His ear seems to have been caught chiefly by *Dryden*, and as Pope's versification was more equably (couplet with couplet being considered, not passage with passage) connected than Dryden's, he thought therefore that nothing could be added to Pope's versification. . . . There are those who cannot relish the noble Diapason of Milton, and who prefer Pope's Couplets, as more harmonious.[2]

Bowles's admiration for Milton's 'noble Diapason' was representative of a conception of verbal style which was unsympathetic towards Augustan versification. It was a notion of style which had little interest in dramatic vitality, the varied tones of declamatory or colloquial speech, or the balanced antithetical movement of the 'line of Pope', but much preferred the effect of

> Spenserian vowels that elope with ease,
> And float along like birds o'er summer seas—

verse, in short, that approximated more to song than to speech. It was a part of the more Romantic tendencies of the early

---

[1] Bowles's Pope, x, 'Concluding Observations'.
[2] *Ibid.* x, 375.

nineteenth century which we cannot find in Warton. 'Fitness
or unfitness for song,' Leigh Hunt claimed in *What is Poetry?*
'makes all the difference between a poetical and a prosaical
subject.' The characteristic versification of Milton's early
poetry (whose 'simple, sensuous, and passionate' appeal
attracted Leigh Hunt and later Arnold) was regarded as antithetical to Pope's, and, in registering his disagreement with
Johnson, Bowles commented:

Shakespear uses an expressive word, 'tuneable'. If I were called
on to say what I thought the most *tuneable* of all Verses in rhyme, I
should answer, Milton's *Lycidas*; but the general structure of its
verse would be totally incompatible with such subjects as Pope has
chosen. We must keep in mind *only the couplet*; and though in this
kind of verse Pope has done a great deal, I cannot for the reasons
given, agree with Johnson.[1]

Bowles realised well enough that Milton's versification enabled
him to penetrate in some respects beyond the frontiers of Augustan poetry. He did not realise as clearly that these gains were
realised at the price of corresponding limitations in the range of
Milton's own expression.

Bowles's criticism of Pope, when compared with Warton's,
illustrates the growing confidence and increased severity of
anti-Augustan tendencies in the early nineteenth century. He
did not go as far as Arnold in denying to Pope the title of poet;
nevertheless, while Warton had never doubted that Pope was
a great poet, and had only wished to suggest that he was not
the greatest, it is plain in Bowles's summing-up of Pope's
achievement (in which he invokes some of Warton's critical
'touchstones') that Bowles regarded Pope as no more than a
polished and able versifier, who had shone in an inferior order
of poetry:

I need not go regularly over his Works; but I think they may be
generally divided under the heads I have mentioned: —Pathetic,
Sublime, Descriptive, Moral, and Satirical. In the Pathetic, *poetic-
ally* considered, he stands highest; in the Sublime, he is deficient;
in descriptions from Nature, for the reasons given, still more so.

[1] Bowles's Pope, x, 378.

He therefore pursued that path in poetry, which was more congenial to his powers, and in which he has shone without rival.[1]

3. WILLIAM ROSCOE'S POPE (1824)

The editor and the public

The third major edition of Pope's *Complete Works* to appear
during this period was brought out by William Roscoe in 1824.
The long-drawn-out controversy regarding the rank and merit
of Pope's verse, revived by Bowles's edition, was now nearing
its end; and Roscoe felt that a re-examination of the grounds
of the controversy was not required of him, as the severely
limiting criticisms of Bowles and Warton, of which he strongly
disapproved, had already been refuted by a host of controversialists.[2] Prominent among the supporters of Pope were
Byron and Campbell, in whose poetry, Roscoe believed, the
'true principles' of the Augustan age survived unbroken:

Accordingly the insults on departed genius have been felt by the
living, and the vindication of the fame of Pope has proceeded from
those quarters where it was most to be expected; from those who
have maintained, amidst the aberrations of public taste, the true
principles of poetic composition, and exemplified in their own im-
perishable productions the sentiments they have advanced.[3]

Despite the 'aberrations of public taste' which Roscoe felt had
affected the reading of Pope in recent times, he claimed that
Pope still remained the favourite of the reading public at large.
Though he was aware of the great changes that were taking

---

[1] Bowles's Pope, x, 372.

[2] 'The defence of the moral as well as the poetical character of Pope has also
been undertaken by several writers of distinguished ability, who have combated
the opinions and refuted the charges of Mr. Bowles, in a manner that must carry
conviction to every impartial mind. By such efforts the attacks upon the memory
of the great poet have been successfully repelled, and Pope yet stands before his
countrymen, not only as a proper object of literary inquiry and consideration, but
as intitled, by his moral and social endowments, to rank with the best and wisest
men that this country has produced.' (Roscoe's Pope, i, 'Preface', p. xix.)

[3] Roscoe's Pope, i, p. xviii.

place in the taste of contemporary readers, Roscoe could still say:

Whatever may be the homage we pay to others, there is no author whose works have been more universally read, or are more fully remembered . . . no poet, excepting Shakespear alone, whose works . . . are quoted on so many different occasions.[1]

As for the relative merits of Dryden and Pope, Roscoe shows a marked tendency to praise Pope at Dryden's expense,[2] thus reversing a tendency which may be traced back to the criticism of Cowper and Churchill and the controversy between Joseph Weston and Anna Seward in 1789.[3] The unhelpful criticism which too often resulted from this 'unnatural civil war between the Drydenists and the Popists', was deplored by Isaac D'Israeli in the *Quarterly Review*. Roscoe's views on this subject are of particular interest because, though his own predilections must be taken into account, he offers to give us some specific information about the relative popularity of Dryden and Pope among the average readers of his time:

On this subject the only decisive judge is the public, and it would not perhaps be too much to assert, that where one person reads Dryden, ten at least read Pope, and that where one line of Dryden is recited by memory, a hundred are repeated from the works of Pope.[4]

---

[1] Roscoe's Pope, II, p. iii.

[2] Roscoe felt that Scott had been unduly partial to Dryden in his edition, and while granting that 'the *Ode for Music* by Dryden excels that of Pope on the same subject', made his own preferences plain: 'What work of original genius has Dryden produced that can compare in fancy, in feeling, in strength, or in dignity with *The Rape of the Lock*, the *Epistle of Eloisa*, *The Dunciad*, or *The Essay on Man?*' (*Ibid.* II, p. xii.)

[3] See the *Gentleman's Magazine*, December 1788 (No. LVIII), for Weston's letter in which he described Pope as a 'jealous tyrant', and so set the controversy going. Anna Seward and two anonymous correspondents who signed themselves 'M. F.' and 'A. S.', defended Pope in a series of letters which appeared in the *Gentleman's Magazine* in April, May, June, August and September 1789.

[4] Roscoe's Pope, II, p. xii. Roscoe's information may be associated with Lockhart's estimate in his *Memoirs of the Life of Scott* of Dryden's popularity in the early nineteenth century. Scott's edition, he claimed, had failed 'to recall Dryden to his rightful station . . . in the general favour of the intelligent public'. For a criticism of Lockhart's view see Chapter I, § 1.

Though this may not provide us with a convincing means of judging the value of either poet, it does throw some interesting light on the reading habits of the age. That a revival of interest in Pope's poetry had occurred in the 1820s was suggested by the reviewer of Roscoe's edition of Pope in the *Quarterly* of October 1825, and a considerable amount of critical energy was devoted to defending Pope's poetry from what were felt to be the extravagances of hostile Romantic criticism. Some of the controversialists were perhaps a trifle carried away by their own enthusiasm: Isaac D'Israeli, for example, in a letter to Byron dated 19 July 1822, declared with every show of confidence: 'Pope has *regained* his due ascendancy.' It is undeniable that after the main tendencies of Romanticism had made themselves challengingly and powerfully felt, in the stock-taking criticism of the 1820s, there was a tendency among some critics to turn back to the Augustan poets in order to define more sharply their sense of the dangers which seemed inherent in the Romantic movement despite its undoubted successes. The greater critical objectivity which these critics sometimes derived from a reference to Augustan standards indicates why the Victorian tendency to dismiss the conservative criticism of the age *in toto* as merely the obstinate repetition of neo-classical shibboleths was unjustified. It is also true that the taste for Augustan poetry of the reading public at large, which remained true to some of its traditional loyalties long after the turn of the century, persisted in spite of the criticism by the Romantic poets. Despite this, the unchallenged supremacy which Pope and the Augustans had enjoyed in the 1790s was never regained.

Critical standards

Although Roscoe's admiration for Pope's poetry is manifest in his Preface and elsewhere, he believed both that the activities of the controversialists had rendered a systematic defence of Pope unnecessary, and that a critical interest in his author was outside the proper scope of an editor, and was an interest

from which Pope had suffered unduly.[1] Roscoe's primary
interest in Pope, therefore, was not critical, and he conceived
his chief duty as an editor to be—'to execute an office which
the author can no longer perform for himself, in the same manner as he would have performed it, if living'. Roscoe, in fact,
regarded his edition as being more than merely an answer to
those of Warton and Bowles. This spirit even prompted him to
include the notes of these two editors whenever he felt they
threw a genuine and unprejudiced light upon their subject.

Yet Roscoe's edition of Pope has some critical interest.
Surveying the critical biographies of Pope that had appeared
since his death, Roscoe briefly examined in his Preface the work
of William Ayres (1745), W. H. Dilworth (1759), Owen
Ruffhead (1769), Dr Johnson (1779), Joseph Warton (1797),
and Bowles (1806). Roscoe was plainly drawn to the criticism
of Johnson among these editors and biographers, though his
attitude towards him was not one of unmixed approval. He
found Johnson's *Life of Pope* 'brief yet decisive, superficial yet
sententious', and commented on the critical part of his Essay
'. . . amongst much unjust and illiberal censure, there are many
judicious and excellent remarks, expressed in the peculiar and
forcible style of the author'.

In an 'Estimate of the Poetical Character and Writings of
Pope' which he included at the beginning of the second
volume of his edition, Roscoe recapitulated the major critical
points made in Pope's defence by Byron, Campbell, D'Israeli,
and the other supporters of Pope. Perhaps the most interesting
and original of his critical notes to Pope's individual poems was
his spirited defence of *The Dunciad* against the well-known disparagement of Warton:

---

[1] Roscoe stated in his Preface: 'But there is one class of notes to which little indulgence has been extended, from whatever quarter they proceed. These are such
as pretend to point out the beauties and faults, accordingly as they appear to the
judgement of the critic. Swift has observed, that "it is the frequent error of these
men (i.e. editors) otherwise very commendable for their labours, to make excursions
beyond their talent and office, by pretending to point out the beauties and the
faults; which is no part of their trade".' (Preface, pp. xxvii–xxviii.)

In rapidity, vigour, and effect of style, *The Dunciad* stands unrivalled. In no other work can there be found such a number of ideas, so concisely and clearly expressed; yet with such infinite variety and brilliancy, that they resemble the coruscations of lightning, following each other in succession without a moment's interval.[1]

Also of interest in Roscoe's criticism was his insistence that the Augustan age was not merely a 'French inter-regnum' in English poetry, but rather the final and natural development of the native English genius. 'In the establishment of the English language,' Roscoe declared, 'Chaucer may be said to have laid the foundation stone of a building, which it was the good fortune of Pope to complete.'

[1] Roscoe's Pope, IV, Notes to *The Dunciad*, p. 10.

PART II
PERIODICAL LITERATURE

CHAPTER III

THE 'EDINBURGH REVIEW'

I. INTRODUCTION

The early nineteenth century was the great age of periodical criticism, and the influence which it wielded over public opinion has scarcely been equalled in any later period. The 'great reviews' of the time revived a periodical tradition which had been established in the early eighteenth century by Addison and Steele in the *Spectator* and the *Tatler*, and developed in the middle of the century in the pages of the *Rambler* and the *Idler* by Dr Johnson. Although the tradition had deteriorated to a certain extent towards the end of the eighteenth century, it was evident that the swiftly growing reading public was in need of guidance and direction, and the new generation of reviewers in the early nineteenth century, like their distinguished predecessors, addressed themselves to the task of disseminating enlightened standards of taste. They aimed not only at fostering and encouraging literary tendencies which they approved of and which seemed beneficial to society, but also at exposing, in terms of the *Edinburgh Review*'s vigilant motto—*Judex damnatur cum nocens absolvitur*—whatever appeared to them false and meretricious. In this aim they were the legitimate successors of Addison, Steele, and Johnson.[1] Although this tradition of periodical criticism had not been uninterrupted in the eighteenth century, the predominantly Augustan and metropolitan literary standards upheld by it had rooted themselves in society throughout England by the middle of the century. Courthope,

---

[1] Even Leigh Hunt, whose views were far from unreservedly pro-Augustan, attempted to model himself upon the periodical reviewers of the early eighteenth century in the *Examiner* which first appeared in 1808: 'I thought only of their wit and fine writing, which, in my youthful confidence, I proposed to myself to emulate.' (*Autobiography*, ed. J. E. Morpurgo, 1949, 'The "Examiner"', p. 173.) The *Edinburgh* and *Quarterly* reviewers attempted to emulate not only the style, but the serious social purpose of their predecessors.

discussing the reading public reached by John Hawkesworth's *Adventurer*, which took the place of the *Rambler*, noted about the *milieu* in which it flourished: 'The ideal of politeness upheld by Addison before the Clubs and Assemblies of London, had penetrated into the country, and was now recognised as a common standard of good-breeding in all parts of English society.'[1] It was therefore not only to upper-class London society, delighting in the cultivated conversation of the *salon* and the drawing-room, that the *Edinburgh* and *Quarterly* reviews addressed themselves. Though its standards were still comparatively homogeneous, the reading public had increased enormously since Addison's time. Scott claimed in 1808 that the *Edinburgh* had become indispensable to every genteel family, and 'genteel' here implied no patronising sneer but merely connoted the educated middle classes. Consulting the reviews had become a common social pastime, and we remember that the company at Sotherton Court in *Mansfield Park* (published in 1814) occupied the hours before dinner 'with sofas, chit-chat, and quarterly Reviews'.[2]

The nature of the critical function performed by the 'great reviews' in the earlier nineteenth century has been summed up by Coleridge in the *Biographia Literaria*. Coleridge himself was often severely criticised by the periodical critics of his time; nevertheless, his praise of their intelligence and powers of discrimination was admirably disinterested:

I most willingly admit, and estimate at a high value, the services which the *Edinburgh Review*, and others formed afterwards on the same plan, have rendered to society in the diffusion of knowledge. I think the commencement of the *Edinburgh Review* an important epoch in periodical criticism, and that it has a claim upon the gratitude of the literary republic, and indeed of the reading public at large, for having originated the scheme of reviewing those books

---

[1] W. J. Courthope, *A History of English Poetry* (1910), vi, Chapter V, 'Influence of the New Whigs', p. 88.

[2] It has often been noted that the tone of Jane Austen's reference to the 'Great Reviews' here is hardly flattering to their literary standards. But the real object of her irony in this instance was the dilettantism of some readers.

only, which are susceptible and deserving of argumentative criticism.[1]

Coleridge's attitude here to the periodical reviewers of his time is entirely just. Though he makes no claim for them as the final arbiters in matters of literary taste and judgement, he unequivocally recognises their essential function; that of drawing the attention of the reading public to whatever work in contemporary literature—even though unfavourably reviewed—was really significant to the life and thought of the age, 'supplying the vacant place of the trash or mediocrity, wisely left to sink into oblivion by its own weight, with original essays on the most interesting subjects of the time'.[2]

Coleridge's appraisal of the valuable services performed by the reviews was unusually disinterested in an age in which moral, literary, and political bias often affected criticism to an excessive degree. Yet, although the reviewers have often been criticised for their partisan loyalties, it is undeniable that the influence they wielded over contemporary opinion was immense. For this reason the criticism of Augustan poetry which appeared in the pages of the great reviews is of great importance in the study of attitudes to the work of Dryden, Pope, and Johnson in the early nineteenth century.

This influence may be appreciated quite simply in the size of the reading public the reviews commanded. The *Edinburgh Review* was launched in October 1802 with a modest circulation of 800 copies. The effect of the first number was later described by Lord Cockburn as 'electrical',[3] and circulation figures rose steeply soon afterwards. By 1814, we learn from a letter from Jeffrey to Moore,[4] 13,000 copies of the *Edinburgh* were being printed every quarter, and by 1818 the review had reached its peak circulation of 14,000. The *Quarterly Review*, which was founded in 1809, got off to a slightly less spectacular start, but

---

[1] *Biographia Literaria*, ed. Shawcross (1907), II, 86.
[2] *Ibid.* II, 86.
[3] Cockburn, *Life of Lord Jeffrey* (1852), I, 131.
[4] *Memoirs, Journal and Correspondence of Moore*, ed. Lord John Russell (1853), II, 40.

the steady widening of its power and influence may be followed in the correspondence of its publisher John Murray. On 12 September 1816 he informed Byron, 'My *Review* is improving in sale beyond my most sanguine expectations. I now sell nearly 9000. Even Perry says the *Edinburgh Review* is going to the devil.'[1] It is not possible to take Murray's comment on the *Edinburgh* here as anything other than wishful thinking, yet the spirit of rivalry and competition between these two reviews was stimulating and kept them both critically alert and vigilant. The circulation of the *Quarterly*, though still slightly behind that of the *Edinburgh*, kept increasing steadily, and Murray informed Byron on 22 January 1817, 'I now this time print 10,000 of my *Review*'.[2] This information is confirmed by other contemporaries. 'Murray,' Southey informed Bedford in 1817, '. . . now prints 10,000, and fifty times ten thousand read its contents, in the East and in the West.'[3] In 1818 the *Quarterly* finally drew level with the *Edinburgh*, and Murray wrote to James Hogg on 24 January 1818, '. . . the *Quarterly Review*—of which, by the way, the number printed is now equal to that of the *Edinburgh Review*, 12,000 . . . I hope to make 14,000 after two numbers'.[4] Élie Halévy, in the third volume of his *History of the English People in 1815*, attempting to assess the size of the public reached by the publishers of London and Edinburgh at the time, noted: 'The combined circulation of the *Edinburgh* and the *Quarterly* extended to 20,000 copies. These 20,000 purchasers, who represented perhaps 100,000 readers, constituted the *élite* of the British public.'[5] Halévy does not, however, take into account the circulation of *Blackwood's Edinburgh Magazine*, which first appeared in 1817 after the two major quarterlies had established themselves among the reading public. After a poor start, *Blackwood's*

---

[1] Samuel Smiles, *A Publisher and his Friends: Memoir and Correspondence of John Murray* (1891), I, 366.

[2] Smiles, *A Publisher and his Friends*, I, 372.

[3] *Ibid.* I, 204.

[4] *Ibid.* II, 4.

[5] Halévy, *A History of the English People in 1815*, tr. E. I. Watkin (1924), III, 'Religion and Culture', p. 134.

expanded rapidly, and John Wilson, who was among its ablest contributors, claimed that at the peak of its power it produced 17,000 copies per month. Indeed, surprising though it may seem today when conditions are so different, quarterly and monthly reviews often enjoyed a wider circulation than daily newspapers at that time. Part of the significance of the circulation figures of three principal periodicals of the time which have been quoted above becomes plain when we remember that the circulation of *The Times* did not exceed 8000 copies in 1816.[1]

The circulation figures of the principal reviews do not indicate the full extent of the reading public whose standards of taste were influenced by the work of the periodical critics. Each copy of a review often passed through the hands of several readers: it provided reading for the whole family, and was often left in the drawing room for the benefit of guests. Southey estimated in 1817 that the *Quarterly* was read by as many as 500,000 readers,[2] and Jeffrey claimed three years later in a letter to Moore that the *Edinburgh* reached an equal number of readers within a month of publication.[3] The full force of these claims can be judged in the light of contemporary estimates of the size of the *total* reading public in the early nineteenth century. Jeffrey, in a review of Crabbe's two-volume *Tales in Verse* which first appeared in November 1812, estimated that readers in the highest ranks of society numbered about 30,000, while the middle classes scattered throughout the country—'all those who are below the sphere of what is called fashionable or public life'—made up a reading public of about 200,000.[4]

The reviewers were not slow to realise the extent to which they could influence the taste and literary standards of the comparatively large proportion of readers who were regular subscribers. Jeffrey's letter to Moore, referred to above, also

[1] Lewis E. Gates, *Three Studies in Literature* (1899), p. 44.
[2] Smiles, *A Publisher and his Friends*, I, 204. This may well be an exaggeration.
[3] *Memoirs, Journal and Correspondence of Moore*, II, 40.
[4] *Edinburgh Review*, XX (1812), 280.

reveals the characteristic spirit in which the early nineteenth-century periodical critic devoted himself to the task of reviewing:

... though you will never understand what gratification this new vocation can give till you set about correcting some prevailing error, or laying down some original principle of taste or reasoning. It is something to think that at least fifty thousand people will read what you write in less than a month. We print now nearly 13,000 copies, and may reckon, I suppose, modestly on three or four readers of the popular articles in each copy: no prose preachers, I believe, have so large an audience.[1]

The tone of this letter plainly reveals the exhilaration with which the reviewers took upon themselves the role of *arbitri elegantiarum*. The strength of their position depended partly upon the fact that the reading public was still relatively homogeneous, so that they could shape and define its taste without appearing dictatorial. 'Almost all the world,' Thomas de Quincey declared, 'has surrendered their opinions and their literary consciences to the keeping of the *Quarterly Review*.' Thomas Carlyle, recalling the literary taste of the same period, said that Jeffrey was at the height of his reputation about 1816, and that the *Edinburgh Review* at that time was commonly regarded as 'a kind of Delphic Oracle, and Voice of the Inspired, for great majorities of what is called the "Intelligent Public"'.[2]

2. FRANCIS JEFFREY

One of the noteworthy features of this periodical criticism was the extent to which the personality of the editor helped to give the review under his charge what has been described as a 'lasting corporate personality': 'The system of anonymous reviewing in periodicals under the guidance and control of responsible editors, themselves men of strong individuality, soon led to the review acquiring a distinct personality of its own.'[3] This feature of the periodical literature of the age is

---

[1] *Memoirs, Journal and Correspondence of Moore*, II, 40.
[2] Carlyle, *Reminiscences*, ed. C. E. Norton (1887), II, 271.
[3] *The Cambridge History of English Literature*, XII, 141.

well illustrated by the work of Francis Jeffrey, the first editor of the *Edinburgh Review*, who was described by John Gibson Lockhart as 'the ablest and most influential critic of the time',[1] and by Lord Cockburn as 'the greatest of British critics'.[2] These claims may now seem the extravagant praise of friends, though there is plenty of evidence to establish that they fairly suggest Jeffrey's prestige in the earlier part of the century, and were more than mere biased personal evaluations. Indeed, the power and authority of Jeffrey's criticism is nowhere more clearly apparent than in the evidence of those whom he had antagonised by severe criticism.[3]

Jeffrey was indeed one of the most influential literary personalities of the time, and his editorship of the *Edinburgh* from 1803 to 1829 enabled him to control taste to a degree unmatched by most of his contemporaries. 'For twenty-five years,' according to Professor Gates, 'Jeffrey was able ... to rule almost arbitrarily a great mass of public opinion in morals, in politics, and in literary and artistic theory.'[4] It is for this

[1] Lockhart, *Life of Scott*, II, 26.

[2] Cockburn, *Life of Lord Jeffrey* (1852), I, 1.

[3] Wordsworth's evidence is particularly relevant here. In 1841 he complained that the difficulty with which readers had been persuaded to accept his poetry had been largely due to the 'tyranny exercised over public opinion by the *Edinburgh* and *Quarterly Reviews*'. (*Wordsworth's Prose Works*, ed. Grosart, III, 437.) Farington noted in his *Diary* that Wordsworth had confided to him that he had decided resolutely to ignore Jeffrey's criticism, as he could not endure to have it 'buz in his thoughts'. Earlier still, enraged by Jeffrey's disparagement in the *Edinburgh* of April 1808, Wordsworth wrote to Scott almost threatening Jeffrey with physical violence: 'If Mr. J. continues to play tricks of this kind, let him take care to arm his breach well, for assuredly he runs the desperate risque of having it soundly kicked.' For a fuller account of Wordsworth's reactions to Jeffrey's criticism, see Russell Noyes, *Wordsworth and Jeffrey* in *Controversy*, Indiana University Publications, Humanities Series, 5, 1941.

[4] '... he was a typically well-equipped and skilful middleman of ideas. He found an increasingly large Liberal or Whig public anxious to have its beliefs expressed plausibly, its feelings justified, and its taste made clear to itself and gently improved. The Whig "sheep looked up" and Jeffrey fed them. He did much the same work in general literary, social, and political theory that Macaulay did later in history. Macaulay's historical essays, also published in the *Edinburgh Review*, were, as Cotter Morison has pointed out, "great historical cartoons", specially adapted for the popularization of history, and specially suited to the knowledge and aspirations of an intelligent middle-class public. Jeffrey's essays in literature had much this same character and value.' (Lewis E. Gates, *Three Studies in Literature* 1899, pp. 11–12.)

reason that his periodical criticism is of special interest to a study of literary taste in the early nineteenth century.

The Augustan poets were a dominant influence upon Jeffrey while he was still a young man in the 1790s.[1] Pope, Swift, and Addison were then the unchallenged models in poetry and were given a place equal in importance to that of the Roman Augustans in the required reading of students. The standards set by the Augustans were generally accepted without question by the bulk of the educated classes. A familiar knowledge of Pope, Swift, and Addison was taken for granted in polite society, and the ability to grace one's conversation with an allusion to one of these poets was a fashionable accomplishment. 'Among those with whom I conversed,' Coleridge wrote of his own acquaintances in the 1790s, 'there were, of course, very many who had formed their taste, and their notions of poetry, from the writings of Pope and his followers.'[2]

It would be a mistake, however, to believe that Jeffrey's critical standards remained a simple reflection of these early influences. Important changes took place in his critical standards, for he was exposed to many currents of taste other than the Augustan. His later attitude towards Dryden, Pope, and Johnson was in consequence far from unqualified. A careful reading of the account given by Jeffrey in 1816—at the very height of his reputation—of the unchallenged supremacy of the Augustan poets during his youth suggests unmistakably that a change had taken place. Contrasting what had seemed to be the unshakeable reputations of the Augustans with the transitory interest aroused by newer additions to literature, Jeffrey observed:

New books, even when allowed to have merit, were never thought of as fit to be placed in the same class, but were generally read and forgotten, and passed away like the transitory meteors of a lower sky; while *they* remained in their brightness, and were supposed to shine with a fixed and unalterable glory.[3]

[1] Introduction, p. 1.
[2] Coleridge, *Biographia Literaria*, ed. J. Shawcross (1907), I, 11.
[3] *Edinburgh Review* (September 1816), p. 1.

The phrase 'were supposed to shine' indicates plainly enough that standards had undergone modification in the intervening years, and clinches some of the ironical overtones which may be observed earlier in the passage.

The nature of the change which had occurred in Jeffrey's standards may be found in the survey of English poetry, which he included in his review of Weber's edition of *John Ford* (*Edinburgh Review*, August 1811). Here it is apparent that Jeffrey had modified his youthful enthusiasm for Pope, Swift, and Addison, and it was instead the Elizabethan age, which now seemed to him 'by far the brightest in the history of English literature—or indeed of human intellect and capacity'. Jeffrey's view that 'In point of real force and originality of genius, neither the age of Pericles, nor the age of Augustus, nor the times of Leo X, nor of Louis XIV, can come at all into comparison'[1] with the Elizabethan age in England, was representative of the great revival of interest in that period which was a striking development in early nineteenth-century taste.

What effect had this new enthusiasm for the Elizabethans upon Jeffrey's estimate of the Augustans, whose supremacy a decade or two previously he had declared unchallenged? Certainly it did not lead him like Southey to denounce the Augustan period as 'the dark age of English poetry'.[2] Jeffrey permitted himself no such extravagance. His views may, however, be compared with those of another critic with pro-Augustan sympathies, Thomas Love Peacock. Peacock, in *The Four Ages of Poetry* (which first appeared in *Ollier's Literary Miscellany* in 1820), shared Jeffrey's view that the Elizabethans represented the supreme manifestations of the English genius in poetry. He described the Elizabethan as the 'golden age' of English poetry, a phrase which Jeffrey himself used.[3] Secondly, their evaluation of contemporary poetry had important features in common. One of Peacock's strongest charges against early

[1] 'Weber's Ford', *Edinburgh Review* (August 1811), pp. 275–6.
[2] Southey, *Specimens of the Later English Poets* (1807), p. xxix.
[3] See Jeffrey's review of Campbell's *Specimens of the British Poets*, *Edinburgh Review* (March 1819).

nineteenth-century poets was that their work was excessively literary and derivative: the march of their intellect as 'like that of a crab, backward', and, in vainly attempting to imitate the splendours of the age of gold, they had only produced an age of brass. Jeffrey too described the progress of Wordsworth, Coleridge, and Southey as crab-like, for they had endeavoured 'to advance beyond the preceding [Augustan] age simply by going back to one still older'. As a result they had succeeded too often in reviving only the more eccentric features of pre-Restoration poetry.[1] Finally, Peacock's account of the Augustan period as the 'silver age' of English poetry, sums up neatly the tempered admiration for the work of the Augustans which is characteristic of Jeffrey's mature criticism.

Jeffrey's approval of the Augustan poets, though not unqualified in his later criticism, always remained steady. Dryden he described as 'beyond all comparison, the greatest poet of his day . . . endued with a vigorous and discursive imagination, and possessing a mastery over language which no later writer has attained'. Yet Jeffrey had two strong criticisms of Restoration poetry: first, he objected to what he called its 'brutal obscenity', and secondly, he felt that the dominance of French influence (a charge made with increasing frequency in the early nineteenth century) had led to the neglect of the native English genius in poetry, best exemplified in the work of the Elizabethans.[2] French influence, Jeffrey claimed, had been largely responsible for the narrowing in the emotional range of poetry which he felt took place at this time. One effect upon Dryden's poetry of this limitation was that he could not find 'one line that is pathetic, and very few that can be considered sublime' in the entire corpus of Dryden's poetry. This criticism is parti-

[1] 'We allude now to the Wordsworths, and the Southeys, and Coleridges, and all that misguided fraternity, that, with good intentions and extraordinary talents, are labouring to bring back our poetry to the fantastical oddity and puling childishness of Withers, Quarles, or Marvel.' ('Crabbe's Poems', *Edinburgh Review* April 1808, p. 133.)

[2] 'But the Restoration brought in a French taste upon us, and what was called a classical and a polite taste; and the wings of our English Muses were clipped and trimmed.' ('Weber's Ford', *Edinburgh Review*, August 1811, p. 278.)

cularly interesting, for it suggests that Jeffrey was not un-influenced by the anti-Augustan critical tendencies of his age. We have already seen that it was the 'sublime' and 'pathetic' which were invoked by Joseph Warton and his followers in relegating Pope to an inferior order of poetry.

During the reign of Queen Anne, Jeffrey discerned a notable improvement of the tradition of poetry inaugurated during the Restoration. Of the post-Restoration poets he declared:

> They corrected its gross indecency—increased its precision and correctness—made its pleasantry and sarcasm more polished and elegant—and spread through the whole of its irony, its narration, and its reflection, a tone of clear and condensed good sense, which recommended itself to all who had and all who had not any relish for higher beauties. This is the praise of Queen Anne's wits—and to this praise they are justly entitled.[1]

The limitations of Addison as a poet were now apparent to Jeffrey ('the solemn mawkishness of Cato'), and he saw that his chief strength lay in the 'delicacy, the modest gaiety, and the ingenious purity of his prose style'. Though the 'higher beauties' of the Elizabethans were not much in evidence, there were many new and pleasing features in the work of the Augustans which were unknown to the Elizabethans:

> That tone of polite raillery—that airy, rapid, picturesque narrative, mixed up of wit and *naiveté*—that style, in short, of good conversation, concentrated into flowing and polished verses, was not within the vein of our native poets, and probably never would have been known among us, if we had been left to our own resources.[2]

Of all the poets of the Augustan age—the 'Queen Anne's wits' as Jeffrey preferred to call them—he reserved his highest praise for Pope, who, possessing 'all the delicacies and felicities and proprieties of diction', seemed to him 'much the best ... of the classical Continental school'. Despite his strongly pro-Augustan upbringing, his approval of Pope was not unqualified. The characteristically Regency qualities in Jeffrey's criticism

---

[1] 'Scott's Swift', *Edinburgh Review* (September 1816), p. 6.
[2] 'Weber's Ford', *Edinburgh Review* (August 1811), p. 281.

are very apparent in his summing-up of Pope's achievement as a poet:

Pope has incomparably more taste and spirit and animation (than Addison and his other contemporaries); but Pope is a satirist, and a moralist, and a wit, and a critic, and a fine writer, much more than he is a poet.[1]

The distinction which Jeffrey makes here between a 'satirist', a 'moralist', a 'wit', and a writer who is primarily a 'poet', indicates plainly that he was directly influenced by that movement in taste which may be traced back to Joseph Warton in the previous century, and which leads to Matthew Arnold's disparaging comment on the poetry of Dryden and Pope in mid-Victorian times: 'their poetry is conceived and composed in the wits, genuine poetry is conceived and composed in the soul'.[2]

Yet the view that Jeffrey in his later criticism completely renounced his early Augustan loyalties,[3] appears to be as untenable as the view that he never modified them. Even as late as 1820, in a review of Spence's *Anecdotes of Pope*, which had just been published for the first time, Jeffrey declared that 'whatever we may think of the greater light of a former age', 'there is scarcely any period in our literature of which we delight so much to dwell, or to which we so often seek to return, as the one to which these pages are devoted'.[4] It is true that he noted, with little outward sign of regret, that the 'wits of Queen Anne's time have been gradually brought down from the supremacy which they had enjoyed, without competition, for the best part of a century'.[5] But this was very far from

---

[1] *Ibid.* p. 281. Jeffrey's criticism of Pope in this passage was extremely influential in the earlier nineteenth century. It was repeated almost *verbatim* in an article entitled 'Lord Byron on Pope', which appeared in *Blackwood's Magazine*, in May 1821, and was also used (without acknowledgement on this occasion) in an article on 'The Augustan Age in England' which appeared in *The Album* in July 1822.

[2] Arnold, *Essays in Criticism*, Series 2, 'Thomas Gray', 1888.

[3] Greig, *Francis Jeffrey of the 'Edinburgh Review'* (Edinburgh, 1948).

[4] *Edinburgh Review* (May 1820), p. 306.

[5] *Edinburgh Review* (September 1816), p. 1.

implying that he had ceased to find anything of value in their work.

Since Jeffrey was the most influential periodical critic of the time, his criticism met both enthusiastic praise and severe disparagement. Representative of the hostile criticism directed against him by his contemporaries would be Southey's comment: '. . . of Judge Jeffrey of the *Edinburgh Review*, I must ever think and speak as of a bad politician, a worse moralist, and a critic, in matters of taste, equally incompetent and unjust'.[1] Southey's disparagement of Jeffrey really shows little more than the extent to which his own views differed from those of the Whig reviewers—'I have scarcely one opinion in common with it [the *Edinburgh*] upon any subject'; just as Macaulay's praise of Jeffrey—'Take him all in all, I think him more nearly an universal genius than any man of our time'—represents little more than the extent of their literary and political sympathy. Our principal concern is with the power and influence of Jeffrey's criticism, and here the evidence of the disinterested contemporary observer is of greater value. We have this perhaps in a letter of the youthful Mrs John Wilson, who, while describing the dinners and evening parties attended by cultivated Regency society in Edinburgh (which rivalled London as the intellectual capital of the country), noted that though personally she found Mr Jeffrey 'a horrid little man', nevertheless, his literary criticism was 'held in as high estimation here as the Bible'.[2]

The actual standards behind Jeffrey's criticism—an odd combination of sympathies and antipathies—are difficult to fit into any neat formula. The combination of qualities which his criticism exhibits, however, shows him to have been thoroughly representative of the transitional complexities which characterised his time. In other words, the puzzle which Saintsbury found in Jeffrey—the 'Neo-Classic inconsistency' in his work

[1] *Life and Correspondence of Robert Southey*, ed. C. C. Southey (1849–50), III, 125.

[2] Quoted in Mrs. Gordon's *Christopher North: A Memoir of John Wilson, compiled from Family Papers and Other Sources* (1879 edn), p. 123.

which made it difficult to discover the boundary line between the ancient and modern elements in his criticism[1]—was a representatively Regency problem. Dr Gordon Cox has found it a puzzling feature of the periodical criticism which appeared in the *Edinburgh Review* as a whole, in the years between 1802 and 1830.[2]

3. AUGUSTAN POETRY AND CONTEMPORARY VERSE

Fuller understanding of the cross-currents in Jeffrey's criticism may be arrived at by a study of the periodical criticism of the review as a whole in the first three decades of the nineteenth century. 'Baron von Lauerwinkel'[3] in *Blackwood's Magazine* of March 1818, noting the strongly adverse criticism of the work of the Romantic poets in the early numbers of the *Edinburgh Review*, also made the very interesting claim that important changes had taken place in the standards of the review itself:

For the first eight or ten years of the *Edinburgh Review*, the school of Pope was uniformly talked of as the true one, and the English poets of the present day were disapproved of, *because* they had departed from its precepts. A true poet has, however, a weapon in his hands, far more powerful than that which is wielded by any critic; and Mr Jeffrey, when he perceived the direction which the public taste was taking, at last found it necessary to become a violent admirer of the old dramatists, and a despiser of the poetry of Pope.[4]

Two principal questions are raised by 'Lauerwinkel' here which seem to be worth considering. First, to what extent did the Augustans provide a critical norm against which the work of the rising generation of poets was judged in the pages of the *Edinburgh*? And secondly, what effect did the newly revived

[1] Saintsbury, *History of Criticism* (Edinburgh, 1900–4), III, 290.

[2] 'Oddly enough, the *Edinburgh* shows 19th century standards to the Augustans, side by side with their opposites.' (R. G. Cox, *19th Century Periodical Criticism*, 1939 (unpublished Cambridge Ph.D. dissertation).)

[3] 'Baron von Lauerwinkel' was one of the many pseudonyms used by J. G. Lockhart, Scott's son-in-law and later editor of the *Quarterly Review*, in succession to Sir J. T. Coleridge.

[4] 'Remarks on the Periodical Criticism of England—in a Letter to a Friend', by Frederick, Baron von Lauerwinkel of Osmanstadt, *Blackwood's* (March 1818), pp. 676–7.

interest in the poetry of the 'old dramatists' really have upon attitudes towards the Augustans themselves in the Review?

As for the first question, 'Lauerwinkel's' claim that the Romantic poets were adversely criticised in the *Edinburgh* because they had departed from the 'precepts' of the school of Pope, is largely borne out by a study of the actual criticism which appeared in the first decade or so in the life of the Review. Jeffrey's lengthy criticism of Southey's *Thalaba, the Destroyer*, in the opening number of the *Edinburgh*, epitomises the Review's initial response to the new generation of Romantic poets. The Augustans, as Jeffrey himself wrote later, had been in the preceding decade 'placed without challenge at the head of our national literature', and the 'fixed and unalterable' standards set by these writers are reflected in the tone in which the *Edinburgh* approached the innovations of the new poets: 'Poetry has this much, at least, in common with religion, that its standards were fixed long ago by certain inspired writers, whose authority it is no longer lawful to call in question.'[1]

Southey is described as the 'champion and apostle' of a new 'sect of poets that has established itself in this country within these ten or twelve years', a group which had dared openly to proclaim themselves 'dissenters from the established systems in poetry and criticism'. It is interesting to see that, at this stage, Southey was regarded as the chief member of the group, and although Coleridge and Lamb were mentioned in this review as collaborators, Wordsworth—who was to provide the real dynamic impulsion to the movement—was as yet unrecognised. The anonymous author of the Preface to the *Lyrical Ballads*, however, was specially arraigned for his 'flagrant hostility' to established authority.

The new movement in poetry was traced back by the *Edinburgh* to a large variety of sources. The 'distempered sensibility' of Rousseau and the German Romanticism of Schiller and Kotzebue were regarded as the principal continental influences, and the movement was alleged to have derived its

---

[1] 'Southey's *Thalaba*', *Edinburgh Review* (October 1802), p. 63.

inspiration in English poetry from the 'homeliness' of Cowper's versification, the 'innocence' of Ambrose Philips (Pope's early rival as a writer of pastoral verse), and the 'quaint' eccentricities of Quarles and Dr Donne. All these influences were calculated to undermine the polish, discipline, and good sense of the Augustan tradition, and the new poets were considered not merely as harmless and bizarre eclectics in search of novelty, but, from their 'very considerable portion of poetical talent' (which the *Edinburgh* was quick to discern), as dangerous innovators: 'They constitute, at present, the most formidable conspiracy that has lately been formed against sound judgement in matters poetical.'[1] The extravagance and indiscipline encouraged by the new sect seemed to the *Edinburgh* to constitute a threat not only to existing standards in poetry, but to the foundations of English society itself: 'A splenetic and idle discontent with the existing institutions of society, seems to be at the bottom of all their serious and peculiar sentiments.'[2]

The 'false taste' of these new 'children of nature' showed itself, according to the *Edinburgh*, in a cult of self-conscious and artificial 'simplicity', a delight in 'low' subjects and debased language, and in an attempt to reach at the same time 'Longinian' sublimities; from the heights of which they were too prone to fall ingloriously.[3] Special attention was paid to the rejection of the ordered discipline of the Augustan heroic couplet. The influence of the careless versification of the new poets could only be harmful, for it must seduce the reader into undervaluing 'that vigilance and labour ... which gave energy and direction to the pointed and fine propriety of Pope'.

The influence of Cowper upon the work of the new poets was regarded as particularly harmful. Jeffrey found it possible to

---

[1] 'Southey's *Thalaba*', *Edinburgh Review* (October 1802), p. 64.

[2] *Ibid.* p. 71.

[3] In contrast to the Augustan poet who was always firmly grounded in the realities of everyday life, the poise of the new poets was found to be precarious: 'A poet who aims at all at sublimity and pathos, is like an actor in a high tragic character, and must sustain his dignity throughout, or become altogether ridiculous.' Dealing with 'low' subjects, the danger of a lapse into bathos was greatly increased, and this was regarded as a major weakness of the Romantics.

praise the 'ease' and 'lightness' of Cowper's prose style, which he found pleasingly reminiscent of the style of Addison and Pope. Nevertheless, Cowper's antipathy towards Pope's versification was well known. Though aware of the deftness and sophistication of Pope's use of the heroic couplet, Cowper observed:

> But he (his musical finesse was such,
> So nice his ear, so delicate his touch)
> Made poetry a mere mechanic art,
> And every warbler had his tune by heart.[1]

These lines anticipate the even more sweeping criticism and rejection of Pope in Keats's *Sleep and Poetry*. It seems necessary to insist that Cowper's criticism would have been more justly directed against Pope's imitators than against Pope himself. The *Edinburgh* itself was intelligent enough to make the distinction. In a review of Erasmus Darwin's *The Temple of Nature* a telling contrast was made between the work of Pope and that of his imitators, and Darwin's own use of the Augustan couplet was shown to have lost much of the subtlety and delicacy of Pope, and to be notable for a 'certain hardness and coldness of execution'.[2] The same reviewer, Thomas Thomson, in a review of Anna Seward's *Memoirs of Dr Darwin*, which appeared in the *Edinburgh* in the following year, developed his criticism of Darwin's versification, 'placing' his *Universal Beauty* as 'an unsuccessful attempt to imitate the fashionable antithetic manner of Pope'. Thomson noted that Darwin's style seemed closer to that of Sir Richard Blackmore[3] than to the style of Pope, and concluded:

Whether or not the poetry of Darwin would, in the age of Pope, have incurred the same hazard of neglect with that of the writer whom we have ventured to exhibit as his prototype, we shall not presume to conjecture.[4]

[1] Cowper, *Table Talk*, lines 652–5.
[2] 'Darwin's *Temple of Nature*', *Edinburgh Review* (July 1803), p. 503.
[3] Blackmore, who died in 1729, was best-known for two tediously long epics, *Prince Arthur* (1695) and *Alfred* (1723), and for his long philosophical poem in Seven Books, *Creation* (1712).
[4] 'Miss Seward's *Memoirs of Darwin*', *Edinburgh Review* (April 1804), p. 241.

Since Cowper was regarded by the *Edinburgh* as a major influence upon the reaction against the 'pointed and fine propriety of Pope', it is specially interesting to examine Jeffrey's review of Hayley's *Life of Cowper* in the *Edinburgh* of April 1803. Not all Jeffrey's criticism of Cowper was adverse. He praised Cowper's originality, which had enabled him to carry 'the dominion of poetry into regions that had been considered as inaccessible to her dominion'; though he also noted at the same time 'that the presumption that belongs to most innovators, has betrayed him into many defects'.[1] Prominent among these shortcomings was the adverse effect of Cowper's attitude to versification.

It is not often noted that Cowper's dissatisfaction with Pope's versification was the reverse side of his admiration for Dryden. Cowper's interest in Dryden was typical of the spirit of the 'Dryden-revival' of the later eighteenth century, which Scott described in the first volume of his edition of Dryden's *Works*. The bounding vigour, the spontaneous, negligent ease of Dryden's versification proved more congenial to the quickening Romantic impulses of the time than the more deliberate and complicated richness of Pope's art. It was at this time that there was inaugurated the prolonged and still continuing 'civil war ... between the Drydenists and the Popists', which Isaac D'Israeli referred to with regret in the *Quarterly Review* of 1820.[2]

[1] 'Hayley's *Life of Cowper*', *Edinburgh Review* (April 1803), p. 81.

[2] 'Spence's *Anecdotes of Pope*', *Quarterly Review* (July 1820), p. 408 n. As Scott noted in his edition of Dryden, Churchill was among those who praised Dryden at Pope's expense. The controversy concerning the relative merits of Dryden and Pope was taken up by Anna Seward and Joseph Weston in the *Gentleman's Magazine* (December 1788–September 1789). The ease with which praise of Dryden, often even unconsciously, implies dispraise of Pope, has been shown even in our own time in Dr F. R. Leavis's point that Mr T. S. Eliot's admirable critical reassessment of Dryden in his *Homage to John Dryden* (1924), was achieved only at the cost of incidental unfairness to Pope. (*Revaluation*, 1936, p. 68.) The dispute over the rival merits of Pope and Dryden was a well-known topic of conversation as early as the 1780s. Hannah More wrote to her sister in 1784: 'On Monday I dined at Lady Middleton's, and in the evening went to Mrs. Ord's, where there was everything delectable in the blue way. Mr. Walpole and I fought over the old ground, Pope against Dryden, and Mrs. Montagu backed him, but I would not give up.' (*The Letters of Hannah Moore*, ed. R. Brimley Johnson, 1925, p. 93.)

Cowper's dissatisfaction with Pope's versification was not extreme, however, and unlike Arnold—nearly a century later— he did not refuse to credit Pope with the title of poet:

I could never agree with those who preferred him [Pope] to Dryden; nor with others (I have known such, and persons of taste and discernment too) who could not allow him to be a poet at all. He was certainly a mechanical maker of verses, and in every line he ever wrote, we see indubitable marks of the most indefatigable industry and labour. Writers, who find it necessary to make such strenuous and painful exertions, are generally as phlegmatic as they are correct; but Pope was, in this respect, exempted from the common lot of authors of that class. With the unwearied application of a plodding Flemish painter, who draws a shrimp with the most minute exactness, he had all the genius of one of the first masters. Never, I believe, were such talents and such drudgery united. But I admire Dryden most, who has succeeded by mere dint of genius, and in spite of a laziness and carelessness almost peculiar to himself. His faults are numberless, and so are his beauties. His faults are those of a great man, and his beauties are such (at least sometimes) as Pope, with all his touching and retouching, could never equal.[1]

Jeffrey, reviewing Hayley's *Life of Cowper* in April 1803, wisely refused to be drawn into the controversy concerning the relative merits of Dryden and Pope. But he expressed forcibly his sense of the danger inherent in Cowper's influence upon anti-Augustan tendencies in his own time. Commenting upon the sentence in which Cowper summed up his attitude—'Give me a manly rough line, with a deal of meaning in it, rather than a whole poem full of musical periods, that have nothing but their smoothness to recommend them'—Jeffrey observed tartly: 'It is obvious, however, that this is not a defence of harsh versification, but a confession of inability to write smoothly.'[2] With Pope's achievement plainly in mind Jeffrey inquired, 'Why should not harmony and meaning go together?' The 'inexcusably negligent' versification of Southey and the new group of poets associated with him, Jeffrey believed, was partly

---

[1] Cowper, Letter to the Reverend William Unwin, 5 January 1782. *Life and Works of Cowper* (1835 edn), ed. Hayley, II, 11–12.

[2] 'Hayley's *Life of Cowper*', *Edinburgh Review* (April 1803), pp. 83–4.

the result of Cowper's rejection of the discipline, polish, and harmony of Pope's style.

The rising generation of Romantic poets underwent no change of heart as a result of the criticism of the *Edinburgh*. Reviewing Southey's *Madoc* in the *Edinburgh* of October 1805, Jeffrey wrote that his 'unlucky facility' in rhyming was among his chief weaknesses, and advised him to 'write in the measure of Dryden and Pope', for then he would be 'sooner struck with his own exuberance and prolixity'. As to the relative merits of the Augustan and the new school of poets, Jeffrey's views were unambiguous:

If we must renounce our faith in the old oracles of poetical wisdom, before we can be initiated into the inspiration of her new apostles— if we must abjure all our classical prejudices, and cease to admire Virgil, and Pope, and Racine, before we can relish the beauties of Mr. Southey, it is easy to perceive that Mr. Southey's beauties are in some hazard of being neglected, and that it would have been wiser in him to have allied himself to a party so respectably established, than to have set himself up in opposition to it.[1]

The *Edinburgh*'s preference for the poetry of the school of Pope over that of the new poets was reaffirmed in Thomas Campbell's review of Bowles's edition of Pope's *Works* in January 1808. The theme of this review was the vindication of the poetry of Pope and the Augustans from the strictures of the new criticism. Bowles's anti-Augustan tendencies have already been discussed in an earlier chapter; but it is necessary to note here that he provided a link between the pre-Romantics in the eighteenth century and Wordsworth, Coleridge, and Southey

---

[1] 'Southey's *Madoc*', *Edinburgh Review* (October 1805), p. 2. At this time the *Edinburgh* believed that the only reasonable future for not only Southey but Wordsworth too, lay in abandoning their 'revolutionary' theories and realigning themselves with the Augustan tradition. Referring to Wordsworth's innovations in the *Lyrical Ballads*, the *Edinburgh* of October 1807 declared: 'We venture to hope that there is now an end of this folly . . . that the lamentable consequences which have resulted from Mr Wordsworth's open violation of the established laws of poetry, will operate as a wholesome warning to those who might otherwise be seduced by his example, and be the means of restoring to that ancient and venerable code its due honour and authority.'

in the early nineteenth century.[1] His influence was regarded by Campbell in his review as both misguided and harmful.

Yet, in this judgment upon the merits of Pope, we conceive Mr Bowles to have failed, and the cause of his failure to be derived from principles of criticism by no means peculiar to himself, but which have obtained too great an influence over the public taste of our age.[2]

Nevertheless, although Pope was being seriously attacked by the vanguard of the Romantic critics, Campbell believed that the reputation of the Augustan poets remained comparatively high in the eyes of the majority of contemporary readers. 'The three writers, of our own country at least,' he observed at the very beginning of his review, 'who seem to bask in the fullest sunshine of reputation, are Pope, Swift, and Johnson.'[3] Noting that Bowles, unlike Pope's previous editors (including Warton), 'almost always evinces an adverse prepossession', Campbell proceeded on behalf of the *Edinburgh* to

vindicate what we deem the cause of poets and poetry, from a narrow and exclusive system. We will not permit the bards of former days to be thus arraigned before a jury of tourists and draughtsmen, for the want of excellences of which their own contemporaries had never dreamed.[4]

The most interesting feature about Campbell's defence of Pope in this review, however, is that the qualities which he himself found most attractive in Pope were far from being purely 'Augustan'. This is apparent in the central passage in the review, in which, through a series of questions and answers, an attempt is made not only to refute Bowles, but to discover whether any of the essentially 'poetical' qualities are wanting in Pope:

Does he [Pope] speak so little to the imagination and the heart? Does he borrow his delineations from manners only, and not from nature? Mr Bowles excepts, indeed, from his position, the *Epistle*

---

[1] For a fuller account of Bowles's influence upon Wordsworth, Coleridge, and Southey, see Chapter VI.
[2] 'Bowles's Pope', *Edinburgh Review* (January 1808), p. 407.
[3] *Ibid.* p. 399.
[4] *Ibid.* p. 412.

of Eloisa, on which he bestows no more praise than is just, when he says, that 'nothing of the kind has ever been produced equal to it for pathos, painting and melody'. But are there no other parts of his works, in which Pope has reached a high tone of real poetry, according to the strictest notion of the term? Is poetry found in the moral sublime, in the excitement of high and dignified emotion, through the medium of harmonious and forcible numbers? The *Epistle to Lord Oxford* displays this reach of noble sentiment, more uniformly, though not, perhaps, more conspicuously, than some other passages of his moral writings. Is the sprightliness of a versatile fancy, the play of varied imagery, a distinguishing characteristic of the poet? Where is this more striking, than in *The Rape of the Lock*,—and, indeed, in many parts of *The Dunciad*? Is the fervour of passion, the power of exciting and expressing emotion, the soul of poetry? We have already pointed to it in the *Eloisa*. What then is it that we want? and for what reason does Mr Bowles, like the vain herd of modern versifiers, carp at the poetical merits of Pope?[1]

The absence of any mention of Pope's range and variety as a satirist, and the greater interest in Pope's 'noble reach of sentiment' and his 'fervour of passion', indicate some of the predilections which were typical of some critics at least in the early nineteenth century, who were broadly in sympathy with the poetry of the Augustans. Although Campbell, like most other reviewers in the *Edinburgh*, was unambiguous in his preference for the poetry of the Augustans over that of the rising generation of Romantic innovators, his attitude to the poetry of Pope was not one of uncritical enthusiasm. While insisting that it was inconceivable that 'any critic of taste could refuse the name of poet to one so highly gifted by nature, and so improved by skill', Campbell wished to make it plain that eulogy should not be substituted for criticism:

But lest, in defending the poetical character of Pope against false principles of criticism, we should inadvertently have appeared to raise it too high, let it be understood, that we do not believe him possessed of that diviner spirit, that energy and enthusiasm, which are required for the epic, the tragic, or the lyric muse.[2]

[1] 'Bowles's Pope', *Edinburgh Review* (January 1808), p. 409.
[2] *Ibid.*, p. 412.

Although, as 'Baron von Lauerwinkel' claimed in *Blackwood's Magazine*, the Augustans provided a critical norm against which the Romantics were judged and found wanting in the pages of the *Edinburgh*, towards the end of the first decade in the life of the Review signs were beginning to appear that the position of unchallenged supremacy which Jeffrey claimed they had enjoyed universally in the 1790s, was now beginning to be questioned.

4. AUGUSTAN POETRY AND PRE-RESTORATION VERSE

'Baron von Lauerwinkel', analysing the change in the attitude of the *Edinburgh* towards Augustan poetry which he believed took place about 1810, claimed that the Review when it 'perceived the direction which the public taste was taking, at last found it necessary to become a violent admirer of the old dramatists and a despiser of the poetry of Pope'.[1] It would be interesting to discover how far 'Lauerwinkel's' claims were justified by a study of the actual criticism which appeared in the *Edinburgh* during this period.

His initial claim that the *Edinburgh* merely followed the lead taken by the reading public appears to be little more than a piece of journalistic extravagance. Although the bulk of the reading public, which was still comparatively homogeneous, shared the same tastes as the reviewers, Jeffrey has himself informed us of the delight with which he addressed himself to the task of controlling and influencing public opinion. The view that the periodical critics of the *Edinburgh* guided and defined the taste of readers, rather than merely reflected it, is supported by the evidence of contemporary observers, including De Quincey and Carlyle.

Secondly, it also appears that 'Lauerwinkel's' claim that an abrupt reversal took place in the *Edinburgh*'s attitude to-

---

[1] 'Remarks on the Periodical Criticism of England', *Blackwood's* (March 1818), p. 676. Lockhart's primary intention in this article was to discredit the *Edinburgh* and the *Quarterly*—whose editors he described derisively as the 'Neri and Bianchi of criticism'—and to indicate the need for a third review, the newly-founded *Blackwood's Magazine*.

wards the Augustans, and that it subsequently 'despised' what it had hitherto admired, was both extravagant and over-simple. Nevertheless, perhaps the most important feature about 'Lauerwinkel's' criticism was that he recognised that the change which did take place in the standards of the *Edinburgh* was due not to a revaluation of the work of the new generation of Romantic poets, but to a revival of interest in pre-Restoration poetry.

A dissatisfaction with the urbanity, polish and refinement of the Augustans was occasionally implied in the criticism which appeared even in the early numbers of the *Edinburgh*. Referring to the poetry of ages which the Augustans had almost taken for granted were 'uncivilised' and 'barbarous', Morehead said in a review of Cary's translation of Dante's *Divine Comedy*:

The rude poetry of early ages possesses some high excellences which can never be attained to an equal degree in the more polished state of the art. That energy and simplicity, which are then its character-istics, are apt to be weakened and effaced, as men advance in the re-finements of society, and in the arts of composition.[1]

It was through the contrast with the merits of Elizabethan and Jacobean poetry—rather than with the poetry of mediaeval times—that it became increasingly common to admit in the pages of the *Edinburgh* that the achievement of the Augustans had its limitations.

One of the principal criticisms directed against the Augustans —the aim of which was to revalue their *status* rather than to reject or disparage their work—was that they had failed to transcend the limitations of the narrow and fashionable society which had provided them with the subject-matter of their poetry. It was felt that their preoccupation with their parti-cular social *milieu* had robbed their work of wider human appeal and deeper human understanding. It was by the con-trasting of Pope not with Wordsworth but with Shakespeare, Spenser and Milton, that his limitations were defined. In a

[1] 'The Divina Commedia of Dante Alighieri', *Edinburgh Review* (January 1803), p. 307.

review of Percival Stockdale's *Lectures on the Truly Eminent English Poets* in April 1808, Campbell observed:

In the knowledge and description of refined life, Pope is the mirror of his times. He saw through human character as it rose in the living manners of his age, with the eye of a judge and a satirist; and he must be fond of exceptions, who should say that such a satirist did not understand human nature. Yet, when we use the trite phrase of Shakespeare understanding human nature, we mean something greatly more extensive than when we apply the same praise to Pope. From the writings of the former, we learn the secrets of the human heart . . . independent of the form and pressure of the times. From Pope we learn its foibles and peculiarities in the 18th century. . . . Amidst all his wit, it has been the feeling of many in reading him, that we miss the venerable simplicity of the poet, in the smartness of the gentleman.[1]

Although Shakespeare's unique greatness had been generally recognised, of course, throughout the Augustan age, the Elizabethan age as a whole was now becoming increasingly preferred to the Augustan in its imaginative and emotional range, and in the depth and profundity of its vision of life. Campbell lavished high praise upon Pope's *The Rape of the Lock*—'There is no finer gem than this poem in all the lighter treasures of the English fancy'—and described it as 'an epic poem in . . . delightful miniature'. Nevertheless its 'fairy brightness' was seen in its charmingly 'Lilliputian' scale when compared with those 'heroic creations of fancy, the agents of Spenser's and Milton's machinery'. Campbell contrasted the 'correctness' of Pope with the 'daring luxuriance of fancy' of Spenser and Shakespeare (itself an indication of the Romantic spirit in which the Elizabethans were now being revived). This growing delight in the exuberance and vitality of the Elizabethans even affected the *Edinburgh*'s attitude to Augustan versification, which in the early years of the review had been consistently praised for its 'pointed and fine propriety', and which the Romantic poets had been exhorted to take as an example.

---

[1] 'Stockdale's *Lectures on the Truly Eminent English Poets*', *Edinburgh Review* (April 1808), p. 78.

Doubt had now replaced the confidence of these recommenda-
tions:

Without entering into an inquiry whether his practice of invariably
closing up . . . the couplet is right or wrong, it is clear that Pope has
made the melody of his general measure as perfect as it can be made
by exactness: whether a slight return to negligence, might not be
preferable to the very acme of smoothness which he has chosen, is a
subject which, interesting as it is, we will not now encroach on the
reader's patience by examining.[1]

The 'slight return to negligence' which is hesitantly referred to
here glances back not only at Cowper's more sweeping disparagement of Pope's versification, but forward to Leigh
Hunt's attempt in *The Story of Rimini* to overthrow the metrical
dictatorship of Pope, and to attempt to introduce a 'freer
modulation' in the heroic couplet, a practice in which he
claimed he was followed by 'all the reigning poets, without
exception'.[2]

The comparative superiority of the Elizabethan and Jacobean ages to the age of the Augustans was decisively accepted
by the *Edinburgh* in Jeffrey's review of the dramatic works of
John Ford in August 1811. Jeffrey's enthusiasm for pre-
Restoration literature led him to read the work of even minor
writers of the seventeenth century with a sense of delighted
discovery. Of Jeremy Taylor's prose folios he observed enthusiastically that they contained more 'of the body and the
soul of poetry, than all the odes and epics which have since
been produced in Europe'. It was the Elizabethan age, however—'by far the brightest in the history of English literature'—
which moved him most often to eloquent praise.

After about 1810 it was generally true that in the judgement
of the *Edinburgh*, the Augustans were decisively overshadowed
by the Elizabethans. Nevertheless, they were far from being
'despised' as Baron von Lauerwinkel claimed. Jeffrey, it will
be remembered, continued to use Crabbe—whose work maintained 'the good old taste of Pope and Dryden'—in order to

---

[1] 'Stockdale's *Lectures*', *Edinburgh Review* (April 1808), p. 78.
[2] Leigh Hunt, 'Free Again', *Autobiography*, ed. J. E. Morpurgo, p. 258.

enforce by contrast Wordsworth's eccentricity. More important, the growth of literary history was now making it increasingly possible for the achievement of the Augustans to be placed in a proper historical perspective. The most comprehensive attempt at accomplishing this may be found, not surprisingly, in the work of the great historian who wrote for the *Edinburgh*, Thomas Babington Macaulay.

In his review of *The Poetical Works of Dryden* in the *Edinburgh* of January 1828, Macaulay included a survey of the history of English literature, interpreted in terms of the conflict and re-concilement of the forces of the creative imagination and the critical intelligence, a process which he believed was found in the history of every literature.[1] Like Peacock, with whose historical notions in this matter he had a great deal in common, Macaulay discerned four principal phases in the development of literature. First, the earliest age of poetry, in which the imagination is unchecked by the intelligence and 'overpowers all the passions of the mind'. Next, the finest age of all—'a short period of splendid and consummate excellence' in which the two forces are reconciled. Thirdly, an age in which the critical intelligence becomes ascendant, and dominates the imagination. And finally, a fourth age which sets out to revive the glories of the second, but which only achieves a pale shadow of its grandeur. Describing the four principal phases of English literature in terms of a seasonal rhythm, Macaulay described the early spring of Chaucer's time giving place to the high summer of the Elizabethans, which in turn was followed by the autumn of the Queen Anne wits, which was finally replaced by what he described, not very flatteringly, as the 'Saint Martin's summer' of his own day.[2]

---

[1] 'The history of every literature with which we are acquainted confirms, we think, the principles we have laid down. In Greece we see the imaginative school of literature gradually fading into the critical. Aeschylus and Pindar were succeeded by Sophocles, Sophocles by Euripides, Euripides by the Alexandrian versifiers. Of these last, Theocritus alone has left compositions which deserve to be read.' ('Dryden's *Works*', *Edinburgh Review*, January 1828, p. 13.)

[2] Macaulay's account of the relationship which was felt to exist between Eliza-bethan and early nineteenth-century poetry may be compared with those of

Macaulay credited Dryden with the founding of the 'critical school' of English poetry. The adjective 'critical' summed up for Macaulay not only the limitations, but the distinctive merits, of the Augustan poets. The peculiar excellencies of this school Macaulay defined as the 'temperate splendours of maturity'—'propriety', 'grace', and 'dignified good sense'. These virtues fell far short, of course, of the 'splendid and consummate excellence' of the Elizabethans; nevertheless, in his insistence that the operation of the critical intelligence was one of the essential conditions of great poetry, Macaulay anticipated some of the central ideas in Arnold's criticism, especially evident in his criticism of the Romantic poets.[1] A balance of critical and creative tendencies produced the *greatest* poetry; yet Macaulay's appreciation of the restrained critical poise of Dryden's verse suggests the extent to which he had inherited the typically eighteenth-century respect for self-discipline, and dislike of emotionalism: 'There are, moreover, occasional touches of tenderness' he observed about Dryden's poetry,

---

Jeffrey and Peacock: 'Pleasing and ingenious imitations . . . of the great masters begin to appear. Poetry has a partial revival, a Saint Martin's Summer, which, after a period of dreariness and decay, agreeably reminds us of the splendour of its June. A second harvest is gathered in, though, growing on a spent soil, it has not the heart of the former. . . . We look on the beauties of the modern imitations with feelings similar to those with which we see flowers disposed in vases, to ornament the drawing-rooms of a capital. We doubtless regard them with pleasure, with greater pleasure, perhaps, because, in the midst of a place ungenial to them, they remind us of the distant spots on which they flourish in spontaneous exuberance. But we miss the sap, the freshness, and the bloom.' ('Dryden's *Works*', *Edinburgh Review*, January 1828, p. 13.)

[1] Though Arnold did not, like Macaulay, praise the critical intelligence as a typically Augustan virtue, it was the virtual disappearance of the critical intelligence in early nineteenth-century poetry which lay at the root of his ultimate disappointment with the Romantics: '. . . life and the world being, in modern times, very complex things, the creation of a modern poet, to be worth much, implies a great critical effort behind it; else it must be a comparatively poor, barren, and short-lived affair. This is why Byron's poetry had so little endurance in it, and Goethe's so much. . . . In other words, the English poetry of the first quarter of this century, with plenty of energy, plenty of creative force, did not know enough. This makes Byron so empty of matter, Shelley, so incoherent, Wordsworth even, profound as he is, yet so wanting in completeness and variety.' (*Essays in Criticism*, Series I, 'The Function of Criticism at the Present Time', 1865, pp. 6–7.)

'which affects us more, because it is decent, rational, and manly.'

Though he was prepared to admit that there were strange and even contradictory elements in Dryden ('most of his writings exhibit the sluttish magnificence of a Russian noble, all vermin and diamonds, dirty linen and inestimable sables'), yet it was this very variety which led Macaulay to prefer Dryden to Pope. It was associated with a warmth of feeling which he found lacking in Pope. Against Pope's moral character Macaulay, like Bowles, had an inflexible prejudice, and in his *Life of Addison* he darkened Pope's motives consistently, describing him in his personal relationships as 'all stiletto and mask'. Macaulay's views here were scarcely representative of the *Edinburgh* as a whole, for Pope was often praised in its pages for the refinement of his moral sensibility.[1]

Criticism of the 'unpoetical' nature of the subject-matter of the 'critical' school was becoming increasingly common among the more Romantic critics of the early nineteenth century, but, as in the case of Scott, the apparent intractability of Dryden's subject-matter only enhanced Macaulay's respect for the transmuting power of his genius:

The advantages which Dryden derived from the nature of his subject he improved to the very utmost. His manner is almost perfect. The style of Horace and Boileau is fit only for light subjects. ... The glitter of Pope is cold. The ardour of Persius is without brilliancy. Magnificent versification and ingenious combinations rarely harmonize with the expression of deep feeling. In Juvenal and Dryden alone we have the sparkle and the heat together. Those great satirists succeeded in communicating the fervour of their feelings to materials the most incombustible, and kindled the whole mass into a blaze, at once dazzling and destructive.[2]

Macaulay's praise of Dryden here looks forward to the extraordinary 'incandescent' force which Gerard Manley Hopkins,

---

[1] Some critics found it possible to praise the moral refinement of Pope's poetry, and, at the same time, to censure what they felt was his want of moral principle in his personal relationships.

[2] 'Dryden's *Works*', *Edinburgh Review* (January 1828), pp. 34–5.

later in the century, singled out as distinctive in Dryden's treatment of his material.[1]

At the very beginning of his review of Dryden's *Poetical Works* Macaulay wrote that 'the public voice had assigned to Dryden the first place in the second rank of our poets', and by the end of the review it is plain that Macaulay concurred with the verdict of the common reader. A preference for Dryden over Pope or vice versa was often a matter of personal predilection, yet it was now generally true of the standards of the *Edinburgh* that the Augustans, though considered admirable within their own sphere, were regarded as having been decisively surpassed by the greater imaginative range and depth of the Elizabethan poets.

[1] One of the principal qualities which Hopkins admired in Dryden may be found in the following passage: '. . . that is what one feels above all things besides in Dryden, who seems to take thoughts that are not by nature poetical—stubborn and opaque, but under a kind of living force like fire they are powerfully changed and incandescent.' (*The Note-Books and Papers of Gerard Manley Hopkins*, ed. Humphry House, 1937, p. 88.)

CHAPTER IV

THE 'QUARTERLY REVIEW'

I. WILLIAM GIFFORD

William Gifford, editor of the *Quarterly Review* from the time of its inception in February 1809 until 1824, combined in his formidable personality some of the characteristic virtues and limitations commonly associated with early nineteenth-century periodical criticism. Gifford's greatest asset, a fiercely uncompromising critical integrity, was liable to deteriorate into stubborn obscurantism or insensitiveness. In his political beliefs, as in his literary leanings, he was a redoubtable conservative, and, before he accepted the editorship of the *Quarterly* —founded primarily as a Tory answer to the predominantly Whig *Edinburgh*—Gifford had already edited, during its short term of life in the 1790s, the aggressively reactionary *Anti-Jacobin*. Gifford's literary standards at this time, which were readily incorporated with his political beliefs, are apparent in the two poems which he published during the same decade: *The Baviad* (1791)[1] and *The Maeviad* (1795). Both these satires, though more remarkable for their destructive gusto than for the polish or poise of Augustan wit, were written in frank imitation of Pope's style. Among his more enthusiastic friends, indeed, Gifford was regarded as a minor Pope of his day; Thomas Mathias remarked after reading *The Baviad*:

> Or pleased with flowers his fancy best can strew,
> I sit, and think I read my Pope anew.

[1] *The Baviad* contains a vitriolic passage denouncing Joseph Weston, a late eighteenth-century versifier and critic, for his disparagement of Pope's claims to greatness in a controversy with Anna Seward. Gifford's main satirical target in the poem, however, was the 'Italianate' verse of the now-forgotten 'Della Cruscan' poets. A leading figure in this group, Robert Merry (1755–98), was a member of the Florentine Academy. For an account of Gifford's condemnation of this school, see J. Longaker, *The Della Cruscans and William Gifford* (1924).

Gifford impressed the stamp of his personality upon the *Quarterly* as decisively as Jeffrey had imposed his upon the *Edinburgh*; yet, while Jeffrey's influence was based on the firm persuasiveness of his critical leadership, Gifford's power was confined largely to the positive—and sometimes dictatorial—exercise of his strictly editorial powers. For Gifford, unlike Jeffrey, was not a ready or prolific literary critic, and he is better remembered today as an editor of Ben Jonson, Massinger and Ford[1] and as a translator of Juvenal and Persius, than as a critic. The total number of literary reviews which Gifford contributed to the *Quarterly* was indeed surprisingly small.[2] His chief control over the critical standards of the *Quarterly* lay in the frequency with which he felt impelled to 'collaborate' with his contributors—adding, altering, and revising their work, whenever their views seemed to threaten the equilibrium and consistency of the review's standards.

As we learn from a letter of Scott's to Gifford (25 October 1808), Jeffrey himself sometimes enlivened the contributions of 'persons of inferior powers of writing' before publishing them in his review, but it was generally true that he did not interfere with the critical judgements of his major contributors. Gifford, on the other hand, rarely hesitated before altering the work of even his more eminent contributors, and the letters of Southey and Lamb, for example, bear witness to their surprise on discovering Gifford's unsolicited 'collaboration'. Excessive dis-

[1] Gifford's editorial interest in Massinger, Ford and Ben Jonson suggests that despite his fundamentally conservative critical orientation he was influenced by the newer trends in early nineteenth-century taste.

[2] Two American investigators, in a recently-published inquiry into the authorship of articles in the *Quarterly*, provide us with detailed information on this point, and also discuss Gifford's primary function as an editor: 'Actually the number of whole articles now attributed to Gifford alone is eight (out of a total of 733 articles examined). In these few—some of them slash-reviews of now-forgotten fiction and poetry—the most serious interest is Roman satire. However, Gifford's main significance as a *Quarterly* writer is not to be found in his individually written articles. It lay rather in the writing and revising he did on other people's contributions, in order to harmonize them with a perhaps vaguely defined but strongly conceived policy and pattern for the periodical.' (H. Shine, and H. C. Shine, *The 'Quarterly Review' under William Gifford* (University of North Carolina Press, Chapel Hill, 1949), Introduction.)

paragement of Pope was among the critical tendencies which Gifford did not find it easy to tolerate—both Hazlitt and Leigh Hunt were taken to task in the *Quarterly* of April 1818 for their dispraise of Pope and Johnson[1]—and perhaps the best-known instance of Gifford's editorial interference may be found in his treatment of Southey's review of Chalmers's *The Works of the English Poets*, which appeared in the *Quarterly* of October 1814. Southey had found occasion here to criticise severely Pope's translation of Homer (preferring Cowper's version); but when the review appeared in the *Quarterly*, Southey reported in a letter to the Reverend Herbert Hill that Gifford had introduced an entirely new passage on Pope's Homer 'praising the translation' and completely reversing Southey's judgement on it.

Although Gifford did not actively participate in the celebrated 'Pope Controversy' of the early nineteenth century, he intimated in his edition of Massinger that he had no very high opinion of Warton and Bowles as editors of Pope.[2] Byron was in Ravenna when he wrote his famous Letter to John Murray on the Reverend W. L. Bowles's Strictures Against the Poetry of Pope, and he directed Murray to consult Gifford as to how much, if any, of the letter was to be printed.[3] Gifford was glad of an opportunity of assisting Byron, and considerably modified the letter prior to publication. Moore noted that Gifford had been specially pleased by the passage in an earlier letter (1817), in which Byron had preferred the poetical system of the school of Pope to that represented by Scott, Southey, Wordsworth, Moore, Campbell, and himself, and informs us that Gifford added as a marginal comment to this passage: 'There is more good sense, and feeling, and judgement in this

---

[1] According to *The 'Quarterly Review' under William Gifford* by H. and H. C. Shine, Gifford wrote this article in collaboration with Eaton Stannard Barrett.

[2] In a not very flattering note on p. cvii of his edition of Massinger, Gifford described Warton as being a pedantic 'knight-errant', and Bowles as his 'attendant' and the 'dullest of mortal squires'.

[3] *The Works of Lord Byron, with his Letters, Journals, and Life*, ed. J. Wright (1832–33), v, 153.

passage, than any other I ever read, or Lord Byron ever wrote.'[1]

However, the ultra-conservative political and literary standards of its editor,[2] and in particular his frequently acknowledged sympathy with the 'school of Pope', must not be confused with the standards of the *Quarterly Review* as a whole in the years between 1809 and 1830. These standards were quite naturally a product of the varied and conflicting currents of taste active at the time, and were sometimes in closer touch with the quickening Romantic impulses of the age. The literary standards of the *Quarterly* were flexible enough to accommodate, for example, the largely nineteenth-century interests of a critic like Southey (whose influence on the review made possible its relatively sympathetic and enlightened reception of Wordsworth's poetry), while preserving the basically eighteenth-century character of its general critical assumptions and principles. Gifford's main importance from this point of view was that he was perhaps the most active and influential agent of the numerous literary and political pressures which succeeded in giving the *Quarterly* its predominantly conservative orientation.

2. AUGUSTAN POETRY AND CONTEMPORARY VERSE

The effect which the revival of interest in Elizabethan and seventeenth-century poetry had upon the reading of Augustan poetry is apparent in the very opening numbers of the *Quarterly Review*. The reinstatement of the Elizabethan and Jacobean poets was often associated with a revaluation of the poetry of the school of Pope, 'which, from the days of Pope to the beginning of this century', the *Quarterly* observed, 'engrossed so much the largest share of the public approbation'.[3] An early

[1] Quoted in R. B. Clark's *William Gifford: Tory Satirist, Critic and Editor* (New York, 1930), p. 204.

[2] R. B. Clark, Gifford's biographer, has summed up his critical position in relation to his age as follows: 'As a writer, Gifford belonged to an old order in a changing era. The norms of drama, poetry, and criticism were for him those of Ben Jonson, Pope, and Dr. Johnson, or in general those of the mid-18th century.' (R. B. Clark, *op. cit.*, pp. 245–6.)

[3] *Quarterly Review* (March 1813), p. 213.

example of the effect of this revaluation may be seen in the *Quarterly* of August 1810, in which Barron Field boldly claimed in his article on Herrick and Carew that 'the reign of Elizabeth, and not that of Anne, was without doubt the Augustan age of English poetry'.[1] Field's claim would have seemed sweeping and unjustified to some of his readers; yet, although the term 'Augustan' was but rarely applied to the Elizabethans at that time, there were few critics in the *Quarterly* who would have doubted that the Elizabethans represented the most powerful expression of the English poetical genius. Less representative of the critical attitude of the *Quarterly Review* as a whole, however, was the assessment made by a sympathetic reviewer of *The Works of William Mason*,[2] who found it possible roundly to assert that, in his opinion, the poetry of 'the school of Pope had expired with himself'.[3] Quite the opposite view of the situation was held by a considerable number of *Quarterly* critics, and a study of their reviews may help to throw some light on the relationship that was felt to exist between contemporary poetry and that of the preceding age.

Unlike most later critics, *Quarterly* reviewers writing during the period of the Regency, were still able to feel that the poetry of their own time maintained direct connections with the Augustan age. Apart from Dryden, Pope, and Johnson, the poet whose work in this tradition was most generally praised in the *Quarterly* was Goldsmith, whose poetry—contrary to the usual practice in the *Edinburgh*—was unequivocally preferred to

---

[1] *Ibid.* (August 1810), p. 166.

[2] Mason's connections with Gray, Joseph and Thomas Warton, and other eighteenth-century critics who were often unsympathetic towards the Augustans, were generally known, and acknowledged by the reviewer.

[3] The *Quarterly* (July 1816), p. 377. Some incidental observations made by Southey in a review of Portuguese literature—*Extractos em Portuguez e em Inglez*—in the *Quarterly* of May 1809, suggest the manner in which the Augustan claim to have brought language and taste to a state of perfection (especially through the 'reform of our numbers under Mr Denham and Mr Waller'), was sometimes sweepingly dismissed in the early nineteenth century: 'That improvement of poetical language which in our country with equal ignorance and absurdity has been ascribed to Waller and to Pope, Camoens affected in Portuguese, nothing before him was so good, nothing after him has been better', pp. 274–5.

that of Crabbe.[1] Not only was Goldsmith regarded as a major influence upon the successors of the Augustan poets in the early nineteenth century, he was also particularly praised in a review of the poems of Mary Russell Mitford in the *Quarterly* of November 1810, for the discrimination with which he had modelled himself upon his great predecessors—'possessing much of the compactness of Pope's versification, without the monotonous structure of his lines; rising sometimes to the swell and fulness of Dryden, without his inflations'. Other qualities which the reviewer found attractive were Goldsmith's evocation of a variety of moods varying from the deftly playful to a gravely contemplative melancholy, and the masterly control and delicacy of feeling of his descriptions. The reviewer's praise of this latter quality partly anticipates some of T. S. Eliot's remarks, in his preface to Johnson's *London*, on the skill with which Goldsmith's 'melting sentiment' is 'just held in check by the precision of his language'.

Among the living poets whom the *Quarterly* regarded as the heirs of the Augustan age Campbell and Rogers were especially prominent. In the work of these two poets the *Quarterly* discerned the direct influence not only of Goldsmith, but of Johnson and Pope as well. In a review of Campbell's poems in the *Quarterly* of May 1809, Scott said that he had successfully avoided mere senseless innovation ('the babbling and jingling simplicity of ruder minstrels') on the one hand, and the uninspired imitation of classical models on the other. His achievement in *The Pleasures of Hope* was characterised as being 'new, but not singular; elegant, but not trite', and the poem had elevated him to 'a pre-eminent station among living poets'. Campbell's Pennsylvanian tale *Gertrude of Wyoming* was also well received by the *Quarterly*; more attention was paid to its

---

[1] Jeffrey, reviewing Crabbe's poems in the *Edinburgh* of April 1808, found it particularly admirable for 'that sort of diction and versification which we admire in *The Deserted Village* of Goldsmith, or *The Vanity of Human Wishes* of Johnson'. Observing that he regarded Crabbe's poem as an effective 'antidote' to Goldsmith's, Jeffrey concluded that although Crabbe was inferior to Goldsmith in 'delicacy' and 'fine finish', he was superior to him in poetic 'vigour' and 'in the variety and truth of his pictures'.

polished versification and animated moral feeling than to its Romantic insipidity and exaggerated pathos. The Augustan affinities of the poem were particularly noted, by Scott, in the effectiveness with which Campbell 'united the sweetness of Goldsmith with the strength of Johnson'. To the modern reader it may well appear that the insistent pathos of Campbell's poem makes it closer in general tone to the disciplined emotionalism of Goldsmith than to the weighty moral strength of Johnson, though the latter's influence is unmistakable. This characteristic of the poem is itself an interesting indication of some of the modifications which the Augustan tradition in poetry sometimes underwent, in adapting itself to the poetical climate of the early nineteenth century.

An even more interesting account of the problems facing the poet writing within the Augustan tradition in the early nineteenth century may be found in the *Quarterly*'s review of *The Poems of Samuel Rogers* in March 1813. Like Byron, who often described Campbell and Rogers in his letters and journals as among the major Regency supporters of 'the Christianity of English poetry, the poetry of Pope',[1] the *Quarterly* too regarded Rogers as being primarily, in Byron's phrase, 'the last of the *best* school'.[2] For, although most of the *Quarterly* reviewers were unanimous in their recognition that the poetry of the Elizabethans had surpassed that of the Augustans, they were more doubtful about the relative value of the influence which these two schools might exert upon the poetry of their own age. For example, Lord Dudley, in the *Quarterly Review* of March 1813, while noting with some misgivings newer influences upon Rogers's work, emphasised what he felt to be his true Augustan descent in poetry:

It was as the faithful, diligent disciple of Pope and Goldsmith, that Mr. Rogers became deservedly a favourite of the public, and it is to the imitation of these splendid and captivating, but safe and

---

[1] Quoted by Arthur Symons in *The Romantic Movement in English Poetry*, p. 70.

[2] Byron's *Journal*: from the entry dated Wednesday, 24 November 1813. *Byron: A Self-Portrait—Letters and Diaries, 1798–1824*, ed. Quennell (1950), I, 220.

correct models of excellence, that he seems most fitted by the bent of his genius, and the direction of his studies.[1]

While to model oneself upon the Augustans was regarded as being in the highest degree 'splendid' and 'correct', Rogers's attempt to achieve a 'style very different from that of his earlier compositions' in *The Voyage of Columbus*, was given a lukewarm reception. It was felt that Rogers, excited by the recent 're-discovery' of the Elizabethans and 'stimulated by the astonishing success of some late writers', had been seduced into renouncing his 'favourite masters'—Pope and Goldsmith—and following 'those mighty geniuses who alone are entitled to be called their superiors', the Elizabethans. Such a venture seemed to the *Quarterly*, of its very nature, fraught with danger. The sensibility of the age, though deeply stimulated by and responsive to 'the flow, the unity, the boldness, and the grandeur that belong to the higher style of poetical composition', appeared to lack the necessary power to recreate these glories in terms of its own experience. More seriously, as in the case of Rogers, it appeared to the *Quarterly* that these attempts at revival were cutting poets off from the Augustan tradition, which, though less magnificent intrinsically, was perhaps a more secure, prosperous and beneficial influence on contemporary verse. Rogers's real genius lay, according to the *Quarterly*, in the natural correctness of his ear—'attuned by practice to the measure of his favourite masters, nice to the very verge of fastidiousness, accurate almost to minuteness'—and in his flair for compassing 'the finer shades of expression, and the most delicate shades of thought'. Yet, while 'harmony', 'elegance', 'correctness' and 'pathos' were within his reach, it was regretted that Rogers, in *The Voyage of Columbus*, had 'resolved to content himself with nothing short of varied cadences, striking traits, awful magnificence, and the lofty flights of a creative fancy'. Longinian sublimities had replaced the 'safe and correct models of excellence' he had hitherto followed:

[1] 'The Poems of Samuel Rogers', *Quarterly Review* (March 1813), p. 212.

Tired of pleasing, he is ambitious to astonish and transport his readers. The consequences of failure are harshness and abruptness, instead of variety in the versification—obscurity for grandeur, and in some instances, mere baldness, where he intended to exhibit the native force of simple and unadorned expression.[1]

Jeffrey, in his review of John Ford in the *Edinburgh Review* of August 1811 and elsewhere, reported more favourably on the attempts made by contemporary poets to revive the glories of Elizabethan and Jacobean times; but he too felt compelled to deplore the artificiality ('there must be nothing moderate, natural or easy about their sentiments') and the affectation ('all their characters must be in agonies and ecstacies, from their entrance to their exit'), which too often marred the results. The *Quarterly*, however, regarded these emotional excesses of the neo-Elizabethan revival as serious, and even alarming, symptoms of a deterioration in the national taste. Newman Ivey White has described in *The Unextinguished Hearth* the unprecedented degree to which social and political bias affected periodical criticism of the time.[2] To the *Quarterly* reviewers, wishing to preserve the *status quo* in a transitional period, poetry which had a disturbing and unsettling effect upon society was not unnaturally regarded with suspicion. In an age of confused values it is plain that the *Quarterly* critics sometimes preferred, as an influence upon contemporary verse, the stability and order of Augustan poetry to the more volatile though brilliant triumphs of the Elizabethan poets, whose influence, the *Quarterly* of March 1813 somewhat extravagantly complained, was threatening to bring about 'the entire depravation of the national taste'. Summing up the relative value of the influence of these two schools upon Rogers's poetry

---

[1] 'The Poems of Samuel Rogers', *Quarterly Review* (March 1813), p. 213.

[2] 'The most striking characteristic of reviewing during Shelley's later life was the strong moral and political bias of the critics. The critical journals of the 18th century furnish numerous examples of the same bias, but without the intensifying fear which made it almost a mania during the Regency. It affected the general tone and policy of the periodicals; it also affected strongly the theory and practice of literary criticism.' (N. I. White, Introduction to *The Unextinguished Hearth*, Chapel Hill, 1938.)

in particular, and contemporary taste in general, the reviewer concluded:

In short, we had looked to Mr Rogers as one of those who were to continue and support that correct and elaborate school of poetry which, from the days of Pope to the beginning of this century, engrossed so much the largest share of the public approbation, and which, we own, we regard with peculiar favour, not only on account of its own intrinsic beauties, but because the cultivation of it appears to afford the best security against that entire depravation of the national taste in poetry which would probably be the consequence of an universal attempt to reach the higher and more perilous kinds of excellence. Unluckily Mr Rogers has taken a different view of this subject.[1]

The reviewer plainly hoped, however, that Rogers would soon realise the folly of writing against the natural 'bent of his genius', and would revert to the style of his 'favourite masters'. This passage is also representative—in the reviewer's plain preference for the 'correct' and 'captivating' achievements of the Augustans over the 'more perilous kinds of excellence' of the Elizabethans—of strongly conservative tendencies in the criticism of the *Quarterly*, which may be observed elsewhere as well.

Yet the new criticism and poetry of the age was not unrepresented in the pages of the *Quarterly*. Wordsworth's poetry, for example, was more generously reviewed by the *Quarterly* than by the *Edinburgh*, not only in the articles by Lamb and Southey, but also in Gifford's review of the *Lyrical Ballads* and *The White Doe of Rylstone* in October 1815.[2] Maintaining that the poetic genius of Pope and Dryden had been unsurpassed in

[1] 'The Poems of Samuel Rogers', *Quarterly Review* (March 1813), p. 213.

[2] Jeffrey's review of *The White Doe of Rylstone* appeared in the *Edinburgh* in the same month as Gifford's. The review begins with the sentence—'This, we think, has the merit of being the very worst poem we ever saw imprinted in a quarto volume'; and, in the remainder of the review the poem is caricatured and reduced to the level of farce. Jeffrey's account of Emily's separation from the doe in the 7th Canto is representative of his destructively ironical treatment of the poem: 'The poor lady runs about indeed for some years in a very disconsolate way in a worsted gown and flannel nightcap; but at last the old white doe finds her out, and takes again to following her—whereupon Mr Wordsworth breaks out into this fine

subjects requiring the animating power of the 'fancy and the understanding', whereas Wordsworth's strength lay, 'when his theories and eccentricities happen to be laid aside', in evoking the immediacy of personal feeling, Gifford suggested that praise of one poet did not necessarily imply dispraise of the others. Nonetheless, Gifford was not uncritical of Wordsworth. He felt that Wordsworth's excessively 'poetical' sensibility had prevented him from responding fully to the feelings and experiences of ordinary life, and that this accounted largely for his lapses into bathos. Gifford also found Wordsworth's attempts to imitate the style of the ballad self-conscious and artificial, and deplored the unnatural cult of 'simplicity' which Wordsworth wished to introduce into contemporary verse.

Praise of the new poetry of the age at the expense of the Augustans may also be found in the *Quarterly*, particularly in Southey's two reviews of Chalmers's *The Works of the English Poets*, the first of which appeared in July 1814, and the second in October the same year. Southey claimed that the 'golden age' of Elizabethan poetry had been followed by the 'silver age' of the Metaphysical school, and described the Restoration as a predominantly 'French' interregnum in the history of English poetry. The development of the heroic couplet at this time had, he felt, a cramping effect upon poetry. Keats was a year or two later to liken the movement of the couplet to the monotonous motion of a rocking-horse; here Southey applied to it, with approval, Aaron Hill's description of the typical movement of the French heroic—'a pert skipping, a kind of

---

and natural rapture:

> Oh, moment ever blest! O Pair!
> Beloved of Heaven, Heaven's choicest care!'

('*The White Doe of Rylstone*; or *The Fate of the Nortons*; a Poem by W. Wordsworth', *Edinburgh Review*, October 1815, p. 362.)

In fairness to Jeffrey, it should be said that this particular review was his most destructive piece on Wordsworth, and that he afterwards rather regretted it. His other reviews of Wordsworth make generous and sometimes perceptive incidental commendations. The note which prefaces the Wordsworth reviews in the collected volume of Jeffrey's essays from the *Edinburgh* shows an honourable and attractive mind.

pause-checked recoil of motion, like the *half-whirl* of a spin-ning wheel'.[1]

The new criticism in militant conflict with the standards of the Augustans may best be seen, perhaps, in Southey's dis-cussion of Pope's translation of Homer in the *Quarterly* of October 1814. Gifford, it has already been noted, considerably modified Southey's review, re-affirming the 'great and general merits of Pope' and shifting the blame upon younger writers who had allowed themselves to be 'dazzled' and 'misled' by the brilliance of his translation. Prominent in Southey's review, however, was his censure of the flagrant 'artificiality' which he found in Pope's descriptions of nature.[2] For this purpose, Southey selected Pope's translation of the description of night in the eighth book of the *Iliad*, which was very popular among early nineteenth-century readers. Dr Rees's *Cyclopaedia*, for example, under the article on 'Poetry', confirming its popularity, informs us that 'perhaps no passage in the whole translation has been more frequently quoted and admired'. It is interesting that Wordsworth, too, selected exactly the same passage from Pope—which he called the 'celebrated moon-light scene in the *Iliad*'—in order to illustrate the extent to which English poetry from Milton to Thomson and beyond, had virtually cut itself off from the imagery of the natural world. Wordsworth's particular criticism of this passage is so similar to Southey's, that it may well be that one was derived from the other. However this may be, they are both repre-sentative of the kind of disparaging criticism that the work of the Augustans was currently receiving from the new generation of poets. In order to enforce his adverse judgement, Southey quoted the passage from Homer in the original Greek, then

[1] 'Chalmers's *The Works of the English Poets*', *Quarterly Review* (October 1814), p. 83.

[2] Disparagement of Pope's imagery because it was not principally derived from the world of nature untouched by man was widespread in the early nineteenth century, and was a central dispute in the 'Pope Controversy'. Warton, it will be remembered, had no such difficulty with Pope's imagery, and had praised him for the skill with which he employed imagery derived from sophisticated life. See Chapter VI.

in Cowper's version (of which he approved), and, finally, in Pope's:

> As when the Moon, refulgent lamp of night!
> O'er Heaven's clear azure spreads her sacred light,
> When not a breath disturbs the deep serene,
> And not a cloud o'ercasts the solemn scene,
> Around her throne the vivid planets roll,
> And stars unnumber'd gild the glowing pole;
> O'er the dark trees a yellow verdure shed,
> And tip with silver every mountain's head;
> Then shine the vales, the rocks in prospect rise,
> A flood of glory bursts from all the skies;
> The conscious swains rejoicing in the sight,
> Eye the blue vault, and bless the useful light.

Southey commented on Pope's translation:

Here are the planets rolling round the moon; here is the pole gilt and glowing with stars; here are trees made yellow and mountains tipt with silver by the moonlight; and here is the whole sky in a flood of glory; appearances not to be found in Homer or in nature. . . . The astronomy of these lines would not appear more extraordinary to Dr. Herschel than the imagery to every person who has observed moonlight scenes.[1]

Southey went on to conclude, in lines which strikingly recall some of Wordsworth's critical remarks in his *Essay Supplementary to the Preface*, which first appeared in 1815:

But images of nature were not in fashion during the prevalence of the 'French' school: from Dryden to Thomson, there is scarcely a rural image drawn from life to be found in any of the English poets, except Gay and Lady Winchilsea.[2]

[1] Wordsworth, discussing the hold which Pope's description of night had upon 'public estimation', remarked in his *Essay Supplementary to the Preface*—'nay, there is not a passage of descriptive poetry, which at this day finds so many and such ardent admirers. Strange to think of an enthusiast, as may have been the case with thousands, reciting those verses under the cope of a moonlight sky, without having his raptures in the least disturbed by a suspicion of their absurdity!' (*Wordsworth's Poetical Works* (Oxford edn), ed. E. de Selincourt, 1952, p. 420.)

[2] Wordsworth remarked in his *Essay*: 'Now, it is remarkable that, excepting the nocturnal Reverie of Lady Winchilsea, and a passage or two in the "Windsor Forest" of Pope, the poetry of the period intervening between the publication of the "Paradise Lost" and the "Seasons" does not contain a single new image of external nature.' (*Wordsworth's Poetical Works* (Oxford edn), 1952, pp. 419–20.)

Discussing the influence of eighteenth-century poetry upon contemporary verse, Southey claimed that, 'notwithstanding the poetical supremacy which Pope so long enjoyed', the most stimulating influence had been derived from a 'different school' of poetry, a school which was associated originally with the work of the Wartons, Gilbert West, and William Mason.[1] Southey linked up the eighteenth-century poetical traditions of this group with the 'New School' of early nineteenth-century poetry, which, he claimed, the 'Aristarchs' of the *Edinburgh Review*, had with 'equal pertinacity and pertness' divided for the past twelve years. 'To borrow a phrase from the Methodists', Southey observed, 'there has been a great revival in our days—a pouring out of the spirit.' Southey was writing here, of course, as one of the leading members of the 'New School', which, though conscious of its roots in the eighteenth century, was attempting to give expression in poetry to what it regarded as the great spiritual revival of its own time.

Yet, although the literary standards of the *Quarterly* were flexible enough to accommodate some of the newer tendencies of the age, we also find side by side with such criticism frequent defences of the Augustan poets from criticism of varying degrees of seriousness. Quoting the following sternly disapproving comment from a *Methodist Magazine*—'Dryden and Pope may amuse, but will rarely edify, and frequently pollute'—the *Quarterly* refused to take it very seriously and regarded it as one more misguided attempt, among certain quarters of the reading public, to disapprove of poetry on exaggerated and therefore irresponsible moral grounds.[2]

[1] Coleridge in the opening chapter of the *Biographia Literaria* refers to Joseph Warton and Gilbert West as two of the poets who influenced him during his formative years. Mason, who was a minor poet of some considerable reputation, was well known as a biographer and editor of Gray. He corresponded frequently with Gray, and also with Horace Walpole, whose critical leanings were sometimes violently anti-Johnsonian. Warton's personal influence was greater than that of either Mason or West. Winchester, under the influence of Joseph Warton, Southey informs us, 'may almost be said to have become a school of poets'. (*Quarterly*, October 1814, p. 89.)

[2] It may perhaps be worth mentioning that such moralistic condemnation was not confined to Augustan poets. The *Methodist Magazine* adds: 'Shakespeare is

More serious was the defence of Pope in a review of Leigh Hunt's *Foliage* in January 1818.[1] The *Quarterly* did not take kindly to Hunt's occasional superciliousness, and he was reprimanded here for a condescending reference to 'that elegant mistake of Pope's in two volumes octavo, called Homer's *Iliad*'.[2] In the very next issue of the *Quarterly*, which appeared in April, Hunt was again criticised in a review of *Endymion* for teaching Keats to cultivate a 'superior' attitude towards Pope and Johnson.[3] It is probable that Keats's dismissal of Augustan poetry as 'a schism nurtured by foppery and barbarism' in *Sleep and Poetry*, which was written in the winter of 1816, was partly a result of his membership of Leigh Hunt's circle in London.

Hazlitt was no favourite of the *Quarterly Review*, and the notices of his work which appeared in July 1818, and in July 1819, were not undiluted in their praise. His views on Pope, especially in his *Lectures on the English Poets*, were regarded as being of mixed value, and were chiefly examined by the *Quarterly* in July 1818. This review includes a defence of Pope against what were felt to be Hazlitt's more irresponsible strictures. 'He, as a matter of course, bestows high praises on Pope', noted the *Quarterly*, 'but they are interspersed with remarks, and modified by limitations, which degrade that

---

still more dangerous; whatever advantages may be derived from perusing him, I suspect few of them will appear in the day of final account.' The *Quarterly* briefly suggested its attitude to such criticism by juxtaposing it with an even more extravagant passage from the *Eclectic Review*, describing Shakespeare's soul in hell, suffering excruciating tortures 'for the evil which his works continue to do in the world'.

[1] This article was written by Croker and John Taylor Coleridge in collaboration, according to H. and H. C. Shine.

[2] '*Foliage* by Leigh Hunt', *Quarterly* (January 1818), p. 333.

[3] In the course of its snobbish though witty destruction of the newly-formed 'Cockney' school of poetry, the *Quarterly* said of its 'hierophant' Leigh Hunt: 'Our readers will recollect the pleasant recipes for harmonious and sublime poetry which he gave us in his preface to "Rimini" . . . and they will recollect above all the contempt of Pope, Johnson, and such like poetasters and pseudo-critics, which so forcibly contrasted itself with Mr Leigh Hunt's self-complacent approbation of
—all the things itself had wrote,
Of special merit though of little note.'
'Endymion: A Poetic Romance', *Quarterly* (April 1818), pp. 204–5.

illustrious genius far below the eminence he must ever occupy.'[1]
Hazlitt's view that Pope 'was in poetry what the sceptic is in
religion' was taken to be little better than a nonsensically
'pretty turn upon words', which implied that Pope was 'no
poet at all'. To his claim that Pope 'goes on describing his own
descriptions, till he loses himself in verbal repetitions', the
Quarterly retorted, with an aptness plain to anyone who has
examined Hazlitt's style in its weaker moments 'This sentence
is not the least descriptive of Pope's poetry, but it is a faithful
description of Mr Hazlitt's prose.' Summing up its attitude
towards Hazlitt's criticism of Pope, and that of others like him,
the *Quarterly* concluded

The truth is that Pope's unpardonable fault, in the estimation of
those who decry him at the present day, consists in his being very
perspicuous; he is always intelligible; every line has its meaning;
every idea which he communicates has its boundaries distinctly
marked; and he is supposed to want feeling because he abounds in
sense. Were some of his finest passages to be translated into the
mystical language of the modern school, the eyes of many would be
opened, who are now blind to his superlative merits.[2]

Yet several critics in the *Quarterly Review*, even as late as the
1820s, were not content with merely defending Pope's poetry
and reputation from unfriendly criticism. Some of them
claimed that a marked revival of interest in Augustan poetry
among the reading public at large was apparent at this time,
and felt that this augured well for the future.[3] In July 1820,
reviewing an edition of Spence's *Anecdotes of Pope* which had
appeared earlier in the same year, and had done much to restore
the public's faith in Pope's personal reputation which had been

---

[1] 'Hazlitt's *Lectures on the English Poets*', *Quarterly Review* (July 1818), p. 432.

[2] 'Hazlitt's *Lectures on the English Poets*' (*Quarterly Review*, July 1818, pp. 432–3.)
The *Quarterly*, however, was not entirely fair towards Hazlitt's genuine efforts to
promote a catholic appreciation of Pope. This particular review was written by
Eaton Barrett and revised by Gifford. For a fuller account of Hazlitt's criticism of
Pope, see Chapter VII.

[3] This observation was made not only by Isaac D'Israeli in July 1820, but also
by the reviewer of Roscoe's edition of Pope in October 1825.

much maligned by Bowles and others,[1] Isaac D'Israeli[2] claimed that Pope's poetry had weathered successfully the disparagement of the new criticism, and was now ready to re-assert its influence upon contemporary verse. Observing that 'a period of languor succeeds a period of glory', and that at such a time poetry is 'left without progressive power', D'Israeli analysed the contemporary situation as follows:

At such a crisis we return to old neglected tastes, or we acquire new ones which in their turn will become old; and it is at this critical period that we discover new concurrents depreciating a legitimate and established genius whom they cannot rival, and finally practising the democratic and desperate arts of a literary Ostracism. In vain, however, would the populace of poets estrange themselves from Pope, and teach that he is deficient in imagination and passion, because, in early youth—

'He stoop'd to truth, and moralised his song.'

It is not the shadows of the imagination and the spectres of the passions *only* which are concerned in our poetic pleasures; other sources must be opened, worthy of the dignity and the pride of the Muse; and to instruct and reform, as well as to delight the world by the charm of verse, is only to 'reassert her ancient prerogative', and to vindicate her glory. A master-poet must live with the language in which he has written, for his qualities are inherent, and independent of periodical tastes. The poet of our age, as well as of our youth, is one on whom our experience is perpetually conferring a new value; and Time, who will injure so many of our poets, will but confirm the immortality of Pope.[3]

What D'Israeli is pleading for here is, of course, a fresh appraisal of the beneficial influence which Augustan poetry could exert upon the poetry of his own age. The exaltation of the 'imagination' and the 'passions' had led to the emergence of a

---

[1] Among the more fantastic allegations made by Bowles was that there had been 'criminality' and 'licentiousness' in Pope's relations with Teresa and Martha Blount. Byron, discussing the licentious intrigue which Bowles surmised from the innocent compliments and gallantries to be found in Pope's letters, declared in his Letter from Ravenna that such accusations constituted a worse indictment of Bowles than of Pope.

[2] Dr R. G. Cox suggests that Croker may have written this review. H. and H. C. Shine in their recent study *The 'Quarterly Review' under William Gifford*, and 'George Paston' (E. M. Symonds) in *Mr Pope*, assign the authorship to D'Israeli.

[3] 'Spence's *Anecdotes of Pope*', *Quarterly Review* (July 1820), p. 434.

too exclusively emotional sensibility, which an acquaintance with the restrained and intelligent moral sensibility of Pope's verse would do much to correct.

An even more emphatic statement of the value which contemporary taste could derive from a more widespread and intimate acquaintance with Augustan poetry, was made a few years later in a review of William Roscoe's edition of Pope in the *Quarterly* of October 1825. The 'three voluminous editions of Pope' to appear in the early nineteenth century,[1] together with the 'long scintillating train of controversialists, commentators, annotators, editors, and biographers' still in attendance upon 'the great luminary' Pope, was according to the *Quarterly* a pleasant sight to all 'lovers of the good old stock-poetry of England'. 'There is evidently a confidence felt by all these,' continued the reviewer, 'that the public taste was beginning to be satiated by the forced meats of modern poetry', and that this trend was accompanied in the reading public at large by a return to favour of Augustan poetry. The reviewer's main evidence for this swing in popular taste was, of course, the marked revival of editorial and controversial interest in Pope in the early 1820s. How far his inference was valid is not easy to say, but it remains plain that it was a tendency in contemporary taste which he wished positively to encourage. It was a tendency which would help to unite 'imagination' with 'intelligence', and would restrain an indulgence in 'exquisite pleasure' unrelated to a concern with moral centrality. It was an alert and lively interest in contemporary poetry itself, which, more persuasively than anything else, suggested the value which the age could derive from renewing its connections with Augustan poetry:

We cannot, we think, be suspected of wanting due sensibility to the merits of our contemporary poets; for there is scarcely a Number of our Journal, which we have not adorned with specimens of their taste, cultivation, or power. But with all this, when we consider the faults, and even the excellencies of those who rank foremost among

[1] The editions are, of course, those of Bowles, Warton, and Roscoe.

them; the defects of their feeble and indiscriminate imitators; and still more the demerits of those who have perverted their talents to serve the purposes of corruption and impiety; we feel convinced that this was a juncture at which an appeal might be made with peculiar propriety to the high name of Pope, and the public be called on to revert to the works of him, who, more than any other poet, united strength of reason with elegance of fancy, and instructed his readers by the moral truth which he taught, while he charmed their attention by the most exquisite pleasures of correct taste. The public seems to have admitted the appeal; a high degree of interest has been revived on the often discussed points of Pope's personal character, and the poetical rank to which he is entitled.[1]

The tendency in contemporary poetry which a renewed connection with Augustan poetry would help to correct, was partly that 'dissociation of sensibility'—that divergence between 'strength of reason' and 'elegance of fancy'—which T. S. Eliot has found typical of the poetry of the Victorian era. It was a movement in nineteenth-century taste which later received its best-known critical expression in Arnold's exaltation of the 'soul' at the expense of the 'wits'.

3. AUGUSTAN POETRY AND PRE-RESTORATION VERSE

The *Quarterly Review* in the period under review consistently regarded the Elizabethan era as the supreme manifestation of the English genius. Observing that the Elizabethan period was 'the most poetical age of this poetical nation', Barron Field remarked in the *Quarterly* of August 1810: 'Certain it is that the poetry of the age in question, possesses a raciness and strength, which was ill-changed in the succeeding reign for mellowness and dilution. The vigour of the Muse in her youth was more enchanting than the graces of her maturity. "This was sometime a mystery, but the time has given it proof." ' Yet the Augustan tendency to under-rate pre-Restoration poetry in general as the product of a sometimes brilliant but often wild and untutored genius, survived into the nineteenth century. Field informs us in 1810 that the greatness of the whole corpus

---

[1] 'Roscoe's Pope', *Quarterly Review* (October 1825), pp. 272–3.

of Elizabethan poetry, 'denied or forgotten in the days of Pope', was 'even now but partially acknowledged'. 'The names of Shakespeare and Spenser', it is true, 'were pronounced with a profounder awe than those of Dryden and Pope', yet the distinguished minor talent of the Elizabethan period and the earlier seventeenth century was often totally unrecognised. For example, while Augustan 'rhymesters' like Halifax, Duke, and Yalden 'are well known and present familiar ideas to the mind', many readers were completely unacquainted with even the names of 'true poets' like Carew, Herrick, and Lovelace. The responsibility for this ignorance among readers Field attributed, perhaps unfairly, to the influence of the 'late very incomplete and careless publication of the English poets, commonly called Johnson's Edition, in which so few of our older classics appear'. Johnson began his edition of the English poets with Cowley—much to Wordsworth's astonishment[1]— and Southey, having censured Johnson for his neglect of the variety and richness of earlier English poetry, in the *Quarterly* of July 1814, praised the editorial labours of Dr Anderson for making this great body of verse accessible to the common reader once again.[2]

The tendency of the Augustans to underestimate the great-

---

[1] Wordsworth's criticism of Johnson's edition of the English poets is to be found in his *Essay Supplementary to the Preface of the Lyrical Ballads* (1815): 'We open the volume of Prefatory Lives, and to our astonishment the *first* name we find is that of Cowley!—What is become of the morning star of English Poetry? Where is the bright Elizabethan constellation? Or, if names be more acceptable than images, where is the ever-to-be-honoured Chaucer? where is Spenser? where Sidney and ... where Shakespeare?—These, and a multitude of others not unworthy to be placed near them, their contemporaries and successors, we have *not*. But in their stead, we have ... Roscommon, and Stepney, and Phillips, and Walsh, and Smith ... etc.' (*Wordsworth's Poetical Works*, ed. E. de Selincourt, 1952, p. 425.)

[2] Southey remarked: 'To good old Dr Anderson the poets and the literature of this country are deeply beholden. ... The booksellers, as their predecessors had done with Dr Johnson's edition, would have begun the collection with Cowley. Dr Anderson prevailed upon them to include some of the earlier and greater writers. ... Many of the Elizabethan poets were thus, for the first time, made generally accessible, and if the good old school of poetry has been in some degree revived, Dr Anderson has been mainly instrumental towards a reformation which was so devoutly to be wished for.' (*Quarterly Review*, July 1814, p. 504.) Anderson's *Works of the British Poets* first appeared in 1792.

ness of the Elizabethan age was often disapproved of in the pages of the *Quarterly*. Southey, in a review of Bishop Burnet's *History of his Own Time*, wrote that 'Dryden had persuaded himself that English poetry had not reached its vigour and maturity in the time of Shakespeare!', and marvelled at his belief that 'even the art of versification had not been understood, till it was introduced by Waller'.[1] Isaac D'Israeli, too, in his sympathetic review of Spence's *Anecdotes of Pope*, was more than a little troubled by Pope's attitude to his predecessors. Quoting Pope's remarks on Shakespeare ('Shakespeare's style is the style of a bad age'), and on Milton ('Milton's style in his *Paradise Lost* is not natural; 'tis an exotic style'), D'Israeli inquired with some uncertainty—'But what are we to conclude, when we find Pope criticising both Milton and Shakespeare in language to which we are not accustomed?'[2] D'Israeli endeavoured to minimise the force of Pope's unfavourable judgements by pointing out that they were 'limited to *style*, and did not touch any of the vital parts of the poetical character of the two master-spirits', and by observing that Pope's strictures were largely determined by the severely 'classical' standards of his age—'in his day there existed no other'.[3] However, though D'Israeli credited Pope with having 'wrought to its last perfection the classical vein of English poetry', he was compelled to grant that 'some of his decisions respecting the highest class of our poets' could only be regarded as 'heresies in our poetical creed'.

Another critical tendency among the Augustan poets of which the *Quarterly* reviewers sometimes disapproved, was their

---

[1] 'Burnet's *History of his Own Time*', *Quarterly Review* (April 1823), p. 208.

[2] *Quarterly Review* (July 1820), p. 432.

[3] Addison, for example, based his criticism of *Paradise Lost* in *The Spectator* of 1712 (Nos. 267, 273, 279 and 285), upon strictly classical 'rules of epic poetry', and relied entirely upon Aristotle, Homer, and Virgil to provide him with critical standards. Richard Hurd, in his *Letters on Chivalry* (1762), found such standards unsatisfactory, and made a strong plea in Letter VIII on *The Faerie Queene* for 'criticising Spenser's poem, under the idea not of a classical but Gothic composition'. Later in the same essay he declared: 'Judge of the *Faerie Queene* by the classic models, and you are shocked with its disorder: consider it with an eye to its Gothic original, and you find it regular.'

proneness to belittle 'Italian' influence upon English taste. In the *Quarterly* of July 1814, Thomas Dunham Whitaker, in a review of Mason's *Life and Writings of Gray*, praised him highly for reviving interest in the noble school of 'higher Tuscan poets' to which Spenser and Milton had been 'deeply indebted', and which, subsequently, had been shamefully 'neglected by the tame spirit of our poets and critics in the "Augustan age of Addison"'. The reviewer protested strongly against Augustan 'attempts to resolve the character, the merits of the language of Italy into opera airs',[1] and against the Augustan antipathy towards Italian influence so strikingly evident in 'the perpetual ridicule with which the English Spectator so unworthily ... abounds on this subject'. The reversal of taste by means of which the 'Italian' school, as opposed to the 'French', was now coming to enjoy increased favour, is plain in the reviewer's concluding exhortation:

We are now called upon, as in the name of an august triumvirate, by Spenser, by Milton, and by Gray, to turn from the *unpoetical* genius of France, and after we have paid our *primal* homage to the bards of Greece and of ancient Latium, we are invited to contemplate the literature and poetical dignity of modern Italy.

This exaggerated emphasis upon 'French' influence in the age of Queen Anne—a notable tendency in early nineteenth-century criticism which partly derived from Warton, and may be found in the work of Bowles, Southey, Coleridge, Leigh

---

[1] In Augustan poetry itself, this tendency may be seen in Johnson's scornful denunciation in his 'imitation' of Juvenal's Third Satire, *London*, of the 'warbling eunuchs' of Italian opera who now 'fill our silenc'd Stage'. Even more contemptuous was Pope's evocation of the 'genius of the Italian opera' in lines 45–60 of Book Four of *The Dunciad*:

> When lo! a Harlot form soft sliding by,
> With mincing step, small voice, and languid eye:
> Foreign her air, her robe's discordant pride
> In patchwork fluttering, and her head aside ...
> O Cara! Cara! silence all that train:
> Joy to great Chaos! let Division reign ...
> To the same notes thy sons shall hum, or snore,
> And all thy yawning daughters cry, *encore*.

For a comprehensive discussion of this aspect of eighteenth-century taste, see *Boileau and the French Classical Critics in England (1660–1800)*, by A. F. B. Clark, Chapter IV, 'The Anti-Italian Tendency in the 18th Century', pp. 337–60.

Hunt, Hazlitt, Jeffrey and many others as well—was not uncritically received by the *Quarterly*. Discussing French influence
upon English dramatic poetry during the Restoration, Charles
Maturin in a review of Richard Sheil's tragedy in five Acts,
The Apostate, wrote

The usurpations of French authority were, however, still confined
to the externals of English drama; its peculiar tone of passion and
its poetry had escaped ... the argumentative and often sublime
poetry of Dryden, the wild, but sometimes thrilling pathos of Lee,
the lulling tenderness, and the simple nature of Southerne, prove
that all was not lost.[1]

What is particularly interesting about this observation is that
the qualities pronounced free from the taint of French influence—the 'wild', the 'sublime', and the 'pathetic'—were
those most widely invoked by Joseph Warton and others in the
reviving 'Romanticism' of the late eighteenth and early nineteenth centuries.

The 'cyclical' theories of poetry, too, which were growing
increasingly popular, and were used by Peacock, Jeffrey, and
Macaulay for 'placing' the achievement of the Augustan poets,
were sometimes criticised in the pages of the *Quarterly*.[2] George
Ellis, in a review of Byron's *The Corsair* and *Lara*, supporting
traditions of restrained emotion and civilised decorum, complained that these 'new and fanciful' theories were encouraging
contemporary poets 'to seek for subj cts in the manners of ruder
ages ... to wander, in search of unbridled passion, amongst

---

[1] 'Sheil's *The Apostate*', *Quarterly Review* (April 1817), p. 257. This article was
written by Charles Maturin, and revised by Gifford.

[2] The *Quarterly* summarised the 'cyclical' theory as follows: 'It is contended that
poetry is destined to complete a certain cycle or great revolution, accompanying
and dependant on a corresponding cycle of the feelings as well as of the manners
of society. That, originating in times of turbulence and anarchy, it was at first
coarse and vehement;—then pompous and stately;—then affectedly refined and
ingenious;—and finally gay, witty, discursive and familiar. That at this stage of
mankind, however, mankind become disgusted with the heartless frivolity of
their gratifications, and acquire a longing for strong emotions, so that poetry,
following the current of popular opinion is compelled to seek for subjects in the
manners of ruder ages. ... Lastly, that this is the period at which we are now arrived: that a growing appetite for turbulent emotion is the peculiar characteristic
of the age.' (*Quarterly Review*, July 1814, pp. 455–6.)

nations yet imperfectly civilised'. In Byron's case, the reviewer maintained, this 'poetical taste of the present times' had encouraged him to believe that his true genius lay in unmasking the minds of great agents, and in exposing 'all the anatomy of their throbbing bosoms' to our gaze. Although Byron's greatest works, the later satires *The Vision of Judgement* and *Don Juan*, whose Augustan affinities are well known, were still to appear, Ellis had already recognised that the sensationalism and emotional extravagance of Byron's middle period were partly an unfortunate concession to popular Regency taste, and implied fairly obviously that in his opinion Byron was capable of much better things. Invoking with effective irony Byron's popular reputation as a 'searcher of dark bosoms', Ellis declared that Byron ought to be regarded as 'least attractive and least popular whenever he attempts to execute this special office'.[1]

Although the reviewers who contributed to the pages of the *Quarterly* often had varied and divergent critical interests, its critical orientation was, on the whole, markedly conservative. In its dealings with contemporary poets in the early nineteenth century, it preferred to recommend to a greater degree even than the *Edinburgh* the more restrained and disciplined virtues of the Augustan tradition as opposed to the emotional excesses too often encouraged by the brilliant triumphs of the Elizabethan poets. But this chapter, like the previous one, has perhaps shown that these two great agencies for influencing educated opinion cannot be dismissed as merely conservative and merely radical. In the main they were conservative in literary matters, and in the main this was because of the influence of their editors. But both editors were to some extent open to new ideas; and both were eager, in the interests of quality and circulation, to have the leading writers of the age (except Wordsworth, Coleridge, Shelley, and Keats) write for them. Therefore the reviews do reflect a process of moderation and reformulation of ideas through controversy.

---

[1] 'Byron's *Corsair* and *Lara*', *Quarterly Review* (July 1814), p. 457.

CHAPTER V

'BLACKWOOD'S EDINBURGH MAGAZINE'

I. EDITORIAL INFLUENCE

Blackwood's Edinburgh Magazine[1] and the *London Magazine*, which appeared a few years later, were the two principal magazines of the early nineteenth century to rival the 'great reviews' as agents shaping and defining the taste of the contemporary public. The distinction between a 'review' and a 'magazine', barely recognised today, was clearly defined at the time. While the scope of a 'review'—though far from being confined to literature—was entirely critical, the scope of a 'magazine' was much wider and more miscellaneous. Critical reviewing remained an important function of the 'magazine', but it also published a wide variety of original contributions, including poetry and fiction.[2] By this means it appealed to more varied interests in the reading public, and sought not only to safeguard intelligent standards of taste—in terms, for example, of the *Edinburgh*'s vigilant motto, *Judex damnatur cum nocens absolvitur*—but also more directly to amuse and entertain its readers.

In 1817 the *Edinburgh* and *Quarterly* reviews dominated the periodical literature of England without rival, but William Blackwood, who was John Murray's agent in Edinburgh, realised that by better exploitation of the varied interests of Regency readers he could produce a flourishing magazine which would seriously challenge his rival Constable's sales in

---

[1] For its first six numbers (April–September 1817) the magazine was called *The Edinburgh Monthly Magazine*.

[2] *Blackwood's* was a great pioneer in the serial publication of novels, which became of great importance in Victorian times. Thirty volumes of *Tales from Blackwood's* appeared in three series between 1858–90. Even after the turn of the century, Conrad first published *Lord Jim* in serial form in *Blackwood's*.

Edinburgh and elsewhere. Blackwood's feeling that the quarterlies were failing to satisfy the potential interests of a large
body of contemporary readers was, as events soon proved,
largely justified. Some readers were indeed a little fatigued by
what they considered the too exclusively critical gusto of the
Edinburgh and the *Quarterly*, and Mrs Jameson, for example,
noted in her *Diary of an Ennuyée*:

Methinks these two reviews stalk through the literary world like
the two giants in Pulci's *Morgante Maggiore*; the one pounding,
slaying, mangling, despoiling with blunt fury like the hearty, ortho-
dox, club-armed Morgante; the other like the sneering, witty, half-
pagan, half-baptised Margutte, slashing and cutting and piercing,
through thick and thin.

This is evidently the exaggerated criticism of an *Ennuyée*, yet
although *Blackwood*'s could match the destructive wit of its two
great predecessors on occasion,[1] its numerous tales and short
stories, its lively dialogue, its copious extracts of poetry ranging
from album-verse to the most recent productions of Wordsworth gave it a considerable appeal among an extremely varied
body of readers. It is well known that the major reviews and
magazines of Regency times provided reading for the entire
family, and some remarks of Charlotte Brontë suggest that
Blackwood's could provide a good deal to interest even a girl
of thirteen. 'Mr. Driver lends us *Blackwood*'s *Magazine*,' she
informs us in 1829, adding at the same time with great confidence that it was 'the best periodical there is'.

Blackwood's enterprise in founding a new magazine was at
first unfavourably received by the reading public, and the first
number was given a very lukewarm reception in April 1817.
After six uninspired numbers under Pringle and Cleghorn,
Blackwood enlisted the services of three high-spirited young
men—John Gibson Lockhart, John Wilson (both fresh from
Oxford) and James Hogg (the 'Ettrick Shepherd'). The

[1] For example, in the violent attack upon Coleridge's *Biographia Literaria* in
October 1817, or in the sustained and devastating ridicule heaped upon Leigh
Hunt and the 'Cockney School'.

notorious *Chaldee MS*,[1] in which they ridiculed the most eminent personalities of Edinburgh in language that was a parody of Scripture, soon involved Blackwood in acrimonious correspondence and threatened law-suits, but the blaze of publicity which attended these proceedings made *Blackwood's Magazine* almost as well known as the *Edinburgh* and *Quarterly*.[2] The calibre of its contributors, who in later years included George Eliot, ensured that *Blackwood's* maintained an honoured position.

Although nominally under the control of William Blackwood, *Blackwood's* possessed no editor like Jeffrey or Gifford who could through the impact of his personality impress what has been described as a 'lasting corporate personality' upon the critical standards of the magazine.[3] The absence of a true editor was in fact one of the means by which Blackwood avoided responsibility for some of the more provocatively personal satire appearing in its pages. As for its general critical standards, *Blackwood's Magazine* was on the whole more favourably disposed towards the 'Romantic' impulses of the age than either the *Edinburgh* or *Quarterly*; yet the conflicting tendencies of the time may be seen, for example, in the criticism of Lockhart (an outstanding influence upon the early career of *Maga*), who

[1] In the *Chaldee MS*, 'the great wild boar from the forests of Lebanon' was plainly Hogg, 'the beautiful leopard from the valley of the palm trees', Wilson; and 'the scorpion who delighted to sting the faces of men' Lockhart.

[2] John Wilson estimated the circulation of *Blackwood's* at about 17,000. John Murray stated in a letter to James Hogg, dated 24 January 1818: '... the *Quarterly Review*, of which, by the way, the number printed is equal to that of the *Edinburgh Review*, 12,000 ... I hope to make 14,000 after two numbers.' According to Mrs Oliphant, *Blackwood's* had a circulation of 6000 copies a month in 1818. See *Annals of a Publishing House* (1897), p. 190. For Wilson's figures, see 'An Hour's Tête-à-tête with the Public', *Blackwood's* (October 1820), p. 78.

[3] 'The system of anonymous reviewing in periodicals under the guidance and control of responsible editors, themselves men of strong individuality, soon led to the review acquiring a distinct personality of its own. By ninety-nine of every hundred readers the criticism expressed would be accepted as that of the review—of the *Edinburgh* or the *Quarterly*—and they would inquire no further. Among regular contributors, as, of course, with the editor, the feeling prevailed that the articles in the review represented something more than the opinion, at the moment, of the individual writer. ... Without the practice of anonymity, combined with responsible and vigorous editorship, a lasting corporate personality could not have been acquired.' (*The Cambridge History of English Literature*, XII, 141–2.)

later became editor of the *Quarterly*, in succession to Sir J. T. Coleridge, in 1825.

From the very outset Lockhart recognised Wordsworth as the greatest poetical genius of his age, but this did not prevent him from maintaining at the same time a high regard for the Augustan poets.[1] He shared his father-in-law Sir Walter Scott's delight in Dryden's poetry, and felt that Dryden's example had had a decisively beneficial influence upon Scott's own verse. Lockhart preferred the heroic couplet to blank verse, and in his *Life of Burns* praised Dryden for his 'masculine wit and sense' and his 'strong and graceful versification'. He was intelligent enough, too, to recognise immediately the originality and power of Coleridge's critical insight, but noted in his review of *Table Talk* that one of Coleridge's signal failures had been his inability to appreciate Pope. Lockhart described Pope in this review as 'one of our best and greatest poets'.[2]

2. AUGUSTAN POETRY AND CONTEMPORARY VERSE

Summing up the spirit of the times in a review of 'Barry Cornwall's *The Flood of Thessaly*, *The Girl of Provence*, *and other poems*, in May 1822, *Blackwood's Magazine* commented:

This is the age of Marmion, and Waverley, and Childe Harold, and Don Juan, and Ruth, and Laodamia, and the ancient Mariner, and Basil, and De Montfort, and Sir Eustace Gray, and Peter Grimes—we will be content with nothing but powerful passion . . .[3]

---

[1] 'His position in regard to the English writers of the century before, however, has a special interest, inasmuch as it has some bearing upon his attitude towards the Romantics. A classically trained mind like Lockhart's, imbued with a sense of order and restraint, would be likely to find something to admire in the writers of the English classical period. He calls Dryden "one of the greatest of our masters" (*Life of Scott*, II, 48), and feels that Coleridge's failure to appreciate Pope . . . was something to be deplored.' (Gilbert Macbeth, *J. G. Lockhart: A Critical Study*, 1935, p. 84.)

[2] Summing up Coleridge's claims to be regarded as Dr Johnson's successor in criticism, Lockhart commented: '. . . he had some early prejudices which warped his judgement as to one or two of our best and greatest poets, especially Pope; but with rare exceptions, he brought to the consideration of literary works, whether old or new, not only a great shrewdness and subtlety of thought and observation, but a most genial and generous tone of feeling.'

[3] *Blackwood's* (May 1823), p. 533.

The kind of poetical interests suggested by this impressive collocation of names regarded sympathetically by the reviewer, helps to explain the customary evaluation of Augustan poetry in *Blackwood's*, in the years between 1817 and 1830. In discussing the famous 'Pope Controversy', the reviewers made it plain that, although not uncritical of Bowles, they sympathised more with his evaluation of Pope than with that of Campbell or Lord Byron. In an article entitled 'Bowles's Answer to Campbell' in July 1819, Bowles's estimate of Pope was found to be on the whole 'rational, judicious, and true'; and, in an article asking the provocative question 'Why are Poets indifferent Critics?', *Blackwood's* declared, in September 1821, that Byron had set himself an impossible task in seeking to persuade the public that 'Pope is, after all, the greatest of poets'. A few months previously, in May 1821, *Blackwood's* had declared in an article on 'Lord Byron and Pope', that the question for the present age was not to inquire 'Whether Pope is a poet?'—for that he assuredly was—'but to ascertain the *order* to which be belongs, that we may assign him a proper place in the poetical calendar.' Protesting that its strictures had been directly provoked by the 'exaggerated panegyrics' that had been lately 'lavished on the little man of Twickenham', and by the attempt to 'establish a sort of Popedom', *Blackwood's* thought that particular care was necessary not to be 'carried by the force of reaction into the opposite extreme'. The review concluded with an attempt to give a balanced appraisal of Pope's achievement:

Let us give to Pope—elegant sensible Pope—the praise that is his due. We sit down to the feast of reason and the flow of fancy which his works present to us with perpetual delight. The variety of his powers securing us against any feeling of satiety, and the exquisite taste with which he embellishes whatever he touches,—

> Leaving that beautiful which still was so,
> And making that which was not—

gives to his reader a peculiar species of enjoyment which no other poet perhaps can communicate. If he does not sweep the strings of

the human heart with that master-touch, which belongs exclusively
to a highest rank of poets, he knows how

      'To wake the soul by tender strokes of art,'

and can at once charm the ear, delight the imagination, and inform
the understanding. These are no slight qualifications, and though
they may not be sufficient to entitle Pope to a place in the highest
rank of poets, will ever cause him to shine pre-eminently in the
second class,—

      —'Velut inter ignes
      Luna minores.'[1]

The touchstone by which Pope was relegated to the second order
of creative writers was Theseus's famous description of the poet
at the beginning of the fifth act of *A Midsummer Night's Dream*,[2]
in which he claims that it is the 'shaping phantasies' of the
'strong imagination' which enable the poet to rise above the
confines of 'cool reason'. Using this description as a norm
against which to judge Pope's achievement, *Blackwood's* concluded: 'Can this be applied to Pope? We think not. He is a
moralist, a wit, a critic, and a fine writer, much more than he
is a poet.' This account of Pope's peculiar inadequacies is
derived almost *verbatim* from Jeffrey's evaluation of Pope in his
review of John Ford in the *Edinburgh Review* of August 1811.
The *Blackwood's* reviewer records his indebtedness to Jeffrey
later in the article; what he evidently did not recognise, how-

---

[1] *Blackwood's* (May 1821), p. 233.

[2] The following description exemplified for the reviewer the qualities associated
with the highest order of poetry:

    'The Poet's eye in a fine frenzy rolling,
    Doth glance
    From heaven to earth, from earth to heaven.
    And as the imagination bodies forth
    The forms of things
    Unknowne; the Poet's pen
    Turns them to shapes, and gives to airy nothings,
    A local habitation, and a name.'

(The vagaries of the quotation are partly the reviewer's.) Crabbe quoted this
passage in the Preface to the volume of *Tales* which he published in 1812, and,
while noting that it had become a popular description of the true poet, commented:
'... still, that these poets should entirely engross the title as to exclude those who
address their productions to the plain sense and sober judgement of their readers,
rather than to their fancy and imagination, I must repeat that I am unwilling to
admit.'

ever, was the extent to which Jeffrey's own views were derived from Joseph Warton. Making a distinction between the Augustans and those who in his opinion belonged to the highest order of poets, Warton had declared in the Dedication to the first volume of his *Essay on Pope*, 'We do not, it should seem, sufficiently attend to the difference there is, between a Man of Wit, a Man of Sense, and a True Poet.' This kind of distinction is one of the most important traditions in the hostile criticism of Augustan poetry, and its culmination will of course be found in Matthew Arnold's confident dismissal of Augustan poetry in his essay on *Thomas Gray*:

The difference between genuine poetry and the poetry of Dryden, Pope and all their school, is briefly this: their poetry is conceived and composed in their wits, genuine poetry is conceived and composed in the soul.[1]

Blackwood's Magazine shows ample evidence of the more 'Romantic' impulses of the age, and, indeed, had a poor opinion of those of Gifford's contemporaries who wrote within the Augustan tradition—they were described in *Blackwood's* as 'imitators of imitations, the third pressing of an exhausted wine-press' and, even more scornfully, as the 'ninth and dwindled farrow of the school of Pope and Addison'. But we also find in its pages spirited defences of Pope against the more violent denunciations of the vanguard of the Romantic critics. Keats's impertinent dismissal of the achievement of the Augustan age in *Sleep and Poetry*, for example, led to a strong protest from *Blackwood's Magazine* against the

long strains of foaming abuse against a certain class of English poets, whom, with Pope at their head, it is much the fashion with the ignorant unsettled pretenders of the present time to undervalue.

The protest, which was as much an attack on the 'Cockney School' as a defence of Pope, went on to ridicule

fanciful dreaming tea-drinkers, who ... presume to talk with contempt of some of the most exquisite spirits the world ever produced,

---

[1] This essay first appeared in 1880, and was prefixed to a selection from Gray's poetry in volume III of Ward's *English Poets*. It was reprinted in *Essays in Criticism*, Series 2 (1888).

merely because they did not happen to exert their faculties in laborious affected descriptions of flowers seen in window-pots, or cascades heard at Vauxhall; in short, because they chose to be wits, philosophers, patriots, and poets, rather than to found the Cockney school of versification, morality, and politics, a century before its time.[1]

Even more emphatic evidence of the extent to which admiration of Pope's poetry survived undiminished even in the 1830s, may be found in the long conversation between the Shepherd, North, and Tickler about the recent 'botheration about Pope', in *Noctes Ambrosianae*, which appeared in *Blackwood's* in March 1825. North had already indicated his attitude towards Bowles by lighting his cigar with his latest pamphlet; but it is the Shepherd, who had previously shown little interest in Pope ('I care little about Pope—except his *Louisa and Abelard*'), who is most eloquent and lively in his praise of Pope, comparing his work with modern poetry to the latter's disadvantage. The Shepherd picks out the following works of Pope as being specially delightful:

... his sound translation o' a' Homer's works, that reads just like an original War-Yepic,—His Yessay on Man, that . . . is just ane of the best moral discourses that ever I heard in or out o' the poupit,— His Yepistles about the Passions, and sic like, in the whilk he goes baith deep and high, far deeper and higher baith than mony a modern poet, who must needs be either in a diving-bell or a balloon,—His Rape o' the Lock o' Hair, wi' a' these Sylphs floating about in the machinery o' the Rosicrucian Philosophism, perfectly yelegant and gracefu', and as gude, in their way, as onything o' my ain about fairies, either in the *Queen's Wake* or *Queen Hynde*,—His Louisa to Abelard is, as I said before, coorse in the subject-matter, but, O sirs! powerfu' and pathetic in execution—and sic a perfect spate o' versification! His unfortunate lady, wha sticked hersel for love wi' a drawn sword, and was afterwards seen as a ghost, dim-beckoning through the shade—a verra poetical thoct surely, and full both of terror and pity—

NORTH: Stop, James—You will run yourself out of breath. Why, you said a few minutes ago, that you did not much care about Pope, and were not at all familiar with his works—you have them at your finger ends.

[1] 'The Cockney School of Poetry', *Blackwood's* (August 1818), No. IV, p. 521.

SHEPHERD: I never ken what's in my mind till it begins to work . . .

North, a little while later, develops the Shepherd's unfavourable comparison of modern with Augustan poetry, and asks:

. . . What poet of this age, with the exception perhaps of Byron, can
be justly said, when put into close comparison with Pope, to have
written the English language at all . . . from what living poet is it
possible to select any passage that will bear to be spouted (say by
James Ballantyne himself, the best declaimer extant) after any
one of fifty casually taken passages from Pope?—Not one.

TICKLER: What would become of Bowles himself, with all his
            elegance, pathos, and true feeling? Oh! dear me,
            James, what a dull, dozing, disjointed, dawdling,
            dowdy of a drawl would be his Muse, in her very
            best voice and tune when called upon to get up and
            sing a solo after the sweet and strong singer of
            Twickenham!

NORTH   Or Wordsworth—with his eternal—Here we go up,
            up, and up, and here we go down, down, and here
            we go roundabout, roundabout!—Look at the nerve-
            less laxity of his *Excursion*!—What interminable
            prosing! The language is out of condition:—fat and
            fozy, thick-winded, purfled, and plethoric. Can he be
            compared with Pope? Fie on't, no, no, no!—Pugh,
            pugh!

TICKLER   Southey—Coleridge—Moore?

NORTH   No; not one of them. They are all eloquent, diffusive,
            rich, lavish, generous, prodigal of their words. But
            so are they all deficient in sense, muscle, sinew,
            thews, ribs, spine. Pope, as an artist, beats them
            hollow . . .[1]

The creative energy and liveliness of *Noctes Ambrosianae*—
some of the most readable criticism of the period—serves to
heighten their critical insight and intelligence. However, the
views advanced in this conversation concerning the relative
merits of Augustan and contemporary poetry are no doubt too
splendidly uninhibited to reflect the average critical standards
typical of *Blackwood's Magazine*. More truly representative of
the standards of the magazine as a whole are some of Croker's

[1] *Blackwood's* (March 1825). Reprinted in *Noctes Ambrosianae* (4 vols), Edinburgh
(1855), I, 13–15.

remarks in his discussion of the 'Cockney School' in *Blackwood's Magazine* of August 1818:

Begging these gentlemens' pardon, although Pope was not a poet of the same high order with some who are now living, yet, to deny his genius, is just as absurd as to dispute that of Wordsworth, or to believe in that of Hunt.[1]

3. AUGUSTAN POETRY AND PRE-RESTORATION VERSE

In its attitude to pre-Restoration poetry *Blackwood's Magazine* from its very outset showed firmly nineteenth-century tastes. 'The poetical genius of this country', it declared in July 1818, produced in Elizabethan times 'an unequalled constellation of great spirits.' The spirit of this revival was sometimes open to criticism, however, and an article in December 1821 on the *Retrospective Review*, which had been founded in the previous year by Henry Southern, while noting that 'the old English drama and poetry have met of late with more attention', also felt compelled to comment that the 'admiration which has hitherto been shewn, has savoured more of undistinguishing enthusiasm, than good taste or careful selection'. But the long series of 'Analytical Essays' on the poetry of Shakespeare, Jonson, Marlowe, Webster, Fletcher, Ford, Dekker, Rowley and many others which appeared in the early numbers of *Blackwood's*, indicates its own enthusiasm for Elizabethan and Jacobean poetry, and was probably intended partly to counter indiscriminate praise.

As in the *Edinburgh* and *Quarterly* and elsewhere, it was the glories of Elizabethan poetry—which, after the long Augustan interregnum, it was felt the age had now to discover afresh—that provided the most effective means of indicating the limitations of Pope and his contemporaries. Invoking the now-familiar charge of excessive 'French' influence upon the poets of Queen Anne's time, the reviewer of Ellen Fitzarthur's *The Widow's Tale, and other poems*, declared in March 1822:

In the Anglo-Gallican school (such it merits to be called, for our palates were then spoiled for the racy taste of our ancestors, by a

[1] *Blackwood's* (August 1818), p. 520.

foolish deference to France), Pope must be allowed to be the very
first in excellence,—'but to class him with great poets, to say that
he is a writer of the *same kind* as Milton and Shakespeare, is absurd;
verse is common to them, and verse is all which they have in common'. He is the poet of the town and of the schools—exquisite in
satire and ethics, in mock-heroics and *vers de société*, in a prologue
or a reflective epistle, in an epitaph or an epigram—but these are
not the moulds into which the highest order of poets naturally cast
their ore. Baser materials than 'thoughts that breathe and words
that burn' will do to be so worked up; and in Pope's poetical
temperament he had no such pulses as must have throbbed along
every vein of him who clothed passion with all the magnificence of
imagination in *Lear*, and wantoned with the many-twinkling wings
of fancy in the *Midsummer Night's Dream* and *The Tempest*.[1]

The relative status of Augustan and Elizabethan poetry was
clearly indicated, too, in the article already referred to entitled
'Why are Poets indifferent Critics?', which appeared in September 1821. Here, while it was granted that Pope was a poet
of 'good sense, wit, and judgement', it was pointed out that his
style was 'plainly the effect of intense labour'—its 'polish' the
result of 'repeated touches', and its 'correctness' of 'anxious
and perpetual pruning'. Commenting on the limitations in
Augustan sensibility implied in its inadequate appreciation of
the Elizabethans, the reviewer added:

A genius like that of Pope could not cordially relish the natural and
luxurious freedom of the older poets. Their thoughts rushed on like
the stream of a mountain torrent, whilst his flowed on with the
equable current of a canal.[2]

A more interesting and original discussion of this subject
may be found in an article, 'On the Progressive Change of
Poetical Style', which appeared in January 1820. The reviewer,
who began his discussion by noting that the 'splendour' of the
Roman Augustan age had 'diminished that of all after literature, and in a great measure blinded posterity to the excel-

---

[1] *Blackwood's* (March 1822), p. 287. The quotation in the body of the passage
is taken from the Preface to Southey's *Specimens of the Later English Poets*, which the
reviewer described as a 'hasty but clever *coup d'oeil* of this department of our
literature'.

[2] *Blackwood's* (September 1821), pp. 183–4.

lencies of succeeding authors', defined his central theme as an attempt to 'point out the similarities between the English poetical style, and that of the Latin classics'. It was more common to describe the Elizabethan period as the 'golden' rather than the 'Augustan' age of English poetry in the early nineteenth century, but the reviewer having suggested that the typical Augustan virtues were related to 'polish', 'simplicity', 'refinement' and 'originality', declared that the 'general style of poetry in the reign of Elizabeth' entitled it to be regarded as 'the *true* Augustan age of Britain'. It is interesting to note that it was largely non-dramatic poetry ('improved by grafts from the ancient classical and modern Italian Parnassus') rather than dramatic poetry (more of 'indigenous growth') that was deemed truly Augustan. Spenser, had he devoted his powers to 'regular Epic' verse, 'might have ranked as the English Virgil'. For the Metaphysical poets and their 'far-fetched conceits' the reviewer had scant praise,[1] though he shared the familiar Augustan notion that a new and improved tradition of poetry had been founded in the work of Waller and Denham. This latter tradition, though without the Elizabethan virtues of 'simplicity' and 'originality', had distinctive virtues of its own. The Elizabethan virtues were replaced by a deceptive 'sophistication', best exemplified in Dryden's style, which, though as far removed from true 'simplicity' as the worst excesses of the Metaphysicals, 'by the better adaptation of the materials to the subject' altogether concealed the art of the poet. After illustrating his point by quoting from half a dozen of Dryden's poems, the reviewer commented: 'Such is the style of Dryden, the great principle of which has, since his time,

---

[1] There was little true appreciation of the merits of Metaphysical poetry in the early nineteenth century (Coleridge's criticism is quite exceptional); and it is an interesting comment on the relative status of Metaphysical and Augustan poetry at this time, that the reviewer, having censured Donne for his 'lumbering conceits' and 'lumbering phraseology', informs us that he was now best known 'by the translations which Pope has made of some of his satires'.

For a fuller discussion of this aspect of early nineteenth-century taste, see A. H. Nethercot, 'The Reputation of the "Metaphysical" Poets, during the Age of Johnson and the Romantic Revival', *Studies in Philology*, xxii (1925).

continued, and probably will continue, to be that of all successful English poets.'[1] What this plainly implied was that—as in
the criticism of the *Edinburgh* and the *Quarterly*—the recognition
of the supremacy of the Elizabethans did not necessarily imply
their acceptance as the best models for contemporary poets. The
special linguistic and other social conditions which made the
Elizabethan achievement possible—'an aggregate of excellencies which it may be difficult to parallel'—were largely
absent in the nineteenth century. The reviewer, noting the
literary and derivative nature of aspects of the Romantic
revival—'criticism which turns back for models to the work of
early poets, is certainly mistaken'—concluded by observing
that 'the regions of poetical simplicity are quickly exhausted
and to expect further discoveries there, is to expect them in a
country which has been surveyed and mapped over and over'.[2]

Criticism in *Blackwood's Magazine*, then, though hospitable
to the newer Romantic tendencies of the age, was far from one-
sided. It condemned the more extreme criticism of Augustan
poetry made by the Romantics themselves, and its standards
were flexible enough to accommodate as well the robustly pro-
Augustan criticism of the 'Ettrick shepherds', North and
Tickler. But in its general tendency to regard the achievement
of the Augustan poets as a triumph in a creditable though inferior order of poetry, *Blackwood's* anticipated the major
Victorian trend.

---

[1] *Blackwood's* (January 1820), p. 369.
[2] 'On the Progressive Change of Poetical Style', *Blackwood's* (January 1820),
p. 369.

CHAPTER VI

THE 'POPE CONTROVERSY'
AND THE MINOR REVIEWS

It is only to be expected that a study of the minor reviews and magazines of the time will furnish few strikingly new tendencies in the criticism of Augustan poetry. Nevertheless, the minor periodical literature of the time should not be entirely neglected, for it is worth noting, for example, that it was in the pages of the less well-known reviews that many of the essays, letters, and pamphlets which went to make up the celebrated 'Pope Controversy' first appeared.

To anyone who has attempted to follow in any detail the interminable repetitions, digressions, and misunderstandings which are characteristic of the controversy, it is a relief to discover that a history of it has already been compiled by J. J. Van Rennes in his *Bowles, Byron, and the Pope Controversy* (Amsterdam, 1927).[1] Van Rennes's principal interest was to assess the intrinsic value of the critical arguments and principles invoked by the controversialists, and, inquiring at this level, he is, not surprisingly, disappointed. From the point of view of our own inquiries the controversy retains a considerable interest as an index of the fluctuations in the critical reputation of Pope among critics and reviewers in the years between 1806 and 1826.

The controversy had three fairly well-defined phases. The first (1806–12) began with the publication of Bowles's edition of Pope's *Collected Works*. Bowles's relegation of Pope to the level of an inferior though polished versifier, was not allowed to go unchallenged for long, and his views were severely criticised

---

[1] Van Rennes has, however, overlooked some important sources of information —for example, the notices of the controversy which may be found in the *Edinburgh Review* and *Blackwood's Magazine*. A detailed bibliography of the controversy has therefore been included in the Appendix to this book.

by Campbell in the *Edinburgh Review* of January 1808. Other defenders of Pope soon appeared, and Byron championed the cause of Pope even more vehemently in *English Bards and Scotch Reviewers*, which appeared in the following year. Here Byron claimed boldly that had Bowles belonged to the age of Pope, he would certainly have been assured of immortality among the Dunces. Leigh Hunt, though he made no mention of Bowles, admonished the defenders of Pope in *The Feast of the Poets*, which was first published in the *Reflector*, No. IV of 1811. It soon became apparent, however, that Bowles himself had been made to realise that his anti-Augustan criticism of Pope had been excessive. The evidence for this may be found in the second edition of his Pope, which appeared in 1812. Most of his adversely critical notes to Pope's poems were drastically reduced, and his biographical *Memoir*, in which he had attacked Pope's moral character, was replaced by Johnson's *Life*.

The controversy subsided in 1812 with the honours largely with the defenders of Pope, but was revived vigorously in 1819 by Campbell's 'Essay on English Poetry', with which he prefaced his *Specimens of the British Poets*. Bowles replied immediately with his pamphlet 'The Invariable Principles of Poetry'. Jeffrey, though he refused to be drawn into the controversy, was not unsympathetic towards Bowles in his review of Campbell's *Specimens* in the *Edinburgh*, and *Blackwood's Magazine* too was favourably disposed towards Bowles's views in 'Bowles's Answer to Campbell' in July 1819. The publication in 1820 of Singer's edition of Spence's *Anecdotes of Pope* which exposed some of Bowles's insinuations as false, greatly heartened Pope's defenders. Octavius Gilchrist published a strongly pro-Augustan review of Spence's *Anecdotes* in the *London Magazine* of February 1820, and this was followed by an even more emphatic defence of Pope by Isaac D'Israeli in the *Quarterly Review* of July 1820. The liveliness of the controversial interest excited at this time by the question of Pope's status as a poet is well illustrated by the articles on this subject which appeared in the *Gentleman's Magazine*, the *Pamphleteer*, and the

New Monthly Magazine (then under the editorship of Campbell), during the remaining months of the same year.

Byron, as we learn from his diary and from his letters, had been watching the progress of the controversy with considerable interest, and he joined the fray himself with his well-known Letter to John Murray on the Rev. W. L. Bowles's Strictures on the Life and Writings of Pope, in February 1821. Extracts from Byron's letter were published in the *Gentleman's Magazine* in April 1821, and the May issue of *Blackwood's Magazine* contained an article entitled 'Lord Byron and Pope'. In this article *Blackwood's*, though plainly anxious to give 'elegant, sensible Pope' his due, was alarmed at what it saw as an attempt to 'raise a sort of Popedom' in contemporary letters. In the following month Hazlitt, in the *London Magazine* of June 1821, reviewed the entire controversy in an article entitled 'Pope, Lord Byron, and Bowles'. Here Hazlitt was scornful of the confused eclecticism and lack of consistent argument which had marred too much of the controversy, and observed that

All this *pribble-prabble* about Pope, and Milton, and Shakespeare, and what foreigners say of us, and the Venus, and Antinous, and the Acropolis, and the Grand Canal at Venice, and the Turkish Fleet, and Falconer's *Shipwreck*, and ethics, and ethical poetry (with the single exception of some picturesque sketches in the poet's best prose-style) is what might be expected from any Bond-street lounger ...

Hazlitt was equally trenchant in his criticism of Bowles's allegations concerning Pope's moral character, and the purpose behind his review was to plead for a more discriminating and unprejudiced appreciation of Pope's merits. Hazlitt's comments do not appear to have materially affected the course of the controversy, and it continued relatively unabated in the pages of the *Pamphleteer* and the *New Monthly Magazine* until 1822.

The final phase of the controversy (1824–6) began with the publication of Roscoe's edition of Pope's *Collected Works*. This provided the occasion for an enthusiastically pro-Augustan review of the edition in the *Quarterly* of October 1825, in which this edition was preferred to those of Warton and Bowles. In the very opening paragraph of the article the reviewer referred to the marked revival of interest in Pope's poetry which had occurred in recent years, and noted that it was a 'juncture at which an appeal might be made with peculiar propriety to the high name of Pope'. Bowles replied in the same year with 'A Final Appeal to the Literary Public relative to Pope', and the controversy concluded with a series of critical exchanges between Roscoe and Bowles in 1826.

The final outcome of the controversy, not surprisingly, was far from conclusive. A large proportion of it was devoted to a discussion of Pope's character as it was reflected in his personal relationships, and here surmise was too often allowed to masquerade as evidence. As for Pope's poetry, the issues disputed were principally two: first, the 'order' to which Pope's poetry was to be assigned on the basis of the poetic *genres* he employed; and secondly, a dispute as to the relative merit of poetic imagery derived from 'natural' and from 'artificial' sources.

On the first of these questions, Byron observed: 'But all this "ordering" of poets is purely arbitrary on the part of Mr. Bowles. There may or may not be, in fact, different "orders" of poetry, but the poet is always ranked according to his execution, and not according to the branch of his art.' Although it is undoubtedly true that some *genres* permit the poet a greater scope and range than others, Byron's attitude appears refreshingly sensible. The dispute concerning the relative merits of 'artificial' and 'natural' images, was, on the whole, unenlightened and confused.[1] Coleridge's insistence in the *Biographia Literaria* that it was the use which a poet made of his imagery rather than the source from which it was derived that

[1] Professor R. Wellek has recently commented upon this aspect of the controversy: 'The polemics defending Pope against Bowles's strictures are hopelessly entangled in the puerile contrast between "natural" and "artificial" subjects in poetry: Bowles arguing that the sun and the sea are more poetic than a ship and Byron countering that the sea without a ship is only an empty desert, and so on.' ('From Jeffrey to Shelley', *A History of Modern Criticism*, II, 123.)

was of fundamental importance, exposes the ultimate barrenness of this aspect of the controversy.

From the point of view of our own investigations, however, the main interest of the controversy is the light which it throws upon Pope's reputation at the time. Later commentators generally tended to agree with Bowles's evaluation of Pope, though they were often doubtful about the fairness of his polemical methods. Ernest Rhys, for example, reviewing the controversy in 1897, wrote '. . . we cannot doubt which of the two is right, but Bowles's bumptious absurdities of expression make it hard to believe him as intelligent as he is'.[1] James Russell Lowell remarked that Bowles 'though in a vague way aesthetically right, contrived always to be argumentatively wrong', and H. A. Beers noted in the second chapter of his *History of Romanticism in the 19th Century* that 'The victory remained with Bowles, not because he had won it by argument, but because opinion had changed, and changed probably once and for all.' It is unlikely that literary opinion ever changes 'once and for all', and the revival of interest in Augustan poetry in the present century provides yet another illustration of the extent to which the 'final' judgements of one age may appear merely relative to the next. In Bowles's own time, however, it is worth noting that the supporters of Pope clearly outnumbered his detractors among the controversialists. Bowles, though he received some support from *Blackwood's*, had to contend virtually single-handed with the reviewers of nearly half a dozen of the major and minor periodical journals of the time; and this suggests the weight of pro-Augustan opinion which still survived in the earlier decades of the nineteenth century.

---

[1] *Literary Pamphlets—Poetry: Sidney to Byron*, Introduction.

PART III

OTHER CONTEMPORARY SOURCES

CHAPTER VII

ANTI-AUGUSTAN CRITICISM

I. INTRODUCTION

In presenting a cross-section of the individual criticism of Augustan poetry in the early nineteenth century, one is committed to dealing with a wide variety of critical opinions of varying degrees of antipathy and friendliness. Although there were recognisable groups, schools, and literary coteries at this time, and similarities and inter-connections are therefore not difficult to trace in the criticism of the age, the pronouncements on Augustan poetry, particularly of the major writers, remain obstinately individual, and resist being reduced to any neat formula. For example, although the poets of the 'Lake School' (originally a derisory coinage not approved of by its members) had many beliefs in common, a detailed examination of the criticism of Wordsworth, Coleridge, and Southey, makes it plain that each reacted to very different elements in the poetry of Dryden, Pope, and Johnson. Hazlitt, too, who was sometimes associated with this group, and claimed that he derived his first 'insight into the mysteries of poetry' from his early 'acquaintance with the authors of the *Lyrical Ballads*'[1] was sometimes severely critical of their views. Hazlitt says several times that a certain narrowness in Wordsworth's sensibility prevented him from achieving a true appreciation of Dryden

---

[1] A walking tour with Wordsworth down the Bristol Channel in 1798 was a great formative experience for Hazlitt—'We walked for miles and miles on dark brown heaths overlooking the Channel, with the Welsh hills behind', conversing all the while.

'He spoke with contempt of Gray, and with intolerance of Pope. He did not like the versification of the latter. He observed that the ears of these couplet-writers might be charged with having short memories, that could not retain the harmony of whole passages. He thought little of Junius as a writer; he had a dislike of Johnson.' ('My First Acquaintance with Poets', *The Liberal*, 1823.) For an account of the positive ideas Hazlitt derived from Wordsworth, see 'On Reading Old Books', *Collected Works*, ed. Waller and Glover, vii, 226.

and Pope.[1] Even when criticism was derivative and nominally in agreement, for example in the criticism of the minor members of the group, fundamental dissimilarities may be found, arising probably from inadequate comprehension. Charles Lloyd's *Poetical Essays on the Character of Pope as a Poet and a Moralist* appeared in 1821, and though obviously Wordsworthian in origin, it substituted the style and reasoning of a debating society for the deeper personal interests which engaged Wordsworth in his best criticism of Pope.

Striking contradictions may be found, too, within the work of even a single critic. Scott's preoccupations with Border minstrelsy and mediaevalism are not always easy to reconcile with his delight in the Augustan strength of Johnson, whose poetry moved him more deeply than that of any other poet. Nor will anyone dispute that the poetry of Byron's middle period—which made him the lion of Regency society, and drove Scott from narrative verse to prose fiction—had nothing in common with his boundless admiration for Pope throughout his life. Even Keats, who dealt scornfully with the Augustans in *Sleep and Poetry*, found Dryden a congenial influence when writing *Lamia*.

These examples suggest the danger of trying to classify individual criticisms of Augustan poetry in terms of simple antagonisms and sympathies. They also suggest that nothing can replace careful individual study of the opinions on Augustan poetry contained in the criticism of each writer of the age. But the critics of the age can be broadly divided into those who were on the whole antagonistic or sympathetic towards the poetry of the Augustan age, without blurring the wide variety of opinions which existed within each of these two classes. This diversity ranged, among sympathetic critics, from the uninhibited enthusiasm of Byron to the ambiguous ironies and pseudo-philistine mockery of Peacock; and, among hostile critics, from the blandness with which Shelley, largely by

---

[1] It is only fair to add that Wordsworth felt that his views on Dryden and Pope had been misrepresented by Hazlitt.

implication, dismissed the whole Augustan tradition in the *Defence of Poetry*, to the destructive fury with which Bowles turned upon the defenders of Pope in his later pamphlets.

2. WORDSWORTH, COLERIDGE AND SOUTHEY

The great pioneer literary historian of the eighteenth century was Thomas Warton, Professor of Poetry at Oxford from 1756—the year in which his brother Joseph Warton's *Essay on Pope* first appeared—to 1767. It was chiefly Thomas Warton's research that provided the background for, and often directly stimulated, the great revival of interest in mediaeval, Elizabethan, and Jacobean literature in the early nineteenth century. Warton's pioneer work of scholarship, his *History of English Poetry* (which appeared in three volumes in 1774, 1778, and 1781) is, in its own way, as astonishing a piece of comparatively unaided literary research as Johnson's *Dictionary*.[1] The exceptional effect which Warton's *History* had upon its first readers has been described as 'difficult to realise and almost impossible to exaggerate', and the reason is not far to seek:

Now for the first time was recovered from the oblivion in which it had hitherto remained the pageant of English poetry as it unfolded itself from the 13th to the 16th century . . . In the survey are included works great and small . . . detailed studies of Chaucer and his contemporaries . . . and the whole panorama of Tudor and Elizabethan achievement. . . . Scattered hints had previously been given that English poetry had not really begun with Mr Waller, and that Chaucer had not stood alone in mediaeval times; but with the marshalling of facts, and the full picture thus presented, facile generalisations, born of ignorance, were no longer possible. . . . In recalling the literary achievements of the Middle Ages he filled a

[1] For Gray's influence, particularly on the plan of Warton's *History*, see *Letters of Gray*, ed. Tovey, III, 277–9, and *Reminiscences of Gray* by his friend Norton Nicholls. In a letter dated 15 April 1770, and written at Pembroke Hall, Gray included a sketch of a *History of English Poetry* which he had considered writing himself. It was divided into five parts: Part I, The Sicilian School; Part II, Chaucer: 1st Italian School; Part III, Wyatt and Surrey: 2nd Italian School; Part IV, Queen Elizabeth's Reign: 3rd Italian School; Part V, School of France. Gray appended a most interesting note to this outline—'You will observe', he informed Warton, 'that my idea was in some measure taken from a scribbled paper of Pope, of which I believe you have a copy.' (*Letters of Gray*, ed. Tovey, III, 278–9.)

yawning gap in literary history, provided material which enlarged the current conceptions of literature, and opened up new fields for critical adventure.[1]

The sense of a discovery of newer and freer standards prompted by these movements in taste had a direct influence upon Romantic criticism of Augustan poetry. For Wordsworth, Coleridge and the Romantic poets of Francis Jeffrey's generation, for whom the Augustan poets had been part of the early literary atmosphere they breathed (in the 1790s 'allusions to them abounded in all popular discourse and ambitious conversation'), this revaluation suggested potentialities in poetry which had been left largely unexplored by the Augustans. There had of course been stirrings of dissatisfaction with the Augustans in the eighteenth century, and some of the Romantics were aware of these tendencies. Southey, for example, who felt that the school of Pope had irrevocably lost the power to produce anything new in poetry, claimed that the innovations of the early Romantics could be traced back to a school 'half-Greek half-Gothick' (consider Gray's mixture of the Pindaric and the Bardic) which, begun by Gilbert West, 'was followed by Mason, Gray, and Warton, and is to be traced in Akenside and Collins'.[2] Too much, perhaps, might be made of the anticipations of Wordsworth's style and subject-matter in Akenside's *Pleasures of Imagination*[3] yet his eighteenth-century affinities are elsewhere evident as well. As for Coleridge, there is ample evidence in his early poems of the influence of Cowper, Collins, Gray, and of typically eighteenth-century 'Miltonic' imitation.[4] It is also well known that a strong early influence upon the poetry of the pioneers of the Romantic generation was

[1] J. W. H. Atkins, *English Literary Criticism in the 17th and 18th Centuries* (1951), p. 214.

[2] Southey, *Specimens of the Later English Poets* (1807), p. xxxii.

[3] See Professor Nichol Smith, Preface to the *Oxford Book of 18th Century Verse*, for an interesting comparison of similar passages.

[4] For an analysis of Coleridge's antecedents, see Dr F. R. Leavis, *Revaluation*, notes on 'Songs of the Pixies', pp. 142–7. Also Coleridge, *Biographia Literaria*, Chapter I.

the work of Bowles, whose violently anti-Augustan criticism has already been explored.[1]

Bowles's poetry is now forgotten—A. J. A. Waldock described him well as 'one of those poets whose chief mission is to be superseded'[2]—yet he was remarkably popular in his own time. His *Fourteen Sonnets*, first published in 1789, had run into seven editions by the turn of the century, and was republished several times in the next. He provided one of the many links between Romantic tendencies in the late eighteenth and early nineteenth centuries. His influence upon the youthful Coleridge is recorded in the opening chapter of the *Biographia Literaria*, and Coleridge claimed that not only did Bowles's poetry save him from the 'unwholesome quicksilver mines of metaphysic lore', but that it *first* revealed to him the unpoetical nature of Pope's verses.

Bowles's own poetry was uniformly musical, and his easy nostalgia invested even the most cheerful scenes with the power to move him to tears: at his best Bowles was not unlike the immature Keats, though without his sensuous strength. The kind of eighteenth-century Romanticism which Bowles communicated to Coleridge is apparent in the first volume of poems which Coleridge published (1796), and even the titles of his monodies, odes, elegies, epitaphs, and sonnets—'Melancholy—a Fragment', 'The Sigh', 'Lines on an Autumnal Evening', 'Elegy Imitated from Akenside'—are full of echoes. A personal visit to Bowles at Donhead in 1802, however, marked the end of Coleridge's discipleship,[3] and the splendid self-parodies in Chapter I of the *Biographia Literaria* are sufficient critical comment.

Coleridge's interest in Bowles was shared by many of his contemporaries including Lamb, Southey, and Wordsworth himself. Lamb's sonnets included in Coleridge's *Poems on Various Subjects* are full of imitations of Bowles; and Southey

---

[1] Chapter VI.

[2] *William Lisle Bowles*, Australian English Association Leaflet, No. 8 (1928), p. 5.

[3] See Coleridge, Letter to Sotheby, 26 August 1802. (*Coleridge's Letters*, ed. H. N. Coleridge, 1895, I, 396.)

confessed in 1832 that for the past forty years he had taken the 'sweet and artless style of Bowles for a model'.[1] It is less well known that Bowles's sonnets exerted a brief though compelling influence upon Wordsworth, and that we owe the *Sonnet on Westminster Bridge* to this influence.[2] His sonnet-sequence *To the River Duddon* was also in some measure indebted to the series which Bowles wrote upon the Tweed, the Cherwell and the Wansbeck, and here Bowles acted as a direct link between the eighteenth-century pre-Romantics and Wordsworth, for his own series was modelled upon Thomas Warton's *To the River Lodon*.

Coleridge's evidence in the *Biographia* defines Bowles's specific importance for us: that of having influenced, at a crucial stage in their early development, some members of the rising generation of poets in the 1790s. Admiration of Bowles's work was fortunately not universal in the early nineteenth century,[3] and Wordsworth and Coleridge soon left him behind in their own development. Bowles's case is instructive, for, although the importance of the critical orientations which the Romantic poets derived from the previous century should not be minimised, they are best regarded as providing no more than an introduction and background to a study of Romantic criticism itself. For the critical intelligence which Wordsworth and Coleridge, for example, brought to bear upon a reading of Augustan poetry, though not unsympathetic towards the ideas of their predecessors, was far more complex and sensitive. This was partly the result of the direct relation which existed between their criticism and the more profound exploration of their

[1] A. Brandl, *Samuel Taylor Coleridge and the English Romantic School* (1887), tr. Lady Eastlake, p. 37.

[2] 'His [Bowles's] *Sonnets* came into Wordsworth's hands (1793) just as he was leaving London with some friends for a morning excursion; he seated himself in a recess in Westminster Bridge, and was not to be moved from his place till he had finished the little book.' (*Ibid.* p. 37.) This account of the origin of the poem is confirmed by Alexander Dyce in his record of a conversation with Wordsworth. See *Recollections of the Table Talk of Samuel Rogers*, p. 213.

[3] Henry Crabb Robinson, for example, briskly dismissed Bowles as 'mawkish and unreadable'. See the entry in his *Diary*, 13 April 1814. *On Books and their Writers*, ed. E. J. Morley (1938), I, 140.

creative work. And this relationship, too, accounts for the greater personal urgency which often lies behind their criticism of Augustan poetry, for, in creating the taste by which they were themselves to be judged, it was the assumptions about the nature of poetry underlying the work of the Augustans, which, more than anything else, prevented their immediate recognition and acceptance by contemporary readers.

The compelling motives behind the hostility of the early nineteenth-century Romantics to the Augustan tradition were sometimes misunderstood, particularly by their own contemporaries. Original poets of any new generation often find themselves quite naturally out of sympathy with the work of their immediate predecessors, and this is perhaps even a necessary condition of their own originality. Yet Hazlitt imputed quite different motives to the Romantics in *The Plain Speaker* and elsewhere. Much to Wordsworth's indignation ('I have ten times more knowledge of Pope's writings and of Dryden's also, than this writer [Hazlitt] ever had'), he claimed that the adverse criticism of the poets of the Lake School originated either in the inadequacies of their own sensibility ('the natural limits of their tastes and feelings'), or in the embittered envy caused by the slow recognition of their own work ('The *forlorn hope* of impotent and disappointed vanity').[1] Byron, despite his lack of sympathy with the Romantic tendencies of many of his contemporaries, achieved a more balanced summing-up of the situation than Hazlitt. He could see that the

[1] An interesting account of the motives behind anti-Augustan criticism may be found in a critical dialogue between Hazlitt and James Northcote, a staunchly pro-Augustan critic ('He is the last of that school who knew Goldsmith and Johnson. How finely he describes Pope'). To Hazlitt's comment on Wordsworth's criticism of Augustan poetry, 'he has no faculty in his mind to which these qualities of poetry address themselves', Northcote retorted: 'You mistake the matter altogether. The acting principle in their minds is an inveterate selfishness or desire of distinction . . . in order to divert the public mind and draw attention to themselves, they affect to decry the old models and overturn what they cannot rival. They know they cannot write like Pope and Dryden, or would be only imitators if they did; and they consequently strive to gain an original and equal celebrity by singularity and affectation.' (Hazlitt, *Collected Works*, ed. Waller and Glover, 1902–6, VII, 102.)

hostile criticism of the Romantic poets was partly inspired by the recognition that, should the conventional valuations of Augustan poetry survive unmodified, their own poetry was likely to go unread; but he was intelligent enough to realise that the rejection of Augustan standards by these poets was a necessary condition of their own originality. This is plain in his Letter to John Murray (7 February 1821) from Ravenna, in which he made a point of distinguishing between *creative* writers like Wordsworth, Coleridge, and Southey, whose 'very natural antipathy to Pope' he respected, on the one hand, and, on the other, the large numbers of those who, following their example, had joined in the disparagement of Augustan poetry without a similar justification:

The attempt of the poetical populace of the present day to obtain an ostracism against Pope, is as easily accounted for as the Athenian's shell against Aristides; they are tired of hearing him called the 'Just'. They are also fighting for life; for, if he maintains his stations, they will reach their own by falling. . . . These three personages, Southey, Wordsworth, and Coleridge, had all of them a very natural antipathy to Pope, and I respect them for it, as the only original feeling and principle which they have contrived to preserve. But they have been joined in it by those who have joined them in nothing else: by the *Edinburgh Reviewers*, by the whole heterogeneous mass of poets, excepting Crabbe, Rogers, Gifford, Campbell . . . and . . . me.[1]

Among the more revolutionary developments in literary theory effected by Wordsworth and Coleridge is the nearly total rejection of the theory of *mimesis*—in the forms in which it had been almost universally accepted by neoclassical theorists since the Renaissance—which is unmistakably implied in their criticism.[2] The writer who claimed to hold a mirror up to life, indeed, was now in some danger of losing his right to the title of poet, and though this attitude is largely implied in the main body of their criticism, it becomes particularly prominent and

[1] Byron, Letter to John Murray, 25 October 1820. (*Byron's Works*, ed. Wright, 1833, v, 13.) The allusion to Aristides is taken from Pope's *Temple of Fame*.

[2] For a discussion of the difference between 'mimetic' and 'imaginative' representation of experience, see Shelley, *A Defence of Poetry*, ed. H. F. B. Brett-Smith (1921), p. 1.

even explicit in their criticism of poets writing within the Augustan tradition. One of their principal objections to the Augustan notion of poetry was that it did not necessarily involve a subjective or emotional transmutation of reality. Not only were the Augustans largely unconcerned with the 'light that never was on sea or land'; in recreating the social life of their age in verse, they were content to represent rather than to reinterpret their experience. Wordsworth's own attempts at presenting the humble realities of ordinary life in the light of an extraordinary vision, and Coleridge's attempts in *The Ancient Mariner* and elsewhere to invest the imagined or fantastic world with all the immediacy and credibility of real life, both suggest the interests which Augustan poetry was now failing to satisfy.

This fundamental dissatisfaction with the Augustan poetical mode may be observed not only in the critical observations upon Dryden, Pope, and Johnson made by Wordsworth and Coleridge, but even more prominently in their criticism of contemporaries writing within the Augustan tradition. Wordsworth's criticism of Crabbe and Jane Austen, whose method of dealing with experience he interestingly associates, is particularly relevant here. Sara Coleridge informs us that Wordsworth (unlike Scott whose great admiration of Jane Austen has already been noted[1]), though impressed by her realism, was convinced that the essentially Augustan mode of dealing with the life she depicted in her novels was a radical disqualification:

though he admitted that her novels were an admirable copy of life, he could not be interested in productions of that kind; unless the truth of nature were presented to him clarified, as it were, by the pervading light of imagination, it had scarce any attraction in his eyes; and for this reason he took little pleasure in the writings of Crabbe.[2]

Wordsworth's reactions to Crabbe's poetry, however, were not simple. There is a good deal of evidence that he was greatly interested by Crabbe's subjects and themes—especially his sense of the tragic dignity which sometimes illumined the lives

---

[1] See Chapter I.
[2] *Memoir and Letters of Sara Coleridge* (1873), I, 75.

of the rural poor.[1] Yet ultimately Wordsworth was dissatisfied, and in explaining his disappointment to Crabb Robinson he said that it was largely the result of Crabbe's 'unpoetical mode of considering human nature and society' in his verse.[2] Despite his interest in Crabbe's subjects, Wordsworth's exasperation at what seemed to him to be Crabbe's inability to 'clarify' the truth of nature 'by the pervading light of imagination', found its most extreme expression in a letter to Samuel Rogers:

The sum of all is that nineteen out of twenty of Crabbe's Pictures are mere matters of fact: with which the Muses have just about as much to do as they have with a Collection of medical reports, or of Law cases.[3]

It will be seen that the criticism of Crabbe which Wordsworth makes here is very different from the simple objections to the subject-matter of Augustan poetry made by his predecessors and by some of the minor critics of his own age. In substance, however, it has a great deal in common with the criticism of Crabbe made by Coleridge, who, although he claimed that an appreciation of Crabbe was a test of a truly catholic taste in poetry, nevertheless found in him 'an absolute defect of the high imagination'.[4] 'Imagination'—perhaps the most frequent term in all their criticism—was one of the major touchstones by which Wordsworth and Coleridge found the Augustan poets wanting. In Coleridge's hands especially it had come to acquire new and specialised meanings, yet its connections with the 'creative and glowing Imagination— acer spiritus ac vis'—invoked by Warton in his Essay on Pope, are quite apparent. It is therefore not surprising that Wordsworth, in selecting those poets of the eighteenth century most gifted with 'Imagination', found it impossible to include Pope. Recognising Pope's unique gifts, Wordsworth agreed with

---

[1] See The Brothers Wiffen, ed. S. R. Pattison (1880), p. 38; and Memoir and Letters of Sara Coleridge, II, 27.

[2] H. C. Robinson, On Books and their Writers (1938), I, 168.

[3] Wordsworth, Letter to Rogers, 29 September 1808. (The Letters of William and Dorothy Wordsworth: The Middle Years, ed. E. de Selincourt, I, 224.)

[4] Coleridge, Table Talk and Omniana, ed. T. Ashe (1917 edn), p. 293.

Warton that he had neglected to exploit in his poetry the full potentialities of his genius:

These three Writers, Thomson, Collins, and Dyer had more poetic Imagination than all their Contemporaries, unless we reckon Chatterton of that age—I do not name Pope, for he stands alone— as a man most highly gifted—but unluckily he took the Plain when the Heights were within his reach.[1]

Although Coleridge transcended the taste of his age in his appreciation of Donne and the Metaphysicals, the growing tendency to regard epigrammatic 'wit' and the critical intelligence as intrusive elements in poetry affected not only his own evaluation of Augustan poetry but that of Wordsworth as well. To Wordsworth, of course, the 'meddling intellect' seemed able to do little more than thwart the 'Imagination', hindering it from communion with the larger powers of nature and the appreciation of a wisdom that began where 'reason' ended. Perhaps it is not too much to say that the principal *raison d'être* of poetry for Wordsworth was its power to soothe and tranquillise and then to elevate the soul, and it was the distracting activity of the critical intelligence in Augustan poetry which prevented Wordsworth from reacting sympathetically. This tendency is best examined by considering some of his adverse criticism of Pope's *Epitaphs*.[2]

A pervasive unity of tone—achieved by a concern with 'those universal feelings and simple movements of the mind which we have called for as indispensable'—seemed to Wordsworth an essential requisite of an epitaph. It was a violation of this simple emotional decorum through the intrusion of the critical intelligence ('we murder to dissect') that prompted

[1] Wordsworth: Letter to Alexander Dyce, 12 January 1829. Wordsworth, in fact, agreed more with Warton, who regarded Pope as a great poet who had neglected fully to exploit the potentialities of his genius, than with Bowles who regarded Pope as a poet of an intrinsically inferior order. For Wordsworth's letter to Dyce, quoted above, see *The Letters of William and Dorothy Wordsworth, 1821–30*, ed. E. de Selincourt (1939), I, 346.

[2] Wordsworth's three essays 'Upon Epitaphs' were written in 1810. The first essay was published in *The Friend* in the same year. The other two essays remained unpublished until 1876.

Wordsworth to declare that 'the epitaphs of Pope cannot well be too severely condemned'. For Wordsworth the presence of irony in particular, in an epitaph, implied not only an unforgivable disturbance of the calm and tranquillising tone appropriate to it, but argued an 'obtuse moral sensibility' in the poet. Wordsworth's objection to this aspect of Pope's epitaphs may best be observed in his disagreement with Dr Johnson on the merit of Pope's epitaph *On Mrs Corbet*. The general effect of the poem Wordsworth found 'cold and unfeeling', and he was particularly disturbed by the line in which Pope, enumerating the lady's virtues, remarked that she

> No arts essayed, but not to be admired.

It seems quite certain that Pope's own intention here—in suggesting his subject's self-effacement and modesty—was plainly complimentary. Yet even the slight touch of irony contained in the suggestion that she employed artifices in order to conceal her virtues seemed to Wordsworth a laborious attempt at discrimination which quite spoilt the total effect of the poem. The sense of love and peaceful admiration she had inspired, which should have been the proper effect of the epitaph, was disturbed by an oblique and ill-timed stroke of satire.[1]

The frame of mind in which the poet addressed himself to the task of writing an epitaph should be such, Wordsworth maintained, that the intrusion of ironical or similarly disturbing touches should not occur to him at all. The Augustan critical sensibility seemed unable to satisfy this demand, and Wordsworth thought that Pope (whose mind had been 'employed in observations upon the vices and follies of men') lacked those 'amiable and ennobling passions' which enabled the poet to rise above the petty discriminations of everyday life. Wordsworth's critical attitude is best illustrated by his own poetry; in 'A Slumber did my spirit seal', for example, it is because he is so completely above the day-to-day transactions of the human situation that Wordsworth rises to that tranquil equi-

---

[1] *Wordsworth's Prose Works*, ed. Grosart, II, 56–8.

poise, in which he reconciles himself to Lucy's death by considering it as part of the background of the vast and permanent forms of nature. But however fine the poem, the conditions of its success are of a specialised kind: nothing is allowed to enter the poem which can run counter to the one-directional flow of feeling. The kind of satisfaction which Wordsworth found in poetry, and which not unnaturally the Augustans had small chance of providing, is suggested by his belief that 'in the mind of the truly great and good everything that is of importance is at peace with itself; all is stillness, sweetness, and stable grandeur'.[1]

Although Coleridge was far from sharing without reservation Wordsworth's distrust of the 'meddling intellect', he regarded with some suspicion what appeared to him the Augustan tendency to substitute for 'poetic thoughts', 'thoughts translated into the language of poetry'. Recording in the *Biographia* his early reactions to the poetry of Pope, Coleridge observed that it seemed more remarkable to him for its dazzling though somewhat mechanical intellectual ingenuity, than for its concern with any deep centre of creative life in the poet:

I saw that the excellence of this kind consisted in just and acute observations on men and manners in an artificial state of society, as its matter and substance; and in the logic of wit, conveyed in smooth and strong epigrammatic couplets, as its *form*: Even when the subject was addressed to the fancy, or the intellect, as in *The Rape of the Lock*, or the *Essay on Man*; nay, when it was a consecutive narration, as in that astonishing product of matchless talent and ingenuity, Pope's Translation of the *Iliad*; still a *point* was looked for at the end of each second line, and the whole was, as it were, a *sorites*, or, if I may exchange a logical for a grammatical metaphor, a *conjunction disjunctive*, of epigrams.[2]

---

[1] *Wordsworth's Prose Works*, ed. Grosart, II, 60–2. Limitations in the kind of tranquillity described by Wordsworth may perhaps be suggested by comparing it with the more difficult tranquillity—often reached only through a painful subjection to all aspects of experience—in the later plays of Shakespeare. It could be argued that Wordsworth's 'rising above' these things could be a weakness, though there are sufficient guarantees (in e.g. *Michael* and the 'Margaret' episode in *The Excursion*) that he had risen to his elevation the hard and painful way.

[2] *Biographia Literaria*, ed. J. Shawcross (1907), I, 11.

It is only fair to note that Coleridge was here describing his
youthful reaction to Augustan poetry in the 1790s, and that he
prefaced his remarks by observing that from 'inexperience of
the world, and a general want of sympathy with the general
subjects of these poems' he doubtless 'undervalued the kind'.
What he was reacting against more powerfully (as Hazlitt
shrewdly pointed out) was the effect which the Augustan
tradition was coming to have upon the writing of poetry in his
own day. It was a time when Darwin's *Botanic Garden* 'was
greatly extolled, not only by the reading public in general' but
even by intelligent critics, and it seemed to Coleridge that
poetry had reached an *impasse* and had deteriorated into a
sophisticated game, which permitted only a repetition and
infinite variation of stereotyped Augustan ideas and expres-
sions, and nothing original or creative.[1] Reacting from the
'logic of wit' Coleridge hoped to discover in poetry a structure
and organisation which was not necessarily dependent upon
intellectual agility, but which had 'a logic of its own, as severe
as that of science; and more difficult, because more subtle, more
complex, and dependent upon more and more fugitive causes'.[2]

That Coleridge had an infinitely higher opinion of Pope than
of his imitators is plain in his later criticism. In considering the
question 'Was Pope a poet?' raised by Warton in his *Essay* (and
answered by Johnson in his *Life*), Coleridge was very far from
sharing Arnold's confident relegation of Pope to the level of a
'classic of our prose', though his criticism was in some measure
influenced by Warton and anticipates Arnold:

In comparing different poets with each other, we should inquire

---

[1] '. . . I have attempted to illustrate the present state of our language, in its
relation to literature, by a press-room of larger and smaller stereotype pieces,
which, in the present Anglo-Gallic fashion of unconnected epigrammatic periods,
it requires but an ordinary portion of ingenuity to vary indefinitely and yet still
produce something, which if not sense, will be so like it as to do as well.' (*Biographia Literaria*, ed. Shawcross, 1907, 1, 26.)

[2] *Ibid.* 1, 4. It has to be pointed out, of course, that the 'logic of wit' is now seen
to be the mainspring of metaphysical as well as Augustan poetry. 'Intellectual
agility' is not sufficient to account for it, and one might well say 'it had a logic
of its own . . .' etc.

which has brought into the fullest play our imagination and our reason, or has created the greatest excitement and produced the greatest harmony. If we consider great exquisiteness of language and sweetness of metre alone, it is impossible to deny to Pope the character of a delightful writer; but whether he be a poet must depend upon our definition of the word; and, doubtless, if everything that pleases be poetry, Pope's satires and epistles must be poetry. This I must say, that poetry as distinguished from other modes of composition, does not rest in metre, and that it is not poetry if it makes no appeal to our passions or our imagination. One character belongs to all true poets, that they write from a principle within, not originating in something without.[1]

Whether by 'a principle within' Coleridge merely intended a contrast between subjective and social poetry, or whether he meant a concern with the deeper springs of creative life, an effort to realise something more inward and mysterious, is difficult to say. He never unambiguously answered the question whether or not Pope—in addition to being a 'delightful writer' —was also a 'true poet'. Comparing Dryden and Pope he declared: 'Only if Pope was a *Poet*, as Lord Byron swears, then Dryden, I admit, was a very *great* poet.'[2] Coleridge does not seem to have been particularly anxious to pronounce the last word on the question raised by Warton, though his doubts and misgivings prepared the way in some measure for the greater certainty of some of the Victorian critics.

Coleridge said in *Anima Poetae* that 'Poetry, like schoolboys, by too frequent correction may be cowed into dullness', and it was for this reason that he preferred the 'force and fervour' of Dryden to the greater discipline and control of Pope's versification. Some of the Romantics believed that the metrical structure of Augustan poetry prevented a free expression of the

---

[1] *Anima Poetae, from the Unpublished Note-Books of S. T. Coleridge*, ed. E. H. Coleridge, p. 189.

[2] On one occasion, however, in a marginal note on Cowley, Coleridge denied to Dryden the title of poet 'in the *strict* use of the term': 'Yet Cowley *was* a Poet, which, with all my unfeigned admiration for his vigorous sense, his agile logical wit, and his high excellencies of diction and metre, is more than (in the *strict* use of the term, Poet) I can conscientiously say of DRYDEN.' (*Miscellaneous Criticism*, ed. Raysor, pp. 284–5.)

poet's feelings, and Southey, who laid the blame entirely on French influence, felt it had led to the suppression of all genius and originality in the previous age.[1] Southey's criticism was extreme, but there was truth in Wordsworth's view—refuting Johnson's claim that 'in blank verse, the language suffered more distortion to keep it out of prose than any inconvenience to be apprehended from the shackles and circumspections of rhyme'—that the heroic couplet, in encouraging the poetry of pondered and deliberate social statement, prevented the living and creative use of language by which the poet could explore his own most deeply personal feelings.[2] Wordsworth's objections to the heroic couplet were part of his dissatisfaction with the whole eighteenth-century attitude to language. The difference is made plain in his remark to De Quincey that it was highly unphilosophical of Dryden to call language the 'dress of thought'; a language that was truly poetical should contain a fresh apprehension of reality and be itself the 'incarnation of thought'.[3]

As for the relative merits of the versification of Dryden and Pope, Coleridge told Klopstock that although he agreed with him that Pope's rhymes were more exact, he preferred Dryden, whose couplets 'had greater variety in their movement' so that the 'general sweep of the verse was superior'.[4] For the 'ardour and impetuosity of mind' which Wordsworth informed Scott

---

[1] 'He so familiarised his countrymen with the mechanism of verse', Southey declared of Pope, 'that the very facility of his versification seems to have prevented the effusions of genius, and the redundancy of poetical phrases to have superseded all originality of language.' The notion of verse-writing as a fashionable and mechanical art, Southey felt, had largely been imported from France: '... since the days of Boileau, who communicated to Racine that notable receipt of making the second line of a couplet first, it has been the fundamental article of critical belief in France. Pope was completely a Frenchman in his taste; he imported *l'art de parler toujours convenablement*, the *étiquette* and *bienséance*, the court-language and full-dress costume of verse.' (*Specimens of the Later English Poets*, p. xxx.)

[2] See the entry in *Alfoxden MS Note-Book* (1798), quoted in *The Prelude*, ed. E. de Selincourt, p. xxx, note 2.

[3] Quoted by Marjorie L. Barstow, 'Wordsworth's Theory of Poetic Diction', *Yale Studies in English*, XVII, 36 n.

[4] Coleridge, 'Satyrane's Letters', *Biographia Literaria* (Everyman's edn), 1947, p. 275. See also *Wordworth's Prose Works*, ed. Grosart (1876), III, 419.

were among Dryden's 'essentially poetical' qualities,[1] were admired by Coleridge too—'Dryden's genius was of that sort which catches fire by its own motion; his chariot wheels *get hot by driving fast.*'[2] These preferences were in keeping with the views of most of the Romantic poets of the early nineteenth century, and may be traced back to the revival of interest in Dryden in the latter part of the eighteenth century described by Scott.[3]

Although Southey's criticism of Augustan poetry may be for obvious reasons of slighter intrinsic interest today, in its own time it exerted considerable influence. Though he considered Pope to have surpassed Boileau and his French models,[4] it is partly to Southey that we owe the excessive emphasis upon French influence in the age of Queen Anne which is a commonplace of Regency criticism. In his *Specimens of the Later British Poets* and in his criticism in the *Quarterly Review*, he popularised the view that 'Pope was completely a Frenchman in his taste' a phrase which presumably caters for nationalist feelings in the period of the Napoleonic wars. Unlike Wordsworth and Coleridge, too, he was positive and unambiguous in his refusal to allow Dryden and Pope the status of poets, and, although he spoke less about the 'soul' than Arnold, his criticism anticipates Arnold's disparagement of the place of the 'wits' in poetry. Discussing what seemed to him 'fatal' developments in taste in the Restoration, Southey claimed

The writers of this and the succeeding generation, understood their own character better than it has been understood by their succes-

---

[1] Letter to Scott, 7 November 1805, *Early Letters of Wordsworth*, ed. E. de Selincourt, p. 540.

[2] *Miscellaneous Criticism*, Raysor, p. 431.

[3] See Chapter I.

[4] 'Pope, though he imitated Boileau, is, in fact, as much superiour to him, as the English language is, in the opinion of an Englishman, superiour to the French. There is in him a bottom of sound sense, not to be found amid all the wit of his master. He is the first of his kind; but to class him with great Poets—to say that he is a writer of the *same kind* as Milton and Shakespeare—is as absurd as it would be to class the *Aeneid* with the *Propria quae maribus*; verse is common to them, and verse is all which they have in common.' (*Specimens of the Later English Poets*, p. xxxi.)

sors; they called themselves Wits instead of Poets, and Wits they were; the difference is not in degree but in kind. They succeeded in what they aimed at, in satire and in panegyric, in ridiculing an enemy, and in flattering a friend; in turning a song, and in complimenting a lady; in pointing an epigram, and in telling a lewd tale; in these branches of literary art, the Birmingham trade of verse, they have rarely been surpassed. Whatever praise may be given to them as versifiers, as wits, as reasoners, they may deserve; but versification, and wit, and reason do not constitute poetry. The time which elapsed from the days of Dryden to those of Pope, is the dark age of English poetry.[1]

Southey's summing up of the Augustan age in English poetry here represents the doctrinaire left-wing of early Romantic criticism. Wordsworth and Coleridge, with whom Southey was conventionally associated as an innovator in his own time, were less one-sided in their criticism, as we have already seen. Wordsworth protested on many occasions at Hazlitt's claim that he had allowed 'none of the excellencies of poetry to Dryden and Pope',[2] and remarked to Scott (who was then busy completing his edition of Dryden)—'I have a very high admiration of the talents of both Dryden and Pope, and ultimately, as from all good writers of whatever kind, their Country will be benefited greatly by their labours.'[3] But although the criticism of Augustan poetry made by Wordsworth and Coleridge was more complex and sensitive than it has often been made out to be, and involved no sweeping dismissal of the claims of Dryden, Pope, and Johnson, it nonetheless marked the most important transitional stage in the history of their reputations. The Victorian assessment of Augustan poetry would not have been possible without their criticism, and the invocation of Warton's critical touchstones in Wordsworth's summing up of the value of the tradition as a whole, indicates the trends to which their criticism had given decisive expression:

[1] *Specimens of the Later British Poets*, pp. xxvii–xxix.

[2] See Hazlitt, *Collected Works*, ed. Waller and Glover, IV, 277; and *Wordsworth's Prose Works*, Grosart, III, 460, and *Letters of the Wordsworth Family*, William Knight, III, 122.

[3] Letter to Scott, 18 January 1808. (*The Letters of William and Dorothy Wordsworth: The Middle Years*, ed. E. de Selincourt, 1937, I, 458 d.)

To this day I believe I could repeat, with a little previous rummaging of my memory, several thousand lines of Pope. But if the beautiful, the pathetic, and the sublime be what a poet should chiefly aim at, how absurd it is to place those men among the first poets of this country! Admirable are they in treading their way, but that way lies almost at the foot of Parnassus.[1]

The criticism of Wordsworth and Coleridge, and to a lesser degree of Southey, in breaking away from the tenets of neoclassical theory still current in their early days and which survived long after the turn of the century, laid the foundations of the modern consciousness in literature.

3. HAZLITT AND DE QUINCEY

But even those literary critics of the early nineteenth century who derived their fundamentally Romantic orientation from the influence of Wordsworth and Coleridge—Hazlitt and De Quincey for example—developed Romantic attitudes that were recognisably individual, and, among other things, they disagreed with Wordsworth and Coleridge in their estimate of Augustan poetry. It was characteristic of Hazlitt to remark:

I believe I may date my insight into the mysteries of poetry from the commencement of my acquaintance with the authors of the *Lyrical Ballads*; at least, my discrimination of the higher sorts—not my predilection for such writers as Goldsmith or Pope.[2]

Hazlitt made the essential point that it was the trivial imitations of the large numbers of undistinguished versifiers who modelled themselves upon the Augustans in the early nineteenth century, rather than the poetry of the Augustans themselves, that had discredited the tradition and merited the disparaging criticism of Coleridge and Wordsworth.[3] Considering the poetry of one of these minor versifiers, the Reverend George Croly, who

---

[1] *Letters of the Wordsworth Family*, ed. William Knight, III, 122.

[2] Hazlitt, *Collected Works*, ed. Waller and Glover, VII, 226.

[3] Hazlitt's point was elaborated later by James Russell Lowell: 'Wordsworth was not in a condition to do Pope justice. . . . Moreover, he was the apostle of the imagination, and came at a time when the school founded by Pope had degenerated into a mob of mannerists who wrote with ease, and who with their congenial critics united to decry poetry which brought in the dangerous innovation of having a soul in it.' (*My Study Windows*, p. 383.)

declared as late as 1831 that among all the English poets 'Pope still retains the pre-eminence' in the public estimation,[1] North-cote observed to Hazlitt in an article 'On Envy' in *The Plain Speaker*:

Such imitators do all the mischief, and bring real genius into disrepute. This is in some measure an excuse for those who have endeavoured to disparage Dryden and Pope. We have had a surfeit of imitations of them. Poetry, in the hands of a set of mechanic scribblers, had become such a tame, mawkish thing, that we could endure it no longer, and our impatience of the abuse of a good thing transferred itself to the original source. It was this which enabled Wordsworth and the rest to raise up a new school (or attempt it) on the ruins of Pope; because a race of writers had succeeded him without one particle of his wit, sense, and delicacy, and the world was tired of their everlasting *sing-song* and *namby-pamby*. People were disgusted at hearing the faults of Pope (the part most easily imitated) cried up as his greatest excellence, and were willing to take refuge from such nauseous cant in any novelty.[2]

Hazlitt recognised that Pope's merits were untouched by the vagaries of fashionable literary taste and the ebb and flow of popular reputations. In an article entitled 'Boswell Redivivus', written in 1826, he wrote: 'Pope's verse is not admired, because it was once the fashion: it will be admired let the fashion change how it will.'[3]

For all Hazlitt's awareness that the Augustan poets, despite

---

[1] Croly, *Beauties of the English Poets*, Introduction. Croly also produced an edition of Pope which appeared in 1836.

[2] *Collected Works*, ed. Waller and Glover, VII, 105. It is only fair to note that, though sympathetic towards Northcote, Hazlitt was far from sharing his extreme views upon the relative merits of Wordsworth and Pope: '. . . do you imagine . . . such trifles as descriptions of daisies and idiot-boys (however well they may be done) will not be swept away in the tide of time, like straws and weeds by the torrent? No; the world can only keep in view the principal and most perfect productions of human ingenuity; such works as Dryden's and Pope's, and a few others, that from their unity, their completeness, their polish have the stamp of immortality upon them, and seem indestructible like an element of nature.' (Hazlitt, *Collected Works*, VI, 336.)

[3] 'Mr Northcote's Conversations', No. 19, *Collected Works*, ed. Waller and Glover, VI, 440. In the same critical dialogue Hazlitt has an interesting comment on the essentially transient nature of fashion: 'Fashion is gentility running away from vulgarity, and afraid of being overtaken by it. It is a sign of two things not very far asunder.' *Ibid.* p. 439.

the hostile criticism levelled at them in the early nineteenth century, were certain of secure and lasting admiration, his own evaluation of their work was fundamentally Romantic. Underlying all his criticism of the whole tradition was the belief, which seemed almost axiomatic to Hazlitt, that the triumphs of the Augustans were essentially triumphs of a secondary order of poetry. Although this feature in his criticism made his praise of the Augustans appear rather sophistical to the *Quarterly Review*, the spirit in which he accepted Warton's classification of the English poets had nothing of the animosity typical of Bowles. Hazlitt contrasted the 'natural' style of Chaucer, Spenser, Shakespeare, and Milton, with what he described as the 'artificial' style of Pope and Dryden, though, in considering the latter in the class to which he had assigned them, he was generous in his praise. His evaluation of their work was tersely summed up in 'A Critical List of Authors', which he appended to his edition of *Select British Poets* which appeared in 1824. In a rapid thumb-nail sketch of Dryden's achievement Hazlitt observed that he had

invention in the plan of his Satires, very little fancy, not much wit, no humour, immense strength of character, elegance, masterly ease, indignant contempt, approaching to the sublime, not a particle of tenderness, but eloquent declamation, the perfection of uncorrupted English style, and of sounding, vehement and varied versification.[1]

This may be fairly taken as a generously 'Romantic' evaluation of Dryden's merits, though it is interesting that Hazlitt—unlike most of the Romantic *poets*—preferred Pope to Dryden and placed him at the head of those who practised the 'Artificial' style. Hazlitt once remarked that there were few persons he would have better liked to be than Pope, and his account of the range and variety of his gifts—coming as it did from a critic who was censured in his own time for hostility to the Augustan tradition—indicates why any broad generalisation about the

[1] *Collected Works*, ed. Waller and Glover, v, 372.

criticism of Augustan poetry in the early nineteenth century cannot be long sustained:

His works are a delightful, never-failing fund of good sense and refined taste. He had high invention and fancy of the comic kind, as in *The Rape of the Lock*; wit, as in *The Dunciad* and *Satires*; no humour; some beautiful descriptions as in the *Windsor Forest*; some exquisite delineations of Character (those of Addison and Villiers are masterpieces); he is a model of elegance everywhere, but more particularly in his eulogies and friendly epistles; his ease is the effect of labour; he had no pretensions to sublimity, but sometimes dis-displays an indignant moral feeling akin to it; his pathos is playful and tender, as in his *Epistles to Arbuthnot* and *Jervas*, or rises into power by the help of rhetoric as in the *Eloisa*, and *Elegy on the Death of an Unfortunate Lady*; his style is polished, and almost faultless in its kind; his versification tires by uniform smoothness and harmony.[1]

In his censure of Pope's versification, of course, Hazlitt was completely in agreement with most of the Romantic poets of his own day, and with a trend in criticism which has been traced back to Cowper in the previous century.[2] Indeed, it is probable that his views on this subject were influenced by his personal association with some of the poets of his own time, particularly Keats and Leigh Hunt. Hazlitt's remark in an article 'On Milton's Versification', which first appeared in *The Round Table* of 20 August 1815—'Dr Johnson and Pope would have converted his [Milton's] vaulting Pegasus into a rocking horse'—not only looks forward to the Keats of *Sleep and Poetry* (first published in *Poems*, 1817), but back to Leigh Hunt's criticism of Pope's versification in *The Feast of the Poets* (which was first published in the *Reflector*, No. IV of 1811).

Despite his own fundamentally Romantic evaluation of the poetry of the Augustans, the general effect of Hazlitt's criticism

[1] *Collected Works*, ed. Waller and Glover, v, 373.

[2] It is interesting to compare Cowper's bold demand for a 'manly rough line' with Hazlitt's account of the characteristic temper of Cowper's own verse. He noted that Cowper looks at nature 'over his clipped hedges, and from his well-swept garden walks; or if he makes a bolder experiment now and then, it is with an air of precaution, as if he were afraid of being caught in a shower of rain'. (*Collected Works*, ed. Waller and Glover, v, 91–2.) Hazlitt's comments here refer to a certain domestic caution in Cowper's temperament, rather than to specific qualities in his versification.

was to promote a more generous appreciation of the work of Dryden and Pope than was accorded them by the first generation of Romantic poets. 'The question whether Pope was a poet, has hardly yet been settled', Hazlitt declared in 1818, 'and is hardly worth settling; for if he was not a great poet, he must have been a great prose writer, that is, he was a great writer of some sort.'[1] Not only did Hazlitt claim that Warton's celebrated question was concerned with little more than purely academic classification, he also hinted broadly that the inability of some poets and critics to relish Pope was largely the result of limitations in their own sensibility.[2] Furthermore, unlike some of the Romantic poets whose criticism reflected that rejection of the tutelage of their predecessors which was a necessary condition of their own originality, Hazlitt was able to look with a more dispassionate eye upon the merits of Augustan poetry. Noting that the 'dispute between the admirers of Homer and Virgil has never been settled, and never will', and that the 'disagreement between the French and English schools of tragedy' would similarly not admit of reconcilement, Hazlitt concluded with a plea for a catholic appreciation of poetry which is eminently disinterested and reasonable:

The controversy about Pope and the opposite school in our own poetry comes to much the same thing. Pope's correctness, smoothness, etc., are very good things and much to be commended in him. But it is not to be expected or even desired that others should have these qualities in the same paramount degree, to the exclusion of everything else. If you like smoothness and correctness of all things in the world, there they are for you in Pope. If you like other things better, such as strength and sublimity, you know where to go for them. Why trouble Pope, or any other author for what they have not, and do not profess to give? Those who seem to imply that Pope possessed, besides his own peculiar exquisite merits, all that is to be found in Shakespear or Milton, are I should hardly think in good

[1] 'On the Question Whether Pope was a Poet?', *Edinburgh Magazine*, February 1818. (*Collected Works*, ed. Waller and Glover, XI, 430.)
[2] 'Many people admire Milton, and as many admire Pope, while there are but few who have any relish for both. Almost all the disputes on this subject arise, not so much from false, as from confined taste.' 'Thoughts on Taste', *Edinburgh*, July 1819. (*Collected Works*, ed. Waller and Glover, XI, 457.)

earnest. But I do not therefore see that, because this was not the case, Pope was no poet. We cannot by a little verbal sophistry confound the qualities of different minds, nor force opposite excellencies into a union by all the intolerance in the world. We may pull Pope to pieces as long as we please for not being Shakespear or Milton, or we may carp at them for not being Pope; but this will not make a poet equal to all three.[1]

De Quincey was more intimately connected with Wordsworth's circle than Hazlitt, yet his own criticism of Augustan poetry—though partly derivative—had its individual features. His best-known critical formula, his distinction between the literature of knowledge and the literature of power, enabled him to relegate the Augustan poets to a 'minor key' in creative literature. More interesting and original are his remarks on the nature of didactic poetry, which throw some light on the essential difference between the achievements of Pope and Wordsworth in this *genre*.

De Quincey's *Encyclopaedia Britannica* essay *The Poetry of Pope* (which Crabb Robinson reckoned among his finest criticism)[2] is based on the assumption that one of the central responsibilities of criticism is the periodical revaluation of past literature in terms of contemporary interests. De Quincey's essay was written after the main tendencies in early nineteenth-century Romantic criticism had made themselves evident, and his essay was in part a reaction to some of these tendencies. The need to 'search and revise' contemporary estimates of Augustan poetry appeared principally to involve for De Quincey the correction of 'three errors which seem current upon this subject:

---

[1] *Table Talk*, 'On Criticism', *Collected Works*, ed. Waller and Glover, VI, 223. James Russell Lowell who claimed that he had been 'brought up in the old superstition that he [Pope] was the greatest poet that ever lived', but had come to dislike him 'on principle', nevertheless argued, like Hazlitt, for a non-partisan appreciation of Pope's merits: 'It is not a matter to be settled by any amount of argument or demonstration. There are born Popists or Wordsworthians, Lockists or Kantists, and there is nothing more to be said of the matter.' (*My Study Windows*, p. 382.)

[2] Crabb Robinson said that De Quincey's criticism of Pope was one of 'the capital articles of *Leaders in Literature*, vol. IX'. See in particular his entries in his *Diary* on a journey to Cromer made on August 9th and 10th 1859. (*Books and their Writers*, p. 789.)

First, that Pope drew his impulses from French literature; *secondly*, that he was a poet of inferior rank; thirdly, that his merit lies in superior "correctness".[1]

De Quincey's denial that Pope's poetry was fundamentally French in character, was not based upon ignorance of the nature and extent of Pope's interest in French literature.[2] Upon this subject he was so well informed that he was able confidently to refute Voltaire's claim that Pope—whom Voltaire had actually met—was hardly able to read French, and 'spoke not one word of the language'.[3] De Quincey, in fact suggested that Pope had declined to speak French before Voltaire as 'the pronunciation was confessedly beyond him'. Nevertheless, fully aware as he was of Pope's French interests, De Quincey's claim that Pope's poetry would have remained essentially unmodified 'even though France had been at the back of China', was a salutary reaction against the excessive and over-simplified stress upon French influence in the reign of Queen Anne which had become a commonplace of Regency criticism.[4] The idea

[1] De Quincey, *Collected Works*, ed. Masson, IV, 278.

[2] De Quincey made the obvious point that Pope's *Essay in Criticism* and *Satires* suggest that he had read Boileau closely (Pope could have done this by consulting the translations and adaptations of Dryden, Soames, Mulgrave, etc.). He also established, through his own inquiries, that Pope, in his translation of Homer, had made extensive use of Madame Dacier's research, and La Valterie's prose-translation of the *Iliad*. He also established that Pope's familiarity with Dacier's *Horace* could only have been through a reading of the original, as no English Translation of the work had appeared even in De Quincey's time. See De Quincey, *Collected Works*, IV, 246-7.

[3] Nevertheless, Voltaire estimated Pope's merit very highly and informed Frederick of Prussia that he considered Pope a greater poet than either Horace or Boileau:

> 'Pope *approfondit* ce qu'ils ont effleuré
> D'un esprit plus hardi, d'un pas plus assuré,
> Il porta le flambeau dans l'abîme de l'être;
> Et l'homme *avec lui seul* apprit à se connoître.
> L'art quelquefois frivole, et quelquefois divin,
> L'art des vers est dans Pope utile au genre humain.'

Quoted in De Quincey, *Collected Works*, ed. Masson, IV, 245.

[4] Yet De Quincey shared the romantic dissatisfaction with French literature, evidence of which may be found in Hazlitt's report that Wordsworth condemned 'all French writers (as well of poetry as prose) in the lump' (*Collected Works*, IV, 277), and in Coleridge's comment 'I cannot say that I know and can name any one French writer that can be placed among the greater poets' (*Anima Poetae*,

that literature was best understood by relating it to the development of society had been advanced by Herder and the German Romantic critics, and De Quincey, who believed in an 'organic' relationship between literature and life, maintained that the character of the poetry of Dryden and Pope had been determined by the essentially English culture and society they represented, and not by any external influence. He went on to make the very interesting point that the undoubted interest in French poetry shown by Dryden and Pope—which was similar to the interest in Italian poetry displayed by Spenser and Milton—was the '*result* and not the *cause* of the determination given to their minds by nature working in conjunction with their social periods'.[1]

As for the second commonplace of contemporary criticism of Augustan poetry which De Quincey wished to correct—the view that Pope was 'a poet of inferior rank'—it soon becomes evident that De Quincey's own views were not as pro-Augustan as they seem at first glance. He shared the common early nineteenth-century view (which may be traced back even to Johnson[2]) that poetry, having reached a peak or golden age, subsequently declines ('Passion begins to wheel in lower flights ... observing, refining, reflecting'), and 'elaborate perfection' comes to take the place of natural genius, the 'point of inferiority' being noted 'not in the finishing, but in the compass and power of the original creation'.[3] It was to this second order of poetry, which could no longer accommodate 'the impassioned movements of the tragic, and the majestic movements of the epic, muse' that Pope's poetry belonged. The point which De Quincey wished to make, then, was that although Pope was not

---

119). De Quincey, too, complained that he found in French literature 'an extraordinary defect of the higher qualities of passion'. (*Collected Works*, ed. Masson, IV, 278.)

[1] De Quincey, *Collected Works*, ed. Masson, XI, 61. My italics.

[2] 'Whatever be the reason, it is commonly observed that the early writers are in possession of nature, and their followers of art; that the first excel in strength and invention, and the latter in elegance and refinement.' (*Rasselas*, ed. Hannaford Bennett, 39–40.)

[3] *Collected Works*, ed. Masson, III, 89.

intrinsically an 'inferior poet', through an accident of history he belonged to an age which circumscribed the power and range of his expression.[1] The difference between De Quincey's criticism and Arnold's was that while the Augustan age was for Arnold an age of prose, it was still possible for De Quincey to regard it as an age which had produced a great deal of genuine and excellent poetry in a 'minor' mode. His estimate was, in other words, more typically Regency than Victorian in character.

Although De Quincey's criticism of those who believed that Pope's merit lay in superior 'correctness' was prompted by understandable impatience with the timidity of versifiers who imitated the externals of Pope's style, his charge that Pope's own poetry was defective in consistency of logic and was careless in construction is, not surprisingly, unconvincing.[2] Much more interesting and original were some of the critical observations which De Quincey made upon the nature of didactic poetry. Edmund Gosse claimed that one of the principal ways in which Joseph Warton anticipated the Romantics was in his recognition of the bankruptcy of the didactic poem, and the Romantic distaste for this *genre* is summed up in Shelley's violent exclamation: 'Didactic poetry is my abhorrence.'[3] Shelley himself, of course, had his own view of didacticism of a

[1] De Quincey also believed (like Warton and Wordsworth) that Pope had been over-preoccupied by the peculiar interests of his own age and time: 'In no part of his poetic mission did Pope so fascinate the gaze of his contemporaries as in his functions of satirist. . . . And one reason, I believe, why it was that the interest about Pope decayed so rapidly after his death (an accident somewhere noticed by Wordsworth) must be sought in the fact that the most stinging of his personal allusions, by which he had given salt to his later writings, were continually losing their edge, and sometimes their intelligibility, as Pope's own contemporary generation was dying off.' (De Quincey, *Collected Works*, ed. Masson, IV, 286 n.)

[2] See, for example, De Quincey's criticism of the emotional 'logic' and consistency of Pope's character of 'Atticus'—'We are to change our mood from laughter to tears upon a sudden discovery that the character belonged to a man of genius; and this we have already known from the beginning.' (*Collected Works*, IV, 280.) An attentive reading of the poetry makes it plain that no such simple and sudden reversal of feeling is appropriate: a sense of the trivial vanities that even genius is heir to is part of the nicely balanced irony that informs the whole portrait.

[3] Shelley, *Prometheus Unbound*, Preface.

higher order; he never gave up his 'passion for reforming the world', and the contradictions and complexities which may be found within the early Romantic movement are illustrated by Wordsworth's remark to Beaumont: 'Every great Poet is a Teacher: I wish to be considered as a Teacher, or as nothing.'[1]

It is incorrect to believe that a rejection of didactic poetry— except of the very simplest kind: the versified encyclopaedia article—took place in the early nineteenth century; what did take place may be much more fairly described as a fundamental change in ideas concerning the manner in which moral beliefs could be assimilated into the language of poetry. De Quincey's distinction between the literature of knowledge and the litera- ture of power provided him with a means of describing this change, for it seemed to him that while the function of the literature of knowledge (exemplified by Pope's verse) in ethical matters was primarily to *teach* by an appeal to the higher understanding, it was the function of the literature of power (exemplified by Wordsworth's verse) to *move* by an appeal to the pleasures and sympathies of the imagination.[2] De Quincey was less than fair to the epigrammatic brilliance and wit which have made Pope's moral *sententiae* almost part of the English language, and he also thought he recognised unequivocally the limitations in the communication of deep or profound moral experience and intuitions implied by his mode. As an alter- native to what he saw as the explicitly didactic mode employed by Pope—at its best a form of enlightened and sensitive moral instruction—De Quincey attempted to define a poetical mode which permitted an exploration of the moral consciousness

[1] Wordsworth, Letter to Beaumont, January/February 1808. (*Letters of William and Dorothy Wordsworth: The Middle Years*, ed. E. de Selincourt, I, 170.)

[2] De Quincey, *Collected Works*, XI, 54. An interesting comparison may also be made with Shelley's account of the moral power of poetry: 'The whole objection, however, of the immorality of poetry rests upon a misconception of the manner in which poetry acts to produce the moral improvement of man. Ethical science arranges the elements which poetry has created, and propounds schemes and proposes examples of civil and domestic life. . . . But poetry acts in another and diviner manner. . . . The great instrument of moral good is the imagination; and poetry administers to the effect by acting upon the cause.' (*A Defence of Poetry*, ed. H. F. B. Brett-Smith, 1921, p. 33.)

through the creative use of language, and which, if it presumed to 'teach' at all, did so in a manner more closely associated with the moral fable than the precept:

Poetry, or any one of the fine arts (all of which alike speak through the genial nature of man and his excited sensibilities), can teach only as nature teaches, as forests teach, as the sea teaches, as infancy teaches,—viz. by deep impulse, by hieroglyphic suggestion. Their teaching is not direct or explicit, but lurking, implicit, masked in deep incarnations. To teach formally and professedly is to abandon the very differential character and principle of poetry. If poetry could condescend to teach anything, it would be truths moral or religious. But even these it can utter only through symbols and actions.[1]

4. HUNT AND KEATS

Leigh Hunt, who was among those attacked by the *Quarterly Review* for allegedly excessive criticism of the Augustan poets, was a younger contemporary of Coleridge and Lamb at Christ's Hospital in London.[2] Coleridge's influence is apparent in the use of the terms 'Imagination' and 'Fancy' in Hunt's most carefully pondered statement of his critical beliefs in his essay *What is Poetry?*; and, although he ridiculed Wordsworth in *The Feast of the Poets* (which first appeared in the *Reflector*, No. IV of 1811), he later confessed that he had derided Wordsworth without being acquainted with his work at first hand. At this stage Hunt's critical beliefs appear to have been largely destructive; as he himself wrote of the reception accorded to *The Feast of the Poets*:

I offended all the critics of the old or French school by objecting to the monotony of Pope's versification, and all the critics of the new or German school, by laughing at Wordsworth, with whose writings I was then unacquainted, except through the medium of his deriders. On reading him for myself, I became such an admirer, that Lord Byron accused me of making him popular upon town.[3]

Like many of the Romantic poets and critics of his time,

---

[1] De Quincey, *Collected Works*, ed. Masson, XI, 88–9.

[2] For an account of Hunt's personal relationship with these two school-fellows, see *Coleridge, Lamb, and Leigh Hunt: The Christ's Hospital Anthology*, ed. S. E. Winbolt.

[3] Leigh Hunt, *Autobiography*, ed. J. E. Morpurgo, 'Literary Warfare', p. 223.

Hunt's early education included a close acquaintance with the Augustan poets—'Pope's smooth but unartistical versification spellbound me for a long time.' Recalling his early years at Christ's Hospital Hunt says: 'I could make little of Pope's *Homer*, which a school-fellow of mine was always reading, and which I was ashamed at not being able to like. It was not that I did not admire Pope; but the words in his translation always took precedence in my mind of the things.' However, this did not stop Hunt attempting to imitate Pope himself, and one of the early poems which he mentions in his *Autobiography* is a mock-heroic imitation of *The Rape of the Lock*, entitled *The Battle of the Bridal Ring*. Through his attempts at imitation Hunt discovered that although the smoothness of Pope's verse was not hard to achieve, his 'closeness' and 'wit'—which Hunt reckoned among his signal merits—were much more elusive.[1] Yet Hunt's early reading was by no means confined to the Augustan poets or to the school-room: 'My favourites, out of school hours, were Spenser, Collins, Gray, and *The Arabian Nights*.'[2]

Some of these Romantic interests found a place in *The Feast of the Poets*, and the most strikingly provocative passage in the poem contained a contemptuous account of Pope's versification. Apollo, musing upon the present state of poetry, exclaims:

> And yet I can't see why I've been so remiss,
> Unless it may be—and it certainly is,
> That since Dryden's fine verses, and Milton's Sublime,
> I have fairly been sick of their sing-song and rhyme.
> There was Collins, 'tis true, had a good deal to say;
> But the rogue had no industry,—neither had Gray.
> And Thomson, though best in his indolent fits,
> Either slept himself weary, or bloated his wits.
> But ever since Pope spoiled the ears of the town
> With his cuckoo-song verses, half up and half down,
> There has been such a doling and sameness,—by Jove,
> I'd as soon have gone down to see Kemble in love.
> However, of late as they've roused them anew,
> I'll e'en go and give them a lesson or two.[3]

[1] *Ibid.* p. 89.   [2] *Ibid.* p. 79.   [3] *The Feast of the Poets*, lines 8–22.

Hunt's reference to a recent renewal of interest in Pope's style was probably a reference to Byron's recently-published heroic couplet satire *English Bards and Scotch Reviewers*. Hunt's subsequent relations with Byron were cordial (he went out to Italy in 1822 to help Byron and Shelley to found the short-lived *The Liberal*); and he also had a high opinion of Byron's later neo-Augustan satire—he considered *The Vision of Judgement* the best satire to have appeared since the days of Pope ('Churchill's satires, compared with it, are bludgeons compared with steel of Damascus'[1]). Hunt's later assessment of Pope, too, was less ungenerous,[2] though his disdain for what seemed to him Pope's mechanically balanced versification was never modified. Hunt always admired his early favourite *The Rape of the Lock* ('the airiest wit that ever raised a joke'); nevertheless, he found in the versification of even this 'exquisite' poem qualities that are not far removed from grotesque comedy:

The reader will observe that it is literally *see-saw*, like the rising and falling of a plank, with a light person at one end who is jerked up in the briefer time, and a heavier one who is set down more leisurely at the other.[3]

In 1816, a year after he was introduced to Wordsworth by Haydon, Hunt made the acquaintance of Keats, and for a while exercised a compelling influence over him. The effects of this influence are plain in *Sleep and Poetry* (written by Keats in the winter of 1816 while he lay 'in a waking trance on the little couch in Hunt's study one night in November'), and are best seen in Keats's scornful dismissal of the versification of Pope and the Augustans, which brought upon his head the wrath of

---

[1] *Autobiography*, 'Genoa' (1822-3), p. 350.
[2] See his Conversations of Pope and Conversations of Swift included in *Table Talk*, and his account of Pope, in stanzas xx and xxi of *The Book of Beginnings*, as a 'true born poet' confined to a 'small sphere'—
> But then so great in that, that he could hide
> Scores of us dwarfs in our savannahs here:
> His rooms were not mere rooms, but worlds beside
> Of spirits, who hung pearls in every ear.

The Liberal, No. III (1823).
[3] *Imagination and Fancy* (1891), p. 44.

Croker and the *Quarterly* critics.[1] Contrasting the work of these poets with the glories of pre-Restoration poetry, Keats voiced the views current in Leigh Hunt's circle in heroic couplet verse:

> Could all this be forgotten? Yes, a schism
> Nurtured by foppery and barbarism,
> Made great Apollo blush for this his land.
> Men were thought wise who could not understand
> His glories: with a puling infant's force
> They swayed about upon a rocking horse,
> And thought it Pegasus . . .
>   Easy was the task
> A thousand handicraftsmen wore the mask
> Of Poesy.[2]

Although even the derisory image of a rocking-horse in this passage was very probably derived from Hunt,[3] his influence upon Keats was not entirely hostile to the Augustan tradition. It was through Hunt, in fact, that Keats was first attracted to Dryden's versification, an interest which was to be of crucial importance in Keats's development towards maturity as a poet.

Hunt's enthusiasm for Dryden was not a particularly early development in his taste. 'Dryden I read too', he declared in an account of his poetical interests in the years between 1804 and 1808, 'but not with that relish for his nobler versification

---

[1] His association with Leigh Hunt (who had slandered the Regent) immediately made Keats a legitimate target for the Tory critics. Shelley claimed in the Preface to *Adonais* that the severity of their criticism led to Keats's premature death. Byron wrote to John Murray shortly afterwards: 'You know very well that I did not approve of Keats's poetry, or principles of Poetry, or of his abuse of Pope; but, as he is dead, omit *all* that is said *about him* in any MSS of mine, or publication. His *Hyperion* is a fine monument, and will keep his name.' (Ravenna, 30 July 1821.)

[2] *Sleep and Poetry*, lines 176–87.

[3] Hunt had a 'magnificent rocking horse' in his house in 1815, and he whimsically likened its movement to Byron's use of the heroic couplet: 'Lord Byron, with childish glee becoming a poet, would ride upon it. Ah! why did he ever ride his Pegasus to less advantage.' (*Autobiography*.) This was a popular anecdote in Hunt's circle. Hazlitt too had heard it, and used it in his *Lectures* delivered at the Surrey Institution in 1818. See Hazlitt, *Collected Works*, ed. Waller and Glover, v. 'On Shakespeare and Milton', p. 63.

which I afterwards acquired.'[1] By 1815, however, shortly after
he regained his freedom and shortly before he met Keats,
Dryden had become a decisive and dominating influence, and
Hunt wrote in his *Autobiography*:

Dryden, at that time, in spite of my sense of Milton's superiority,
and my early love of Spenser, was the most delightful name to me
in English poetry. I found in him more vigour, and more music
too, than in Pope, who had been my closest poetical acquaintance;
and I could not rest till I had played on his instrument.[2]

Yet it is undeniable that Dryden's influence upon Hunt was not
always beneficial, and exhibited many of the features which
Scott had criticised in the 'Dryden revival'. Reacting against
what seemed to him the cramping limitations of Pope (carried
to their extreme limit in the monotony of Darwin's style), Hunt
found in Dryden warrant for laxity in his metrical organisation
and uninhibited freedom in his use of colloquial speech. Hunt's
reaction was plainly excessive, and the lapses into flaccid diffuse-
ness and almost incredible bathos which it led him into, for
example in *The Story of Rimini*, shocked Byron, whose own
language by contrast—though sometimes slapdash and uneven
—has a richly colloquial vigour which is all too often absent in
Hunt. Hunt himself was aware of some of his own defects,[3] yet

---

[1] 'Essays in Criticism', *Autobiography*, p. 150. Some notes in the *Reflector* of
1812, indicate the direction in which Hunt's taste was already moving: '. . . perhaps
there never was more favourable time than the present for an attempt to bring
back the real harmonies of the English heroic, and to restore to it half the true
principle of its music, variety. I am not here joining the cry of those, who affect
to consider Pope no poet at all. He is, I confess, in my judgement, at a good
distance from Dryden, and at an immeasurable distance from such men as Spenser
and Milton; but if the author of *The Rape of the Lock*, *Eloisa to Abelard*, and of the
Elegy on the Unfortunate Lady, is no poet, then are fancy and feeling no properties
belonging to poetry. I am only considering his versification: and upon this point
I do not hesitate to say, that I regard him, not only as no master of his art, but as
very indifferent practicer, and one whose reputation will grow less and less.'

[2] 'Free Again', *Autobiography*, p. 258.

[3] Some of these, Hunt believed, were partly compensated by the more 'romantic'
interests of his poetry: 'My versification was far from being so vigorous as his
[Dryden's]. There were many weak lines in it. It succeeded best in catching the
variety of his cadences; at least so far as they broke up the monotony of Pope.
But I had a greater love for the beauties of external nature; I think also I partook
of a more southern insight into the beauties of colour . . .' ('Free Again', *Autobiography*, p. 258.)

he prided himself upon having overthrown Pope's metrical dictatorship in the heroic couplet, and he wrote in 1816: 'I had the pleasure ... of seeing all the reigning poets, without exception, break up their own heroic couplets into freer modulation (which they never afterwards abandoned) ...'[1]

Although it was undoubtedly through Hunt that Keats was first attracted to Dryden, it is worth insisting that the true value of this for Keats was that, instead of encouraging him to follow Hunt's own experiments in versification, it sent him back to a close and sustained reading of Dryden himself. This is confirmed by the evidence of Keats's poetry itself, and also by the accounts of contemporaries and friends. *Lamia* was the first poem in which Dryden's influence is unmistakable, and Woodhouse, who had discussed the poem with Keats, told Taylor that Keats had intended its metre to be a form of 'Drydenian heroic'[2]; and Charles Armitage Brown, who was almost constantly with Keats during the composition of *Lamia*, has put it on record that Keats 'wrote it with great care, after much studying of Dryden's versification'.[3] This is particularly relevant because the differences in the effects of Dryden's influence upon Hunt and Keats could hardly be more striking. Whereas for Hunt it had implied an emancipation pure and simple from the inhibitions of strict metrical control, for Keats it represented a means by which he might achieve that poetic discipline and restraint, without which subjection to a 'life of sensations rather than thoughts' would deteriorate into a mere indulgence of feeling. Keats's distinction was that his poetry was more than merely 'simple, sensuous, and passionate', and his interest in Dryden was part of his reaction against the Miltonic mode. The varied richness of metrical control which Keats derived largely from the study of Augustan versification: the antithetical use of line-halves, the

---

[1] 'Free Again', *Autobiography*, p. 258.

[2] Woodhouse: Letter to Taylor, 20 September 1819. Woodhouse's Letter, now in the Morgan Collection, is quoted by Amy Lowell in *John Keats* (1925), II, 317–20.

[3] Charles Armitage Brown, *Life of John Keats*, ed. Boduntha and Pope (1954), p. 56.

variation of such balance by the use of triptology, the effective use of triplet and alexandrine, the variation of initial and medial inversion within the line, the exclusion of feminine rhymes and the 'clinching effect' of the stressed rhyme-word—all of which may be found in *Lamia*—was an integral part of his growing maturity as a poet. W. J. Bate, in a recent intensively technical and statistical analysis of Keats's metrical development, has come to the conclusion that there was 'a general inclination throughout Keats's entire technical development to return gradually, in a degree surpassing most of his contemporaries, to the skeletal integrity of the Augustan line'.[1] This metrical discipline—which could, in Johnson's words, 'admit change without breach of order', and could 'relieve the ear without disappointing it'—was in Keats's case part of a more inclusive poetical discipline which pointed forward to the great achievements of the *Odes* and *The Fall of Hyperion*. The richly sensuous and tactual vitality, firmly restrained and held in check, which links the characteristic achievement of Keats with that of Hopkins, is the principal feature which sets them apart from most poets of the nineteenth century. Their great admiration of Dryden is therefore of unmistakable significance and interest.

5. SHELLEY AND POE

Of all the Romantic poets of the early nineteenth century Shelley, in his deepest beliefs about the nature of poetry, was at the farthest remove from the assumptions underlying the Augustan tradition. There is in fact almost no direct reference to the Augustan poets in his literary and philosophical criticism, or even in his letters. The principal aim of *A Defence of Poetry*, which contains the most complete statement of his critical beliefs, was more to counter the Utilitarian criticism of poetry of his friend Peacock in *The Four Ages*, than to attempt any discussion of basic incompatibilities between his own view of poetry and that of the Augustans. This absence of open hostility to the Augustan tradition has been explained in terms of historical

[1] W. J. Bate, *The Stylistic Development of Keats* (Harvard, 1945), p. 86.

causes.[1] It was partly a question too of Shelley's temperament; what did not appear directly to challenge his passionately held convictions he was quite content to ignore. Yet the *implications* of Shelley's criticism are particularly relevant, because they illustrate some of the fundamental and revolutionary changes in beliefs about the nature of poetry which had taken place since Augustan times, and in this way they help to explain Shelley's indifference. The Horatian notion of the poet as a formal and dedicated craftsman, whose native genius could best express itself through diligence and industry—a view which Pope and the Augustans would have regarded as only just and natural—is almost totally disregarded in Shelley's account of the poetic process. For Shelley poetic composition was involuntary, effortless, and often unanticipated, a creative process in which the operation of the everyday human will had little place: 'for it acts in a divine and unapprehended manner beyond and above consciousness'.[2] Although in Shelley's account of the relation of poetry to the unconscious or the 'super-conscious' neo-Platonic ideas of divine possession are unmistakably present,[3] he also suggested that within the poet there existed a kind of schizophrenic *alter ego*, beyond the power of his will, which was responsible for poetic creation.[4] The idea

[1] In distinguishing between the criticism of the first and second generations of Romantic poets, Alois Brandl suggested that the latter were able to regard the Augustan tradition more accommodatingly because it was no longer through a denial of the Augustan claims that their own could receive recognition. This can perhaps be pressed too far, though a parallel with more recent literary history is instructive. Debunking of the Victorians is less common today, because less necessary, than it was three decades ago. Lytton Strachey's iconoclastic portraits of the Victorians, in fulfilling their function, have 'dated' and belong now to the history of taste.

[2] Shelley, *A Defence of Poetry*, ed. Brett-Smith, p. 31.

[3] We learn from the lists of Shelley's reading included by Mary Shelley in her *Journal* (edited by F. L. Jones and published in 1947), that Shelley consulted Plato's *Ion* during the period in which he wrote his answer to Peacock's *Four Ages*. Earlier, he drew Peacock's attention to the discussion of 'poetic madness' in the *Phaedrus*, as an antidote to 'false and narrow systems of criticism.' (*Literary and Philosophical Criticism*, ed. Ingpen and Peck, p. 213.)

[4] 'The poet and the man are two different natures; though they exist together, they may be unconscious of each other, and incapable of deciding on each other's powers and efforts by any reflex act.' (Shelley, Letter to the Gisbornes, 19 July 1821. *Shelley's Letters*, ed. Ingpen, 1914, II, 883.)

that genuine poetry was written, not through the loving care and conscious industry which the Augustans devoted to their materials, but through the operation of inward and spontaneous forces not under the full control of the poet himself, may be seen in the work of other Romantic poets as well. There is some support in the genesis of *Kubla Khan*; though as Professor Livingston Lowes demonstrated in *The Road to Xanadu*, much of Coleridge's material for the poem was derived from his wide and eclectic reading, Coleridge himself was only aware that it had originated in the interrupted recollection of a dream.[1] The direction taken by Shelleyan notions of the poetic process later in the century, in their relation to criticism of the Augustan tradition, are quite obvious: they lead up to Arnold's confident pronouncement that genuine poetry could never originate in the 'wits', but could only be 'conceived and composed in the soul'.

The recurrent image used by Shelley in the *Defence* to describe the effect which poetry had upon the 'inward being' or 'soul' of the poet was the Aeolian lyre, or wind-harp, a musical instrument now almost forgotten, though a popular piece of household furniture in the late eighteenth and early nineteenth centuries.[2] Since its music could quite literally be attributed to

[1] Such notions of the unconscious workings of the poetic mind fitted in with the revived mediaevalism of the age, and the notion of the poem as a dream-vision. The tendency may be noted outside poetry, in the novel, as well. Horace Walpole, whose interest in the 'Gothick' anticipated Romantic tendencies, claimed that *The Castle of Otranto* had its origin in a dream which he set down immediately after waking. On reading it for the first time himself he found it as unfamiliar and surprising as the work of a total stranger.

[2] In the mid-1790s Coleridge suggested the wind-harp as a metaphor for the thinking mind:

> 'And what if all of animated nature
> Be but organic harps diversely framed,
> That tremble into thought, as o'er them sweeps
> Plastic and vast, one intellectual breeze,
> At once the Soul of each, and God of all?'

> (*The Aeolian Harp*, pp. 44–8.)

Coleridge himself was dissatisfied with the metaphor, though it was popular enough to enable Robert Bloomfield to publish in 1808 an anthology of wind-harp poetry entitled *Nature's Music*. The instrument itself was first devised by Athanasius Kircher in 1650. For an account of its history see Erika von Erhardt Siebold,

nature rather than to art, it was for Shelley an attractive analogy for the poetic mind possessed of a creative power independent of the poet's will. Elsewhere in the *Defence* Shelley noted that 'the mind in creation is as a fading coal, which some invisible influence, like an inconstant wind awakens to transitory brightness', but the metaphor which he returned to most often was his account of the poetic mind as 'an instrument over which a series of external and internal impressions are driven, like the alterations of an ever-changing wind, over an Aeolian lyre, which move it by their motion to ever-changing melody'.[1]

Although Shelley made fun of Wordsworth in *Peter Bell the Third*, he recognised Wordsworth's originality and greatness ('But his was *individual* mind'), and if they may be said to have anything in common it is their belief that the intrusive 'will' and the 'meddling intellect' could thwart the spontaneous life of the 'soul'. Remote though he may seem from the work of these early nineteenth-century poets, we find in D. H. Lawrence too an intense awareness of the power of misplaced 'reason' and the perverse 'will' to thwart the spontaneous fulfilment of the deepest urges in human life, though it seems almost too obvious to insist that there is in him no preoccupation with the Romantic 'soul'. Nevertheless there is some point in mentioning Lawrence, for his criticism particularly of Edgar Allan Poe (whose work in certain respects represents the development of Shelley's notions) is directly related to some of the dangers attendant upon regarding the wind-harp as an adequate metaphor for the poetic mind.

It is plain from Poe's remarks in *The Poetic Principle* and *The Philosophy of Composition*, that he regarded poetry as a spontaneous visitation of the kind described by Shelley which 'intensely excites by elevating the soul', and which like 'all intense excitement' was 'through psychal necessity, brief'. Like all critics influenced by Longinian notions of 'elevation'

'Some Inventions of the pre-Romantic period and their influence upon literature', *Englische Studien*, LXVI, 347–63.

[1] *A Defence of Poetry*, ed. Brett-Smith, p. 23.

and the 'transport' (John Dennis and Joseph Warton, for example, in the eighteenth century), Poe described poetry in terms of its *effects* ('that intense and pure elevation of the soul— *not* of intellect or heart—upon which I have commented'[1]); the actual process of composition was for him a spontaneous process outside the will or control of the poet himself. Spontaneous life was invariably for Lawrence 'felt in the blood and felt along the heart' ('The blood as it runs has its own sympathies and responses to the material world, quite apart from seeing. And the nerves we know vibrate all the while to unseen presences, unseen forces'), and yet it was a problem to him whether spontaneity of the kind represented by Poe (the spontaneity of the wind-harp as Lawrence himself noted) had any necessary connection with the deepest impulses of life:

It is a question how much, once the true centrality of the self is broken, the instrumental consciousness of man can register? When man becomes selfless, wafting instrumental like a harp in an open window, how much can his elemental consciousness express?

The dangers inherent in a surrender to the promptings of the merely 'mechanical consciousness' seemed to Lawrence forcibly exemplified in the poetry of Poe:

The absence of real central or impulsive being in himself leaves him inordinately, mechanically sensitive to sounds and effects, associations of sounds, associations of rhyme, for example—mechanical, facile, having no root in any passion. It is all a secondary, meretricious process. So we get Roderick Usher's poem, *The Haunted Palace*, with its swift yet mechanical subtleties of rhyme and rhythm, its vulgarity of epithet. It is all a sort of dream-process, where the

---

[1] Longinian influence may be noted in the criticism of Augustan poetry in our own day. A. E. Housman, who did not have a high opinion of Augustan poetry, contrasted it with genuine poetry which was 'lofty or magnificent or intense'. Housman's definition of poetry in terms of its effects—it transports with rapture and shakes the soul—is purely Longinian. In Housman's own case the effects of genuine poetry were partly recognisable by their physiological symptoms —a bristling of the skin, a precipitation of water to the eyes, and a sensation like a spear through the pit of the stomach. (*The Name and Nature of Poetry*, 1933, pp. 12, 34–5, 46–7.)

association between parts is mechanical, accidental as far as passional meaning goes.[1]

This is of course a criticism of Poe, and not of Shelley or Wordsworth. It is unlikely that Lawrence would have criticised Shelley in quite these terms, and almost certain that he would not have found in Wordsworth any 'absence of real central or impulsive being'. Yet his criticism is salutary, because it brings into sharp focus the dangers which the 'Romantic' rejection of the Augustan concept of the conscious and dedicated craftsman unavoidably entailed.

Finally, it is worth noting of the implications underlying Shelley's criticism, that his assumptions regarding the relationship between the poet and his readers were at the farthest possible remove from those characteristic of the Augustan age. Whereas the Augustan poet invariably regarded himself as a social being who addressed his fellows in the broad light of the waking consciousness, this was Shelley's account of the relationship of the poet and his audience:

A poet is a nightingale, who sits in darkness and sings to cheer its own solitude with sweet sounds; his auditors are as men entranced by the melody of an unseen musician, who feel that they are moved and softened, yet know not whence or why.[2]

---

[1] D. H. Lawrence, 'Edgar Allan Poe', *Studies in Classic American Literature* (1924), p. 88. In the light of accounts of the origin of their poems given by some of the Romantics, Lawrence's association of 'mechanical consciousness' and a 'dream-process' is particularly interesting.

[2] *A Defence of Poetry*, ed. Brett-Smith, p. 31.

CHAPTER VIII

PRO-AUGUSTAN CRITICISM

A study of the innovations of the early Romantic poets and critics suggests that one of the principal changes which took place during this period was a disparagement of the powers of reason (associated with the 'wits'), and exaltation of the intuitive profundity of feeling (associated with the 'soul'). But this estimate of the relative importance of 'reason' and 'feeling', when considered in relation to the life and thought of the age as a whole, may be actively misleading. For although Wordsworth and Shelley and Keats and the other Romantics gave expression in their work to the new stress on the exploration of 'feeling', the Benthamite tradition in the early nineteenth century ensured that the eighteenth-century emphasis upon 'reason', far from declining, seemed now endowed with an even more vigorous lease of life.[1] As for the theoretical expression of this dualism, Coleridge on the one hand and Bentham on the other—as John Stuart Mill noted in his essays—represent the central antithesis in the life and thought of the age.

A concern for 'reason', however, could no longer be regarded necessarily as a concern for the preservation of the Augustan virtues in the early nineteenth century. For the 'reason' of the Augustans and the 'reason' of the Utilitarians often implied strikingly different preoccupations. Whereas 'reason' for Pope and his contemporaries usually meant the guiding principle which gave to all aspects of civilised human existence their due proportion and emphasis, and was thus part of an integrated and inclusive 'wisdom', 'reason' for the Utilitarians was almost invariably confined to the practical and

---

[1] The extreme rationalistic tendencies of the age are well exemplified in James Mill who, according to his son, 'regarded as an aberration of the moral standard of modern times . . . the great stress laid upon feeling'. (J. S. Mill, *Autobiography*, 1908 edn, p. 28.)

materialistic aspects of human life. This narrowing of interests is reflected in an extreme form in the answers which Bentham found to the two questions which principally interested him with regard to poetry: first, 'Is it true?' and secondly, 'Is it of any use?' With regard to the first, Bentham, who considered language primarily as a means of stating objective and logical truth rather than as a form of complex social behaviour (and who could see no point in the metaphorical resources of poetical language), arrived at his well-known aphoristic conclusion: 'All poetry is misrepresentation.' As for the usefulness of poetry, Bentham maintained that for the purposes of his 'felicific calculus' the pleasure derived from poetry was equal in value to that derived from push-pin, or, if anything, less valuable, because, as he went on to explain: 'everybody can play at push-pin, poetry and music are relished only by a few'.[1]

The only justification for the wide currency of such Benthamite 'philistinism' (to use the word Arnold later coined) among those who under James Mill's leadership supported the *Westminster Review*, was that to men who were quite genuinely and passionately devoted to reform, the enormity of the political and social evils of the day made a concern for literary culture appear an expensive luxury. J. S. Mill wrote in his *Autobiography* that Peregrine Bingham's article in the opening number of the *Westminster Review* 'did a good deal to attach the notion of hating poetry to the writers in the *Review*'[2]; but he emphasised that not all Utilitarians were enemies of poetry. His own development is indeed a classic example of this, and the crucial role which Wordsworth's poetry played in the great spiritual crisis which he underwent, led directly to the reconciliation and balance of emotion and intelligence which he later strove to achieve. In 1836 he wrote to E. Lytton Bulwer that he had now come to consider 'feeling at least as valuable as thought, and

---

[1] J. S. Mill noted that Bentham's antipathy to poetry sprang from his belief that words were 'perverted from their proper office when they were employed in uttering anything but precise logical truth'. ('Bentham', *Early Essays*, 1838, pp. 379–80.)

[2] J. S. Mill, *Autobiography* (1908 edn), p. 64.

Poetry not only on a par with, but the necessary condition of, any true and comprehensive Philosophy'.[1]

I. PEACOCK

'Had the intellectual seriousness of the Benthamites been accompanied by a more educated taste and sensibility', Dr R. G. Cox has pointed out, 'the *Westminster* might have proved an important check to the excesses of Romanticism.'[2] Although most of the contributors to the review were unable to see how the pursuit of poetry could lead to the improvement of cotton-spinning or the abolishing of the poor-laws, there was at least one among them who had an educated sensibility as well as an uncompromisingly rational intelligence: Thomas Love Peacock. Peacock's peculiar merits are reflected in his friendship with Shelley on the one hand and with James Mill on the other, and he was undeniably the ablest contributor to that section of the *Westminster* which Bentham grudgingly agreed might be devoted to 'literary insignificancies'.

It would be a mistake to take Peacock's Utilitarian arguments in *The Four Ages of Poetry* at their face-value. For although his essay is a devastatingly amusing criticism of some of the Romantic tendencies in the poetry of his own time, Peacock was able through an equally destructive exercise of his wit to expose the limitations of the Utilitarians themselves.[3] Part of his purpose in *The Four Ages*, as we gather from his correspondence with Shelley, was to be witty and provocative at Shelley's expense,[4] and one may even ask whether the caricature of the Romantic position contained in the essay represents Peacock's own views, or whether it may not be more suitably taken to

---

[1] *Letters of J. S. Mill*, ed. H. S. R. Elliot (1910), I, 104.

[2] *19th Century Periodical Criticism*, p. 182.

[3] The Social Science Association, for example, was delightfully parodied by Peacock in *Gryll Grange*, where Lord Facing-both-ways and Lord Michin Malicho appear as the leaders of the Pantopragmatic Society.

[4] See, in particular, Peacock's *Memoirs of Shelley* (1909), pp. 205–6, and 208.

represent the views of Peacock's Mr MacQuedy, representative of the Steam Intellect Society in *Crotchet Castle*. The answer to this question is not simple, though it is worth insisting that Peacock's attack in *The Four Ages* is not directed against poetry *per se* but against tendencies in *contemporary* poetry. Peacock was far from being a single-minded Utilitarian, and he may merely have *used* the Utilitarian arguments to give point and force to his provocative criticism.

Peacock's 'cyclical' theory of literary history was not entirely new in the early nineteenth century, and reference to it may be found in the work of other contemporaries,[1] although Peacock's version is perhaps the most comprehensive. In tracing the inevitable development of poetry in any civilisation, Peacock discerned four principal phases in its history. First, an original age of iron devoted to the celebration of the exploits of tribal heroes. Next, through a refinement of the materials provided by this iron age, a Homeric age of gold (the age of Shakespeare in the modern world), in which poetry, having outstripped its rivals history, philosophy, and science, 'is cultivated by the greatest intellects of the age, and listened to by all the rest'. In this age poetry reaches its highest point, and it is left for the succeeding age to spend its powers 'in recasting, and giving an exquisite polish to, the poetry of the age of gold'. This is the silver age of poetry, which produced the work of Menander and Aristophanes, of Virgil, Horace, and Juvenal. Peacock assigned the Roman Augustan poets to this third period in the ancient world, and he appropriately assigned their modern counterparts, the English 'Augustan' poets, to the silver age of modern times, which he described as 'beginning with Dryden, coming to perfection with Pope, and ending with Goldsmith, Collins, and Gray'. The 'recasting' and 'exquisite polishing' of the poetry of the age of gold, which is the primary business

---

[1] F. H. B. Brett-Smith, in the introduction to his edition of *The Four Ages*, noted that there is an interesting similarity between Peacock's 'cyclical' theory and Macaulay's views in his essay on Milton. Similar views may be found in Macaulay's article on Dryden in the *Edinburgh* in the mid-1820s, and in Jeffrey's review of John Ford, a decade before the appearance of *The Four Ages*.

of the succeeding age, could not continue indefinitely; poetry then entered a period of crisis: 'It is now evident that poetry must either cease to be cultivated, or strike into a new path.' This was the problem which faced poets in the early nineteenth century. Though they had chosen the second alternative (originality), Peacock felt that in 'rejecting the polish and learning of the age of silver' and professing 'to return to nature and to revive the age of gold', the Romantic poets had not succeeded in creating anything new, but had only completed the cyclical development of the whole tradition by 'taking a retrograde stride to the barbarisms and crude traditions of the age of iron' in which poetry had originated. This return to the traditions of the age of iron Peacock found in the 'Romantic' interest in the Middle Ages (which he himself described in Augustan terms as a compound of 'barbarous manners, obsolete customs, and exploded superstitions'), an interest reflected in the 'Gothick' revival and in the many attempts to imitate the style and subject-matter of the mediaeval ballad. Whereas 'good sense' and 'elegant learning' had made the Augustan poet *par excellence* 'the poet of civilised life', the mediaeval preoccupations of the Romantic poet led Peacock to describe him as 'a semi-barbarian in a civilised community'. His main objection was that, unlike the Augustan poet who wrote from the centre of his life and experience, the preoccupations of the early nineteenth-century poet prompted him to turn away from the realities of the everyday world, or to falsify or glamourise them. Peacock's criticism of this tendency in Moore's 'Persian' and Campbell's 'Pennsylvanian' tales, 'both formed on the same principle as Mr Southey's epics, by extracting from a perfunctory and desultory perusal of a collection of voyages and travels all that useful investigation would not seek for and that common sense would reject', has, in its concern for the common-sense realities of human experience and its weighty and antithetical style, a Johnsonian ring.

Although Peacock was outrageously (and perhaps consciously) unfair to the genius and originality of Wordsworth,

Coleridge, and their contemporaries in *The Four Ages of Poetry*,[1]
it is undeniable that his insistence on the extent to which their
poetry involved a turning away from everyday life and from
the interests and concerns of the normal, adult world, was a
serious criticism. Whereas in Homeric and Augustan times 'all
the associations of life' in their fullest and widest application
were the legitimate province of the poet, Peacock felt that there
was a tendency among the poets of his own time to neglect 'the
real business of life' and 'to cultivate poetical impressions
exclusively'. It was this tendency in their work which disturbed Peacock most deeply, because he felt it was leading increasingly to a neglect of poetry itself, not only by the *Westminster* reviewers, but by the intelligent and educated sections
of the community as a whole: 'intellectual power and intellectual acquisitions have turned themselves into other and better
channels, and have abandoned the cultivation and the fate of
poetry'.[2] Peacock's method of ironical caricature undoubtedly
led him at times into exaggerating and distorting the Romantic
position, yet the underlying interest informing his diagnosis of
literary tendencies in his time was more than merely light-
hearted and mocking. Although he would in all likelihood have
disagreed with Arnold's unfavourable assessment of *Augustan*
poetry, Peacock's belief that the principal weakness of early
Romantic poetry was its tendency to lose touch with the life
and thought of the age as a whole, anticipates Arnold's own

---

[1] Much more generous estimates of the work of the Romantics may be found
elsewhere in Peacock's writings. 'Wordsworth, Coleridge, and Southey', he once
noted, 'are true to nature ... even in their wildest imaginings' (*Gryll Grange*,
1861, p. 204), and on another occasion Peacock observed that although Wordsworth's genius was 'neither epic, nor dramatic, nor dithyrambic', he had 'deep
thought and deep feeling, graceful imaginings, great pathos, and little passion'.
('The Flask of Cratinus', *Fraser's Magazine*, October 1857.)

[2] In a letter dated 4 December 1820, which Peacock sent to Shelley together
with a presentation copy of *The Four Ages*, Peacock stated: 'The truth, I am convinced, is, that there is no longer a poetical audience among the higher class of
minds; that moral, political, and physical science have entirely withdrawn from
poetry the attention of all those whose attention is worth having.' (Quoted by
H. F. B. Brett-Smith in his introduction to Peacock's *The Four Ages of Poetry*, 1921,
p. xi, from a privately printed volume of *Letters and Fragments* by Peacock, edited
by Richard Garnett for the Bibliophile Society, Boston, in 1910.)

relegation of Wordsworth, Scott, and Keats to a 'minor current' in literature (despite his admiration for them), because their verse was insufficiently concerned with the powerful application of 'modern ideas' and the 'modern spirit' to literature.[1] In Peacock's case, unlike Arnold's, this awareness of disturbing tendencies in early nineteenth-century poetry was partly the result of his sense of the contrasting virtues of the Augustan poets.

2. ROGERS AND CAMPBELL

The early nineteenth-century tendency, noted by Peacock, for the rational intelligence to dissociate itself from poetical composition influenced the work not only of overtly 'Romantic' poets but also of poets commonly regarded by their contemporaries as the legitimate descendants of the Augustan age. This may be seen particularly in the work of Rogers and Campbell, who were praised by the *Quarterly Review*, by Byron, by William Roscoe, and many others, for maintaining some of the traditions of the school of Pope in Regency times. Their great appeal to conservative tastes may be attributed largely to the fact that the Augustan tradition had undergone considerable modification in their work, and was now perfectly adapted to the changed poetical climate of the new century.[2] To some contemporaries, indeed, the work of Campbell and Rogers ap-

---

[1] Summing up the achievement of the early nineteenth-century Romantic poets, Arnold observed: 'The greatest of them, Wordsworth, retired (in Middle Age phrase) into a monastery. I mean, he plunged himself in the inward life, he voluntarily cut himself off from the modern spirit. Coleridge took to opium. Scott himself became the historiographer royal of feudalism. Keats passionately gave himself up to a sensuous genius, to his faculty for interpreting nature; and he died of consumption at twenty-five. Wordsworth, Scott, and Keats have left admirable works; far more solid and complete works than those which Byron and Shelley have left. But their works have this defect—they do not belong to that which is the main current of the literature of modern epochs, they do not apply modern ideas to life; they constitute, therefore, *minor currents*, and all other literary work of our day, however popular, which has the same defect, also constitutes but a minor current.' (Essay on Heine, *Cornhill Magazine*, August 1863, pp. 242–3.)

[2] A recent editor of Rogers, Morchard Bishop, says '. . . *The Pleasures of Memory* gauged the taste of the time to a nicety; it said nothing much, but it said it very smoothly, with the result that, by 1816, 19 editions of it had been sold.' (*Table Talk of Samuel Rogers*, 1952, Introduction, p. xv.)

peared to combine the best of both worlds, and *The Album* of culy 1822 said that ' *The Pleasures of Hope* may be considered the Ionnecting link between the past and present school of poetry. Jt is written in the metre and manner of the first, and with the glow, animation, and energy of the other'.[1]

A study of the poetry of Campbell and Rogers soon reveals that what they derived from the Augustan tradition was smoothness and polish of versification and elegance and refinement of diction, rather than satirical power, 'wit', or play of intelligence. In dealing with the *Quarterly Review*'s reaction to their work, it has already been mentioned that Campbell and Rogers seemed closer in spirit to the disciplined emotionalism of Goldsmith ('his melting sentiment just held in check by the precision of his language') than to the more masculine good sense and intellectual weightiness of Johnson. This tendency in their poetry is reflected in their criticism too, and was noted by Lord Brougham, in his comments upon what seemed to him Campbell's unfair preference for Goldsmith over Johnson as a poet. Referring to the introductory essay with which Campbell prefaced his *Specimens of the British Poets*, Brougham observed:

Towards Dryden he is *wholly unjust*, nor had he apparently a *due* value for the poetry of Johnson. He includes *The Vanity of Human Wishes* among the specimens, but he never mentions Johnson among the poets whom he commemorates. Bestowing so disproportionate a space upon Goldsmith, *renders it plain that he undervalued Johnson.* For though Goldsmith is superior to him, they are *too near in merit*; and come from *schools too much alike*, to authorise him who sets the one so high to *neglect or undervalue* the other.[2]

Though Brougham exaggerated the pejorative force of Campbell's criticism of Dryden and Johnson, it is nevertheless a revealing indication of the nature of Campbell's interest in the Augustan tradition that he was much more readily attracted by the work of Goldsmith than by that of either Johnson or Dryden.

Yet it was undoubtedly Pope whom Campbell admired most

---

[1] 'The Augustan Age in England', *The Album* (July 1822), p. 211.
[2] Quoted in *Literary Reminiscences and Memoirs of Thomas Campbell*, edited Cyrus Redding (1860), I, 82.

among the Augustan poets. Unlike many of his 'Romantic' contemporaries, he tended to praise Pope at Dryden's expense, or at least sympathised with those who did.[1] A considerable part of Campbell's critical energies were devoted to defending Pope against the hostile criticism of the age, and he was the first of the pro-Augustan critics to reply to the disparaging criticism of Pope in Bowles's edition. Campbell's eloquent and lively defence of Pope in the *Edinburgh Review* of January 1808[2] did not exhaust his views on this matter, and he developed them at an even greater length in the *Essay on English Poetry*, which he placed at the beginning of his *Specimens*, which appeared eleven years later. Campbell's wish to defend Pope, particularly against the strictures of Bowles, was so marked that he completely sacrificed the balance and structure of his *Essay* to this purpose. Instead of giving a history of eighteenth-century poetry, as he had set out to do, Campbell devoted the entire concluding section to an elaborate defence of Pope. The earlier part of his discussion confirms that Brougham had exaggerated Campbell's antipathy towards Dryden. Campbell's criticism of Dryden, though not ungenerous, was fairly conventional. Like Wordsworth and most contemporary readers, he was particularly attracted by the *Fables*, and found Dryden's style 'bold and graceful and generally idiomatic and easy'. His principal deficiencies were his lack of interest in the 'tender' and 'pathetic' movements of the heart, and a certain bluntness of sensibility—'had the subject of the *Eloisa* fallen into his hands, he would have left but a coarse draft of her passion'.

Although the main ground of Campbell's defence of Pope—that the criticisms made against him were more appropriately applied to the work of his imitators rather than to Pope himself

---

[1] The following anecdote indicates Campbell's predilections: 'He observed that there was much shrewdness in Wolcot's remark, when discriminating between Dryden and Pope. "Dryden comes into a room like a clown, in a drugget jacket, with a bludgeon in his hand, and in hobnail shoes. Pope enters like a gentleman, in full dress, with a bag and a sword." ' (*Ibid.* II, 49–50.) Although this account of Dryden as a rustic churl is grotesquely unfair, Campbell's approval of the anecdote suggests the high regard in which he held Pope's polish and refinement.

[2] See Chapter III.

—had been used by several other contemporaries, some particular features in his criticism are worth noting because they suggest some of his special interests in Augustan poetry. One noteworthy feature of his defence of Pope is that he never praises him for the brilliance of his 'wit' or for the range and variety of his satirical powers. On the other hand, perhaps the most interesting and original part of his defence is his rebuttal of Bowles's claim that Pope was deficient as a painter of the world of nature. Pope's keen eye for the minutiae of natural life Campbell found abundantly demonstrated in *Windsor Forest*, though he contented himself with quoting a passage of delicate observation from the *Essay on Man*, about which he claimed, 'every epithet is a decisive touch':[1]

> From the green myriads in the peopled grass:
> What modes of sight betwixt each wide extreme,
> The mole's dim curtain, and the lynx's beam . . .
> The spider's touch, how exquisitely fine,
> Feels at each thread, and lives along the line.

Nevertheless, the qualities which Campbell admired most in Pope were the 'rich economy of his expression', and the disciplined tightness and precision of his versification: 'Pope gave our heroic couplet its strictest melody and tersest expression

D'un mot mis en sa place il enseigne le pouvoir.'[2]

Campbell—in striking contrast to most Romantic poets and critics—was a great admirer of French poetry (he claimed that Racine in some respects surpassed even Shakespeare),[3] and he felt that Pope had successfully recreated in terms of an essentially English sensibility all the 'regularity', 'elegance', 'gracefulness' and 'poise' which he associated with the best poetry of the French classical tradition.

As for the emotional content of Pope's verse, Campbell was particularly attracted by the 'pathetic' elements in the *Elegy to the Memory of an Unfortunate Lady* and *Eloisa to Abelard*, and was fond of reciting passages from the second poem from

[1] Campbell's *Specimens*, Vol. I, p. 267 (1819).
[2] *Ibid.* p. lxxxvi.
[3] *Literary Reminiscences and Memoirs*, II, 228–9.

memory. The specialised nature of Campbell's interest in the Augustan tradition is apparent in Redding's account of his attitude towards *The Rape of the Lock*:

Campbell could repeat a great deal of it, and yet nothing could be more foreign to his own style of writing and manner of treating a subject. He could not get his muse to dally in a like playful humour, for he did not possess a particle of that rich vein of wit which Pope exhibited.[1]

In fact, Campbell shared the 'Romantic' underestimate of satire and 'wit', and believed that Pope's claims to be regarded as a true poet were based on quite different qualities:

But his wit is not all his charm. He glows with passion in the Epistle of Eloisa, and displays a lofty feeling, much above that of the satirist and the man of the world, in his Prologue to Cato, and his Epistle to Lord Oxford. I know not how to designate the possessor of such gifts but by the name of a genuine poet—

qualem vix reperrit unum
Millibus in multis hominum consultus Apollo.[2]

It is plain from this passage that Campbell and his critical adversary Bowles were largely in agreement as to the qualities in Pope which were essentially poetical. Where they differed was upon the status that was to be assigned to Pope for his possession of these qualities.

Samuel Rogers, who was some years older than Campbell and directly influenced him, was even more widely praised in his day as a descendant of the Augustan age. The *Quarterly* claimed that his best work showed him to be the 'faithful and diligent disciple of Pope and Goldsmith'; and Byron, constructing his well-known *Gradus ad Parnassum* in the Journal which he kept between November 1813 and April 1814, wrote that although Scott was undoubtedly the 'Monarch of Parnassus' in the eyes of the public, he himself preferred Rogers for his Augustan affinities—'I value him more as the last of the *best* school.'[3]

[1] *Ibid.* II, 48.
[2] Campbell's *Specimens*, pp. 270–271 (1819).
[3] *Byron's Works*, Murray, 1898, 'Letters and Journals', II, 344. Also *Byron: A Self-Portrait*, ed. Quennell (1950), I, 220.

Yet the qualities which Rogers derived from the Augustans were of a specialised kind, and may be observed in the poem which first made him the favourite of the conservative critics, *The Pleasures of Memory*, which first appeared in 1792. It was upon this poem that Campbell based his own *Pleasures of Hope* (1799), which brought him recognition among the *élite* of Edinburgh literary society, enabling him to make the acquaintance of Scott, Lord Brougham, Jeffrey and many others. The elegant versification and diction, the style of moral and philosophical elevation, which Rogers derived from Pope and Johnson, and transmitted to Campbell, may be found in the following representative passage from *The Pleasures of Memory*:

> Survey the globe, each ruder realm explore;
> From Reason's faintest ray to Newton soar.
> What different spheres to human bliss assigned!
> What slow gradations of the scale of mind!
> Yet mark in each these mystic wonders wrought;
> Oh! mark the sleepless energies of thought.

The elevated tone struck in the opening line, with its obvious echoes of *The Vanity of Human Wishes*, is scarcely sustained in the lines that follow. The declamatory style and energetic antithesis cannot conceal the emptiness of the platitudes being offered as the findings of the philosophically contemplative mind. The creative impulsion behind Rogers's lines is nothing more urgent than the interests of a tasteful and too obviously well-read mind addressing itself to a congenial literary pastime, and those who admired such stuff were responding more to what was familiar and admired in others than to anything personal to the poet. In *The Voyage of Columbus* (1812) and *Jacqueline* (1814), much to the disappointment of the *Quarterly Review* and Byron,[1] Rogers attempted to develop more strikingly

---

[1] Rogers had appeared prominently among the select few whom Byron had praised in *English Bards and Scotch Reviewers* (March 1809):

> 'And thou, melodious ROGERS* rise at last,
> Recall the pleasing memory of the past . . .
> Restore Apollo to his vacant throne,
> Assert thy country's honour and thine own', etc.

In a letter to John Murray from Venice, dated 15 September 1817, at a time

'Romantic' interests, yet it was soon apparent even to himself that the 'Longinian' sublimities and other extravagances of personal feeling which he aimed at in these 'experimental' poems, were plainly outside his natural range as a poet, and he reverted to the safer and more decorous style of Pope, Johnson, and Goldsmith in *Human Life* which appeared in 1819.

It was as a fastidious imitator of these Augustan poets that Rogers gained his great popularity during the Regency. This fastidiousness was so extreme that it led him at times to criticise even Pope's versification, which he had chiefly used as a model. Considering the uniformity, bordering upon monotony, of Rogers's own poetry, it is a little surprising to find him remarking:

The want of pauses is the main blemish in Pope's versification: I can't recollect at this moment any pause he has, except that in his *Prologue to Cato*:

> *The triumph ceas'd*, tears gush'd from every eye;
> The world's great victor pass'd unheeded by.[1]

A possible explanation of this criticism is that Rogers was intending to contrast Pope's style with that of Dryden. For shortly afterwards he went on to remark:

Pope is not to be compared with Dryden for varied harmony of versification; nor for ease;—how naturally the words follow each other in this couplet of Dryden's in the *Second Part of Absalom and Achitophel*:

> The midwife laid her hand on his thick skull,
> With this prophetic blessing—*Be thou dull!*

and in that touching one in his *Epitaph to Congreve*,

---

when Byron's own poetry was undergoing considerable changes, he noted in a vivaciously debunking tone: '. . . Rogers, the Grandfather of living Poetry, is retired upon half-pay, (I don't mean as a Banker),—

> Since pretty Miss Jacqueline,
> With her nose aquiline,

and has done enough, unless he were to do as he did formerly.' (*Byron: Letters and Diaries, 1798–1824*, ed. Quennell, 1950, p. 419.)

[1] *Recollections of the Table Talk of Samuel Rogers*, by Alexander Dyce, ed. Morchard Bishop (1952), pp. 16–17. Rogers was probably attempting to recall really memorable or striking pauses in Pope's verse. His difficulty in recollecting 'any pause' at all in Pope is less easy to understand.

> Be kind to my remains; and, O, defend,
> Against your judgement, your departed friend![1]

Although Rogers's own versification was almost totally without the robust energy and vigour of Dryden, his preference for Dryden over Pope in this matter links him with Leigh Hunt and Keats and some of his other confessedly 'Romantic' contemporaries.

Yet there is ample evidence that Rogers rated the poetry of the Augustan age infinitely above the work of his contemporaries. Defending Pope rather gushingly against the censures of those who had dared to question the profundity of the power of 'Reason' in Pope's work, he declared: 'People are now so fond of *the obscure* in poetry, that they can perceive no *deep thinking* in that darling man Pope, because he always expresses himself with such admirable clearness.'[2]

In all their critical utterances Rogers and Campbell were invariably pro-Augustan. There can be little doubt, too, that in their own poetry they strove deliberately to continue the Augustan tradition. But the extent to which this tradition had itself undergone modification in the early nineteenth century is immediately remarkable. For although in theory both Rogers and Campbell looked back to the Augustans for their models, their poetry showed unmistakable signs of the new Romantic tendencies of their time. Their proneness to sentimentality and pathos is far removed from the discipline and restraint of their Augustan predecessors. Their poetry can best be described as developing some of the characteristics of the Augustan tradition, and not others. For example, it is generally true of the work of Rogers and Campbell that their language (though too often prone to lapse into the kind of 'poetic diction' which Wordsworth campaigned against), retained something of the refinement and elegance of the Augustans. As regards the subject-matter of their verse, it is also true that the didactic and moralising interests which may be found in the work of Pope, Johnson,

[1] *Recollections of the Table Talk of Rogers*, Dyce, p. 17.
[2] *Ibid.* p. 17.

and Goldsmith, survived recognisably in Rogers and Campbell, and these features in their poetry may be traced back to the *Eloisa to Abelard*, the *Essay on Man*, *The Vanity of Human Wishes*, and *The Deserted Village*. Undoubtedly some characteristics of the Augustan tradition survived, yet what was lost was possibly even more striking and distinctive than those features that were kept. The extent of this loss comes home to the reader if he chances to remember—and in reading Rogers and Campbell he can easily forget—that the poets upon whom they modelled themselves belonged to what was undoubtedly the greatest tradition of satirical poetry that the language has produced. The distinctive virtues have all but disappeared in the work of Rogers and Campbell.

But the admiration which these two poets always felt for the Augustans was genuine and influential, and helped to keep alive the reputation of the Augustan poets in the early nineteenth century. As we have already learned from the evidence of Jeffrey and Coleridge and from many other sources, the Augustans were unrivalled in their popularity among the majority of readers right up to the turn of the century, and these literary loyalties were slow in dying out. As an anonymous reviewer said in *The Album* of July 1822:

The elders of the present generation cling with the tenaciousness of habit to the favourites of their youth. They still consider Addison the model of prose style, and look, with almost Catholic horror, on any doubts regarding the infallibility of Pope.

When Leslie Stephen observed that eighteenth-century standards of literary taste survived after the turn of the century in the 'upper currents of opinion', he was probably referring to the literary coteries which assembled at Holland House, at Lady Blessington's in Kensington, and at the numerous fashionable houses in Edinburgh, Bath, Bristol and elsewhere. Interest in Pope and the Augustans survived to a considerable extent at such gatherings.[1] We know, for example, that Lord Holland

[1] Observing that there was a considerable interest in Pope and Swift among 'fashionable' readers, Hazlitt noted in 'Trifles Light as Air' (*The Atlas*, September 1829) that Pope and Swift required 'a little *modernising*' to accommodate them to

himself was a great admirer of Pope. His favourite passage of poetry was taken from Pope's *Imitation of the Second Epistle of the Second Book of Horace*, which he declared to be as fine as anything which could be found in the work of the Roman poet. Rogers informs us that Lord Holland was particularly fond of hearing him repeat this passage, which began

> Years following years, steal something every day,
> At last they steal us from ourselves away;
> In one our frolics, one amusements end,
> In one a mistress drops, in one a friend.[1]

Rogers, whose delight in Pope was well known, exerted a considerable influence upon the taste of his contemporaries, and was described by Macaulay as 'the Oracle of Holland House'. He liked to regard himself as 'the self-appointed dictator of English letters', and his celebrated literary breakfasts at 22 St James Place in London were attended at one time or another by almost all the leading literary personalities of the time.[2] Some of the literary conversation that was natural upon such occasions was fortunately recorded by Alexander Dyce and was subsequently published.

It is from this source that we learn that Fox was 'so fond of Dryden that he had some idea of editing his works', and that Richard Porson the classical scholar, who was a friend of Rogers, was 'passionately fond of Swift's *Tale of a Tub*, and ... could repeat by heart a quantity of Swift's verses'. Dyce also tells us of Porson: 'His admiration of Pope was extreme. I have seen the tears roll down his cheeks while he was repeating Pope's lines *To the Earl of Oxford, prefixed to Parnell's Poems*'.[3] The dis-

---

'ears polite'. He was probably referring here to the growing prudishness of nineteenth-century taste. Of other changes which had affected the reading of Dryden's poetry, Hazlitt noted '. . . a bluestocking belle would be puzzled in reciting Dryden's sounding verse with its occasional barbarous old-fashioned accenting, if it were the custom to read Dryden aloud in these serene morning circles'.

[1] *Recollections of the Table Talk of Rogers*, Dyce, p. 16.

[2] Among those who were present at such gatherings were Wordsworth, Coleridge, Byron, Campbell, Moore, Sheridan, Porson, Fox, and Jeffrey. Among Rogers's literary guests later in the century were Tennyson, Dickens, and Thackeray.

[3] *Recollections of the Table Talk of Rogers*, Dyce, p. 181.

pute about the relative merits of the translations of Homer made by Pope and Cowper was very much in the air at the time, and Porson, whose classical scholarship gave authority to his criticism, declared firmly that the finest passages in Pope's translation were immeasurably superior to anything in Cowper's.[1] Porson's admiration for Pope was little short of idolatry, and during the course of a visit which he paid to Pope's villa at Twickenham in the company of Rogers and Dyce, he exclaimed: 'Oh, how I should like to pass the remainder of my days in a house which was the abode of a man so deservedly celebrated!' Sheridan, whose most celebrated plays belonged to the age of Johnson, also attended Rogers's literary breakfasts after the turn of the century, and he shared Fox's great admiration for Dryden. He sympathised with the early nineteenth-century enthusiasm for Dryden's *Fables*, and was specially attracted by *Palamon and Arcite*. Sheridan's recitation of passages from this poem made a great impression upon Dyce, and in preparing his records of literary conversation for publication many decades later, he wrote: 'I seem now to hear him reciting from them.' The following lines, in particular, Dyce said, were 'great favourites with Sheridan':

> Vain man! how vanishing a bliss we crave!
> Now warm in love, now withering in the grave!
> Never, O, never more, to see the sun,
> Still dark, in a damp vault, and still alone![2]

Porson, Fox, and Sheridan were literally survivals of the previous century, and it is hardly surprising that they clung,

---

[1] Rogers, somewhat surprisingly, was unable to agree with Porson in this matter: 'My father used to recommend Pope's *Homer* to me: but, with all my love of Pope, I never could like it. (I delight in Cowper's *Homer*; I have read it again and again)'. *Ibid.* p. 17. Coleridge described Pope's *Iliad* as 'an astonishing product of matchless talent and ingenuity' (*Biog. Literaria*, p. 11). Pope's translation was severely criticised by both Wordsworth and Southey, but was defended by Byron.

[2] *Recollections of the Table Talk of Rogers*, Dyce, p. 18. It is interesting that the passages from Pope and Dryden which Dyce quotes as being most popular in Rogers's circle, were derived from the moralistic and didactic rather than the satirical strain in Augustan poetry.

in the words of the anonymous reviewer in *The Album,* 'with the tenaciousness of habit to the favourites of their youth'.

3. CRABB ROBINSON AND JANE AUSTEN

Yet the supporters of Pope were far from being confined to the members of an outmoded generation who had fortuitously outlived their time. Many distinctively early nineteenth-century personalities retained unimpaired their admiration for the Augustan poets, as we have already seen, and even the most radical innovators among the new generation of Romantic poets kept some of the admiration for the Augustan tradition which had been almost universal in their youth.

Scott's poetry, for example, in strong contrast to his criticism, is notable for its Romantic preoccupations. Yet his earliest poems were entirely Augustan in style. According to his biographer Lockhart, Scott's translations from Horace and Virgil at Edinburgh High School, preserved by his mother, were in heroic couplets reminiscent of Pope, in diction, imagery, and movement:

> In awful ruins Aetna thunders high,
> And sends in pitchy whirlwinds to the sky
> Black clouds of smoke, while, still as they aspire,
> From their dark sides there bursts the glowing fire.[1]

Despite his youthful inexperience, Scott's use of the run-on line, and the variation in his pauses, reveal a confident familiarity with the technical resources of the 'line of Pope'. His epithets— 'awful', 'pitchy', 'glowing'—and his use of the word 'aspire' in its present context, are also typically eighteenth century. The practice of using Pope as a model for writing verse was evi-

---

[1] Lockhart, *Life of Scott*, I, 77. J. S. Mill wrote of his own early education: 'The verses I was required to write were English. When I first read Pope's *Homer*, I ambitiously attempted to compose something of the same kind, and achieved as much as one book of a continuation of the *Iliad*.' (*Autobiography*, 1908, p. 8.)

W. Haller, in his biography of Southey, says that his earliest models in poetry were Dryden, Pope, and Goldsmith: '*The Retrospect . . .* is in heroic couplets and reminds one of the tone and manner of Goldsmith. *Rosamund to Henry* plainly harks back to *Eloisa*, and *The Triumph of Woman* to *Alexander's Feast*.' (*The Early Life of Robert Southey*, 1917, p. 73.)

dently fairly common in schools at the time, and even the earliest lines of Wordsworth which have survived also copy the balanced, antithetical style of Pope's heroic couplet:

> Oft have I said, the paths of Fame pursue,
> And all that Virtue dictates, dare to do;
> Go to the world, peruse the book of man,
> And learn from thence thy own defects to scan;
> Severely honest, break no plighted trust,
> But coldly rest not here—be more than just.[1]

These lines, which faithfully imitate the didactic and moralising interests of the *Essay on Man*, were the work of a fourteen-year-old schoolboy. The moral and 'philosophical' interests which distinguish Wordsworth's mature poetry employed an entirely different mode; yet the taste which made it natural for him to imitate Pope's heroic couplets as a boy survived long after the originality of Wordsworth's genius had been widely recognised, and may be found even in the work of those who were most profoundly influenced by his poetry.

In support of the view that an appreciation of the innovations of the Romantic poets did not necessarily imply a neglect of the Augustans, the evidence of Henry Crabb Robinson—whose standards may be described as those of the alert and well-informed reader slightly in advance of his day—is particularly relevant. He wrote to Wordsworth's son-in-law Quillinan in 1843:

Before I had heard of the *Lyrical Ballads*, which caused a little revolution in my taste for poetry, there were four poems which I used to read incessantly; I cannot say which I then read the oftenest or loved the most. They were of a very different kind, and I mention them to show that my taste was *wide*. They were *The Rape of the Lock*, *Comus*, *The Castle of Indolence*, and *The Traveller*. Next to these were all the ethic epistles of Pope; and, with respect to these, they were so familiar to me, that I never for years looked into them—I seemed to know them by heart.[2]

[1] *Wordsworth's Poetical Works*, ed. E. de Selincourt, I, 261. This passage was composed by Wordsworth for a purely formal occasion: the second centenary of his school. See also the extremely perceptive chapter on 'Early Poems' in *The Early Life of William Wordsworth* by Emile Legouis (2nd edn, 1921), pp. 120ff.

[2] *The Life and Times of Henry Crabb Robinson*, ed. E. J. Morley (1933), p. 141.

Crabb Robinson, in fact, never lost his youthful admiration for Pope. Indeed he is justified in saying that his taste was *wide*, for the four poems unite the two opposing tendencies of eighteenth-century poetry; and many readers only had a taste for one. As we learn from his *Diary*, he could return to Pope's poems nearly half a century after the publication of the *Lyrical Ballads*, and still recapture the delight with which he had originally read them. Recording a visit to the Hutchinsons on 11 September 1837, Crabb Robinson wrote that Wordsworth was unable to compose because of an inflammation of the eyes. The evening was therefore spent in reading poetry aloud, a domestic practice which was still widely current:

In the evening I read Mr Monkhouse[1] Pope's *Dunciad*, Book IV, and the Prologue and Epilogue to the *Satires*. We were both sufficiently well-read in Pope to enjoy this like the renewal of an old intimacy, and I relished this as I did forty years ago.[2]

Crabb Robinson, then, despite the 'revolution' which he claimed had been affected in his taste through a reading of the *Lyrical Ballads*, retained unimpaired his capacity to enjoy the best poetry in Pope. Those readers in his own time who were less directly exposed than he was to the influence of the new generation of Romantic poets, naturally retained their interest more readily in the work of Pope and the Augustans. Jane Austen may be taken as representative of this latter class of readers. Her standards were not fundamentally different from Crabb Robinson's, and the four poets whom he read 'incessantly' in his youth were among those referred to most often by Jane Austen in her novels and her correspondence,[3] though her

[1] Crabb Robinson does not mention whether or not Wordsworth was present at this reading.

[2] *Henry Crabb Robinson on Books and their Writers*, ed. E. J. Morley (1938), 3 vols, p. 537. *The Dunciad* was often criticised for its 'indecency' in Regency times; nevertheless, the fourth book of *The Dunciad*, which Crabb Robinson read out to Monkhouse, was highly praised by some critics in Victorian times. Thackeray, for example, in *Lectures on the Humorists*, described the end of *The Dunciad* as the most sublime passage in English literature.

[3] For an interesting account of Jane Austen's reading and her literary interests, see R. W. Chapman, *Jane Austen: Facts and Problems* (1948), Chapter III, 'Reading and Writing'.

standards seem comparatively unaffected by the work of the Romantic innovators. In addition to Pope and the other poets whom Crabb Robinson enjoyed, Jane Austen also mentioned Johnson, Gray, Cowper, Scott, Byron, and Crabbe with approval. There is in fact no evidence in Jane Austen's work that she regarded the age in which she lived as being in any way a revolutionary epoch of creative literature and criticism. Undoubtedly the themes of her early novels were consistently anti-Romantic, yet it is worth observing that her satire was directed less against Wordsworth's contemporaries than against tendencies in the pre-Romantic novel of the late eighteenth century. Her burlesque in *Northanger Abbey*[1] of the stock situations of the 'gothick' or 'terror' novel and her debunking in *Sense and Sensibility* of the emotionalism of the 'sentimental' novel (at its best in Sterne, at its worst perhaps in Henry Mackenzie) seem to be worth closer examination. For the taste which indulged itself in these two types of novel was related to anti-Augustan tendencies in the eighteenth century, and their characteristic extravagances, as Walter J. Bate has pointed out, originated partly in a reaction against what was conceived to be the 'tameness' and 'coldness' of neo-classical discipline and restraint.[2] Bate does not, however, make the point, which is of central importance to our own inquiries, that the interests satisfied by the 'sentimental' and the 'terror' novel were closely related to the principal limitations in Pope's poetry noted by Joseph Warton: Warton's invocation of the 'sublime' (which in the later eighteenth century connoted the 'awful' and the 'terrifying' rather than merely the 'elevated') had obvious affinities with the taste which, at a lower level, found the 'gothick' and 'terror' novel congenial; and it is equally plain that the emotionalism encouraged by an interest in the 'pathetic' found relatively free and uninhibited expression in

---

[1] It is possible that Jane Austen's use of Northanger Abbey for the purposes of her anti-Romantic satire suggested to Byron the possibilities of using Norman Abbey in the final cantos of *Don Juan*.

[2] See, in particular, the final chapter of W. J. Bate, *From Classic to Romantic* (Cambridge, Mass., 1946).

the tear-drenched pages of such novels as Mackenzie's *The Man of Feeling*.

In strong contrast to such tendencies in the pre-Romantic eighteen-century novel, Jane Austen herself, as Charlotte Brontë observed, had little in common with the 'stormy sisterhood of the passions'. The 'limitations of Pope', it is true, were prominent among Marianne Dashwood's 'four topics of discourse' in *Sense and Sensibility*, yet her history in the novel is instructive. After her uncritically Romantic faith in 'sensibility' has led her into disillusionment, it is part of her greater maturity at the end of the novel that she reaches a truer and less prejudiced evaluation of theAugustan virtue of 'good sense'. *Sense and Sensibility*, though an early novel and comparatively simple in its themes, is in many ways representative of the positive moral and emotional interests behind Jane Austen's art. The habit of mind she stands for in Regency England had obviously derived a good deal of its strength from the Augustan tradition of Johnson and Pope in particular. In her attitude to the poetry of her own age, it is only natural therefore that while Wordsworth is only mentioned once,[1] and Coleridge, Southey, Shelley, and Keats are not mentioned at all, Jane Austen found particularly congenial the poetry of Byron and Crabbe.

4. CRABBE AND BYRON

For it was in the work of these two poets, rather than in that of Rogers and Campbell, that the Augustan tradition received its most important development in the earlier nineteenth century. This was partly because Byron and Crabbe were not content with being accomplished imitators of the Augustan poets. No one would take Crabbe's *Inebriety*,[2] or Byron's *English Bards and Scotch Reviewers* as representative of their best work, and their true status as original poets was achieved long after they had

[1] In Jane Austen's last novel, unfinished at the time of her death in 1817, *Sanditon*.

[2] For detailed information about the passages in *Inebriety* (1775) in which Crabbe imitated parallel passages in *The Essay on Man* and *The Dunciad*, see *Poems by George Crabbe*, ed. A. W. Ward (1905), I, 11–36.

developed beyond the apprentice-work in which they modelled themselves closely upon Pope. In examining their connections with the Augustan tradition it is worth insisting upon the distinction between the 'conventional' poet, and the poet who writes creatively within a tradition: while the former never attempts to go beyond the achievement of his predecessors, the latter brings something distinctively new to the tradition, and in the process of maintaining the tradition achieves a personal modification of it. The true distinction of Byron and Crabbe was that in adapting the Augustan tradition to the interests and preoccupations peculiar to the early nineteenth century—which required a much more radical alteration of the tradition in Byron's case than in Crabbe's—they succeeded in keeping alive much of the characteristic vitality and strength of the poetic tradition of which they were the last true descendants.

The difference between Crabbe and Byron may be traced to the fact that Crabbe, unlike Byron, was quite literally a survival in Regency times of the age of Johnson. Burke, to whom Crabbe appealed in dire hardship, immediately recognised Crabbe's unusual talent, and it was through his assistance that *The Library* was published in July 1781. It was through Burke too that Crabbe made the acquaintance, later in the same year, of Reynolds, Charles James Fox, and several notable figures of the age who were impressed by his work. Two years later, Reynolds brought Crabbe's first major poem, *The Village*, to the personal notice of Dr Johnson. Johnson was delighted with the poem, and its predominantly Augustan style agreed so well with the temper of his own verse that he added some lines to the poem himself, though he noted in a letter to Reynolds that he did not consider his own additions an improvement upon Crabbe.[1] Crabbe's early links with the Augustan tradition,

[1] Johnson wrote to Reynolds on 4 March 1783: 'I have sent you back Mr Crabbe's poem; which I have read with great delight. It is original, vigorous, and elegant. The alterations which I have made, I do not require him to adopt; for my lines are, perhaps not often better [than] his own: but he may take mine and his own together, and perhaps, between them, produce something better than either.—He is not to think his copy wantonly defaced; a wet sponge will wash all the red lines away, and leave the pages clean.—His Dedication will be least liked:

then, were directly personal as well as literary, and the guidance and encouragement which he derived from this source left a permanent impression upon the poetry which he wrote throughout his life.

Yet, after the publication of *The Newspaper* in 1785, at the very beginning of which Crabbe wrote that the age seemed unpropitious for original composition, there followed a period of over two decades in which he wrote little or no poetry.[1] The final phase of his work, which is of particular interest here, belonged entirely to the early nineteenth century. Crabbe resumed the writing of poetry in 1802, and in 1806 *The Parish Register*, though still in MS, was read to Charles James Fox. In 1807, together with Crabbe's earlier poems, it was published, and was enthusiastically reviewed by Jeffrey in the *Edinburgh Review* of April 1808.[2] *The Borough*, upon which Crabbe had begun working in 1804, appeared in 1810. Crabbe's art developed rapidly at this stage, and two years later he produced what may be described as his truly mature work, his first volume of *Tales in Verse*. We may find in this volume all the distinctive Augustan qualities which had distinguished *The Village* nearly thirty years previously. We have a similar Augustan neatness and economy of language, a measured and antithetical balance in the versification, a similar exploitation of sardonic irony and epigrammatic 'wit'. Yet all this Augustan strength in Crabbe's verse was now applied with astonishing deftness to a new interest: the art of the short story (or more exactly, the moral fable).

Leigh Hunt claimed in 1816 that he had overthrown the

it were better to contract it into a short, sprightly address.—I do not doubt of Mr Crabbe's success.' (Quoted in *Poems by George Crabbe*, ed. Ward, 1905, I, 92.)

[1] These years were not wasted from the point of view of Crabbe's poetry, for his work as a clergyman in various country parishes brought him into close touch with rural life, and provided him with that rich fund of human experience which formed the basis of his later work.

[2] Jeffrey saw that Crabbe, who was in this respect unlike Campbell and Rogers, reacted away from the development which the Augustan tradition underwent in the hands of Goldsmith. ' *The Village*,' Jeffrey said, 'was commonly considered as an antidote or answer to the more captivating representations of *The Deserted Village*.' ('Crabbe's Poems', *Edinburgh Review*, April 1808.)

metrical dictatorship of Pope, and that as a result of his innovations, he had the pleasure of 'seeing all the reigning poets, without exception, break up their heroic couplets into freer modulation'.[1] Crabbe's use of the heroic couplet is the outstanding exception to Hunt's generalisation. Crabbe kept all the tightness and discipline which had distinguished Pope's use of this verse form, though now applied to new interests and new subjects,[2] and it was only the idiosyncratic elements in his versification which were so admirably caught by James and Horatio Smith in their parody of Crabbe in *Rejected Addresses* (1812). In his later work, indeed, Crabbe extended the potentialities of the Augustan heroic couplet, and the movement of his mature versification, as he adapted it for the purposes of dramatic dialogue and narrative exposition, has often a new flexibility and range. There is little in the Augustan tradition before Crabbe with which his achievement here may be compared, as Dr F. R. Leavis has pointed out in *Revaluation*, if we except the brilliant narrative-interlude of Sir Balaam and the Devil which Pope included in his third *Moral Essay*. But Crabbe did not derive the art of the short story from Pope. It took him nearly a lifetime to discover his own peculiar talent in this mode, and the slow emergence of the form may be traced back to his earliest work.[3] In his mature work it is

---

[1] Hunt, *Autobiography*, ed. J. E. Morpurgo, 'Free Again', p. 258.

[2] Crabbe's preoccupation with realism and the poor, as Wordsworth pointed out, was partly anticipated by John Langhorne. Passages in Langhorne's heroic couplet satire *The Country Justice*, which appeared in three parts between 1774 and 1777, are so strikingly reminiscent of Crabbe that they could easily be mistaken for the latter's work. Wordsworth preferred the work of 'our Westmoreland Poet, Langhorne', to that of both Goldsmith and Crabbe, and wrote of *The Country Justice*: 'As far as I know, it is the first Poem, unless perhaps Shenstone's *Schoolmistress* be excepted, that fairly brought the Muse into the Company of common life, to which it comes nearer than Goldsmith, and upon which it looks with a tender and enlightened humanity—and with a charitable, (and being so) philosophical and poetical construction that is too rarely found in the works of Crabbe. It is not without many faults in style from which Crabbe's more austere judgement preserved him—but these are to me trifles in a work so original and touching.' (Letter to S. C. Hall, 15 January 1837. *The Letters of William and Dorothy Wordsworth: The Later Years*, ed. E. de Selincourt, 1939, II, 829.)

[3] Crabbe's interest in the possibilities of narrative-art led him at one time to experiment in prose-fiction. Shortly after the turn of the century he wrote three

associated not only with a development in his versification, but with a capacity for acute and objective psychological penetration, and a refinement of moral sensibility (qualities in which Crabbe was akin to Jane Austen) and with a flair for exploiting the symbolic potentialities of the domestic and natural settings he employed. John Speirs's account of Crabbe as an eighteenth-century equivalent of Chaucer draws attention to the best elements in his work,[1] and it is his achievement in the verse-*nouvelle* which makes Crabbe's later work a vital and living development of the Augustan tradition.

A detailed study of Crabbe's poetry is outside the scope of this book, and our primary interest is in his critical reactions to the Augustan tradition. Crabbe's close familiarity with the work of Dryden, Pope, and Johnson, which is evident in almost every line of poetry which he wrote, is confirmed by his son's account of Crabbe's reading. According to the younger Crabbe, his father had a 'strong partiality for Latin poetry' (especially the Roman Augustan satires of Horace), and, among the English poets, in addition to the verse of the 'Augustans', particularly enjoyed reading Chaucer, Shakespeare, and Samuel Butler. Crabbe's interests were those of a poet rather than a literary critic, yet his carefully-pondered defence of his own poetry and of the Augustan tradition as a whole, which may be found in his Preface to the *Tales* of 1812, merits close examination.

It is clear that Crabbe knew that he was no longer writing in the age of Johnson, and that the authority of the Augustan standards was now being seriously questioned:

Nevertheless, it must be granted that the pretensions of any com-

---

novels, the first of which was entitled *Reginald Glanshaw, or the Man who commanded Success*. On his wife's advice he abandoned prose-fiction in favour of the verse-tale. Unfortunately, Crabbe burnt the MSS of his prose-novels, so that no comparisons are now possible. For a brief account of the novels, see 'The Life of Crabbe', by his son in Vol. I of *The Poetical Works of George Crabbe*, published by Murray in 1834.

[1] For a comparison between Chaucer and Crabbe, and an analysis of Crabbe's use of symbolism in his treatment of landscape, see J. Speirs, *Chaucer the Maker*, p. 205.

position to be regarded as poetry will depend upon that definition of the poetic character which he who undertakes to determine the question has considered as decisive; and it is also confessed that one of great authority may be adopted, by which the verse now before the reader, and many others which have probably amused and delighted him, must be excluded: a definition like this will be found in the words which the greatest of poets, not divinely inspired, has given to the most noble and valiant Duke of Athens—

> The poet's eye, in a fine frenzy rolling,
> Doth glance from heaven to earth, from earth to heaven;
> And as Imagination bodies forth
> The forms of things unknown, the poet's pen
> Turns them to shapes, and gives to airy nothing
> A local habitation and a name.[1]

Although Crabbe, with characteristic modesty, conceded that the kind of poetry described here by Theseus was superior to anything he could himself produce ('theirs is a higher and more dignified kind of composition'), he objected to the view that only those who addressed themselves to the 'fancy and imagination' should 'entirely engross' the title of poet. If this were granted, Crabbe observed, 'a vast deal of what has hitherto been received as genuine poetry would be no longer entitled to that appellation'.

Wordsworth, as we have already seen in an earlier section,[2] had censured Crabbe in a letter to Rogers of 29 September 1808, for his 'unpoetical mode of considering human nature and society', and for his inability to 'clarify' the truth of nature 'by the pervading light of imagination'. Part of Crabbe's purpose in his Preface to the *Tales* of 1812 was to defend his own poetry (and that of the other Augustan poets as well) from criticism of this kind. In justifying the predominantly realistic preoccupations of his own verse, Crabbe found support in a whole tradition of realism in English poetry which went back to Chaucer. Discussing the 'naked' and 'unveiled' (i.e. realistic

[1] *Poems by Crabbe*, ed. Ward, Preface to 'Tales in Verse', II, 8. This same passage from *A Midsummer Night's Dream*, Act V, was invoked by a reviewer in *Blackwood's Magazine* in relegating Pope to the second order of creative writers: 'Lord Byron and Pope', May 1821, p. 233. See Chapter V.
[2] Chapter VII.

rather than fancifully draped) character of Chaucer's poetry, Crabbe referred to the 'many pages of coarse, accurate, and minute, but very striking description' typical of Chaucer's Tales. Crabbe admired the language of 'fancy' and 'imagination' as he found it in Shakespeare (whether he admired it equally in Wordsworth is much less certain), yet he wished to insist that the realistic tradition which employed the 'strong language of truth and nature', was also capable of producing valuable poetry, and he found his best examples of the successful use of this mode in the work of the Augustan poets:

In times less remote [than Chaucer's], Dryden has given us much of this poetry, in which the force of expression and accuracy of description have neither needed nor obtained assistance from the fancy of the writer. . . . And to bring forward one other example, it will be found that Pope himself has no small portion of this actuality of relation, this nudity of description, and poetry without an atmosphere; the lines beginning 'In the worst inn's worst room', are an example, and many others may be seen in his *Satires*, *Imitations*, and above all in his *Dunciad*.[1]

Crabbe, quoting Johnson's celebrated retort to Warton—'To circumscribe poetry by a definition will only shew the narrowness of the definer, though a definition which shall exclude Pope will not easily be made', concluded with some tartness, that if the language of 'imagination' and 'fancy' were the only true test of a poet, he could reconcile himself 'to expulsion from the rank and society of Poets, by reflecting that men much his superiors were likewise shut out, and more especially when he finds also that men not much his superiors are entitled to admission'.

The frequent references made to the criticism of Byron throughout the course of this study have made it plain that he was perhaps the most ardent supporter of the poetry of Pope in the early nineteenth century. Nevertheless, the obvious discrepancies between much of Byron's 'popular' poetry and the standards of the Augustans whom he admired have often been a puzzle to his critics. Crabb Robinson, for example,

---

[1] *Poems by George Crabbe*, ed. Ward, II, 10.

having noted the disparity, remarked in his *Diary* on 22 October 1832, shortly after the appearance of Moore's edition of Byron: 'It is, I think, impossible that this love for Pope could have been genuine. It would have produced fruits . . .'

A careful study of Byron's criticism makes it difficult to support Crabb Robinson's view, for the energy and consistency with which Byron championed the cause of the Augustans throughout his life hardly suggests a factitious or superficial interest. Nor was Crabb Robinson correct in his assertion that Byron's interest in Pope had had no effect upon his own poetry. After the disastrous *Hours of Idleness*, the satire in which he answered his critics, *English Bards and Scotch Reviewers*, though partly indebted to the influence of Gifford's *Baviad* and *Maeviad*,[1] was largely an attempt to imitate the style of Pope. Although *English Bards and Scotch Reviewers* does not always rise above the level of effective *pastiche*, it contains many local approximations to the manner and movement of Pope's heroic couplet. Byron continued to maintain his interest in the Augustan tradition, and when he returned in July 1811 from his visit to Portugal, Spain, and the Middle East with John Cam Hobhouse, he brought back with him not only the first two cantos of *Childe Harold*, but also an 'Imitation' of Horace's *Ars Poetica* entitled *Hints from Horace*. It is interesting that Byron himself unhesitatingly preferred his neo-classical 'Imitation'—which was partly based upon Pope's *Epistle to Augustus*— to the more romantic *Childe Harold*.[2] However, the tremendous

---

[1] Gifford's own satires were modelled on a large number of imitations of Pope's *Dunciad*, which appeared in the latter half of the eighteenth century. These imitations, which were often very inferior in quality, included Churchill's *Rosciad* (1761), Thomas Morell's *Churchilliad* (1761), Pye's *The Rosciad of Covent Garden* (1761), John Hill's *Smartiad* (1752), Christopher Smart's *Hilliad* (1752), Arthur Murphy's *Meretriciad* (1764), Chatterton's *Consuliad* (1764), William Combe's *Diaboliad* (1777), etc. These imitations, which often were merely personal attacks, cannot always be dignified with the title of satires.

[2] Byron continued to value *Hints from Horace* very highly. On 8 June 1820 he wrote to John Cam Hobhouse: 'I wish you would ferret out at Whitton the *Hints from Horace*', and wrote to Murray on 6 October and 9 November of the same year regarding plans to have it published. As Elisabeth Boyd has pointed out in *Byron's Don Juan* (1945), Byron's desire to publish his neo-classical 'Imitation' was a logical part of his campaign in support of Pope at the time.

enthusiasm with which the reading public acclaimed *Childe Harold*, which surprised Byron himself ('I woke one morning and found myself famous'), was undoubtedly partly responsible for the energy with which he devoted himself in the years that followed to tales of diabolic passion, violence, remorse, and revenge, which made him the most sought-after and popular poet in Regency times.

Although there is nothing in the emotional extravagance of the poetry of Byron's middle period which may be reconciled with his admiration for the Augustans, there was one feature in his work which distinguished it from that of his Romantic contemporaries. This was the scrupulous realism which Byron always maintained in rendering the costumes, natural settings, and backgrounds of his exotic verse-tales. Though it may appear little more than affectation, it is plain that Byron himself set great store by such accuracy. The importance of Byron's beliefs here, from the point of view of our own inquiries, was that it led him not only to criticise the falseness of Campbell's Pennsylvanian settings,[1] but to defend strongly, against the censures of Southey, Wordsworth, and Leigh Hunt, the accuracy of Pope's celebrated 'moonlight scene' at the end of Book VIII of the *Iliad*.[2] Referring to Wordsworth's 'attack on Pope' in his *Essay Supplementary to the Preface*, Byron said in a letter to Hunt of 30 September 1815:

By-the-way, both he [Wordsworth] and you go too far against Pope's 'So when the Moon', etc.; it is no translation, I know, but it is not such a false description as asserted. I have read it on the spot; there is a burst and a lightness, and a glow about the night in the Troad, which makes the 'planets vivid', and the 'pole glowing'. The moon is—at least the sky is, clearness itself; and I know no more appropriate expression for the expansion of such a

---

[1] 'The secret of Tom Campbell's defence of *inaccuracy* in costume and description is, that his *Gertrude* etc., has no more locality in common with Pennsylvania than with Penmanmaur. It is notoriously full of grossly false scenery, as all Americans declare, though they praise parts of the poem.' (*Byron: Letters and Diaries, 1798–1824*, ed. Quennell, 1950, pp. 561–2.)

[2] For the passage in Pope's translation referred to here. and the criticism of Wordsworth and Southey, see Chapter IV.

heaven—o'er the scene—the plain—the sky—Ida—the Hellespont
—Simois—Scamander—and the Isles—than that of a 'flood of
glory'.[1]

The tone of this letter suggests why it is difficult to accept
Crabb Robinson's claim that Byron's delight in Pope was
merely the result of 'affectation and caprice'. Byron himself
was scarcely ever in doubt regarding the relative merits of the
Augustans and the Romantic poets of his own generation, and
observing to Murray in 1817 that all his contemporaries, with
the exception of Crabbe and Rogers, were 'upon a wrong
revolutionary poetical system', Byron concluded:

I am the more convinced in this by having lately gone over some of
our classics, particularly Pope, whom I tried in this way—I took
Moore's poems and my own and some others, and went over them
side by side with Pope's, and I was really astonished (I ought not
to have been so) and mortified at the ineffable distance in point of
sense, harmony, effect, and even *Imagination*, passion, and *Invention*,
between the little Queen Anne's man, and us of the lower Empire.
Depend upon it, it is all Horace then, and Claudian now among us,
and if I had to begin again, I would model myself accordingly.[2]

As a matter of fact, Byron did attempt a 'new beginning' in
his later work, especially in *The Vision of Judgement* and *Don
Juan*, in which he modelled himself partly upon his Augustan
predecessors. Yet many other influences which were strikingly
non-Augustan in character—for example, the verse of the
Italian serio-comic poets, Pulci, Berni, and Casti—also modified
his later work in important ways. One of the results of these
influences was that Byron decided, at least for a time, against

---

[1] *Byron: Letters and Diaries, 1798–1824*, ed. Quennell, p. 319.

[2] Letter to John Murray, Venice, 13 September 1817, *ibid.* pp. 418–19. Although
the term 'Augustan' was occasionally applied to the Elizabethans in the early
nineteenth century, it was more usually applied to the age of Pope as Byron does
at the conclusion of the passage quoted above. The association may be found in
the criticism of the early eighteenth century itself. Joseph Spence, who was
Thomas Warton's predecessor as Professor of Poetry at Oxford, noted in his
Quelques Remarques Historiques sur Les Poètes Anglois, which was written in the
1730s: '. . . notre age Augustain, qui commence avec lea Restauration de Charles
2'. For a discussion of Spence's *History*, see 'The First History of English Poetry',
by James M. Osborne, in *Pope and his Contemporaries: Essays presented to George
Sherburn*, ed. J. L. Clifford and L. A. Landa (1949).

the dignified and formal imitation of Pope which is to be found in *English Bards and Scotch Reviewers*.[1] The radical modification which the Augustan tradition underwent in Byron's later satire was, however, a necessary development, for it resulted in the effective adaptation of the tradition to the peculiar interests and preoccupations of Regency England. Byron's use of the *ottava rima* stanza in place of the heroic couplet provides a good illustration of this. While the movement of the first six lines of the stanza provided him with all the flexibility and freedom which he required, he was nonetheless often able, in the spruce finality of his final couplet, to achieve an authentic Augustan ring reminiscent of Pope

> And having voted, dined, drank, gamed, and whored,
> The family vault receives another lord.

---

[1] But after the exuberance and high spirits of *Don Juan*, he returned to the more disciplined movement of the heroic couplet in *The Age of Bronze*.

CHAPTER IX

CONCLUSION

The considerable body of evidence concerning early nineteenth-century attitudes towards the Augustan poets assembled
and discussed in the present study, has largely confirmed the
view that taste and criticism during this period were extremely
varied and complex, and reflected a great variety of critical
and creative preoccupations. With the data now before us we
may attempt to sum up the principal conclusions concerning the
forces which affected the reading and assessment of Augustan
poetry at that time, which have emerged during the course of
the inquiry. Our task here is twofold: first, to recapitulate
briefly the main tendencies which may be observed in the anti-
Augustan criticism of the early nineteenth century, and to
indicate their relationship with the criticism of earlier and later
periods; and secondly, to determine the nature and extent of
the persistence of Augustan standards during the period, and
the value which they had for the poetry and the criticism of the
time.

We think of the early years of the nineteenth century as an
age of transition, and unambiguous critical beliefs are rare
enough in any age. Both pro-Augustan and anti-Augustan
tendencies may often be observed existing side by side in the
attitudes of many critics and readers of the time. The diversity
which existed even in the opinions of individual critics who were,
on the whole, sympathetic or hostile to the Augustan tradition
should not be overlooked, and an attempt has been made in the
body of the work to indicate characteristic complexities of
response to the work of the Augustans. Nevertheless, some
broad tendencies directly favourable or unfavourable to the
critical reputations of the Augustan poets may be observed in
the criticism of the age, and their implications merit careful
consideration.

Early nineteenth-century criticism was often related to general developments in the social and moral temper of the period, and the growing frequency with which aspects of earlier literature came now to be disapproved of, upon prudish moral grounds, often affected attitudes towards the Augustan poets. Although such criticism is undoubtedly an interesting symptom of the changing moral climate of the time, its importance from the point of view of the Augustan tradition should not be exaggerated. Shakespeare was the object of similar disapproval at the time, and it was not until his work had been suitably edited by the Reverend Thomas Bowdler in 1818, that it was generally accepted as unexceptionable reading in mixed society.[1]

Among the more fundamentally critical objections to the poetry of the Augustans, perhaps the most widespread was the claim that the subject-matter of their work had too often been of its very nature unsuitable for poetry. 'The depreciation of Dryden', said T. S. Eliot, defending Dryden's work against nineteenth-century criticism, 'was not due to the fact that his work is not poetry, but to a prejudice that the material . . . out of which he built is not poetic.' Such objections to the 'unpoetical' subject-matter of the Augustan poets, which varied from the violent disparagement of Bowles to the more restrained and moderate criticism of Hazlitt, had their origins in the critical observations of Joseph Warton in the middle of the previous century. The shortcomings which these critics found in the subjects and themes usually dealt with by the Augustan poet were principally two. The first was that Augustan poetry was unduly 'occasional' in its appeal: in other words, its meaning was too largely dependent upon a knowledge of the personalities, factions, and incidents of its own time, and its meaning would therefore 'date' badly and become increasingly

---

[1] The Bible suffered the same fate. A Quaker of York produced an edition 'principally designed to facilitate the audible or social reading of the Sacred Scriptures' in 1828. Passages unsuitable for a mixed audience (i.e. capable of bringing a blush to the cheek of the young person) were printed at the foot of the page.

unintelligible to succeeding generations of readers. Associated with this criticism was a more comprehensive objection to the 'unpoetical' nature of Augustan poetry: it was asserted that the conventions and modes of behaviour of the fashionable society which the Augustans had often depicted in their verse were, of their very nature, 'artificial', and that they had therefore provided subject-matter which was intrinsically unsuitable for the creation of genuine poetry.

The first of these objections is partly historical, for it draws attention to a peculiarly critical phase through which the work of the Augustans passed in the late eighteenth and early nineteenth centuries. As Warton first observed, and De Quincey after him, personal and topical interest must surely have added an edge to the pleasure with which the Augustans had been read by their own contemporaries, and the immediacy of such interest inevitably diminished with the passing of time. Yet it seems worth pointing out that these critics were referring to a feature which is common to the satire of all ages. While imaginatively distanced or exotic themes and subjects are usually congenial to the Romantic poet, it is evident that the poetry of the satirist must inevitably originate in the immediate realities of his personal and social experience. This undoubtedly explains the unpopularity of the satirical mode during the Romantic period; nevertheless, it is less easy to explain the facility with which Romantic poets and critics assumed that the appeal of the Augustan poets would largely disappear with the diminution in the liveliness and piquancy of their merely contemporary interest. It is strange, for example, that Joseph Warton, who greatly enjoyed the work of the Roman Augustan satirists at first hand, did not seem to realise that their greatness, too, had been based upon the degree to which their poetry had transcended its purely local and contemporary interest.

Viewed impartially, it is also evident that the 'artificiality' of the fashionable life of the Restoration and the eighteenth century was often heightened and exaggerated by nineteenth-century critics. It is a truism worth repeating that any generation tends to regard its own predilections as natural, and those of its predecessors as artificial. Leslie Stephen, who was unusually objective in his defence of the Augustans upon this matter, was forthright in his criticism of the 'habit of absurdly exaggerating the difference between ourselves and our ancestors, and speaking as if everybody was "artificial" in the reign of Pope, and "natural" in the reign of Wordsworth'.

Nevertheless, the social and literary life of any age tends to determine the temper of its poetry, and it was often claimed in the early nineteenth century that the poetical conventions which were the rule in the Restoration and the eighteenth century had seriously limited the range and depth of Augustan poetry. It was especially felt that the lively operation of the critical intelligence and the 'wits', which had been encouraged by the social life of the time had inhibited the poetic exploration of more deeply personal levels of feeling; and Warton's observation that Pope was more a 'Man of Wit' and a 'Man of Sense' than a 'True Poet' was very influential in later criticism. The critical distinction made by Warton here was repeated almost *verbatim* by several later critics, including Southey and Francis Jeffrey, and the influence of the anti-Augustan line of criticism here initiated may be seen in Coleridge's disparagement of the 'logic of wit' in poetry, and Wordsworth's distrust of the 'meddling intellect'. Although Wordsworth and Coleridge themselves took particular care not to be tempted into a sweeping dismissal of the value of Augustan poetry, it was through a development of these tendencies that the Augustans were decisively rejected later in the century. The direction in which Warton's criticism of Augustan poetry tended in late Victorian times is, of course, unmistakable; the entire tradition reached its decisive culmination in Matthew Arnold's disparagement of the 'wits' and exaltation of the 'soul' in his celebrated condemnation of the Augustan tradition in his essay on the poetry of Gray:

The difference between genuine poetry and the poetry of Dryden and Pope, and all their school, is briefly this: their poetry is conceived and composed in their wits, genuine poetry is conceived and composed in the soul.

Nevertheless, the most striking difference between Arnold's criticism of the Augustan poets and that of his predecessors, from the point of view of the development of taste, was that while Arnold's disparagement produced scarcely a murmur of protest, the anti-Augustan criticism of the late eighteenth and early nineteenth centuries provoked a storm of fierce controversy. As we learn from the periodical criticism of the time, the reputations of Dryden, Pope, and Johnson were still near their zenith in the final decade of the eighteenth century, and continued to remain high after the turn of the century. Evidence of the surviving admiration for the work of the Augustan poets is everywhere apparent in the criticism of the age, and a noteworthy feature of the 'Pope Controversy', for example, was that the supporters of Pope were substantially more numerous than his detractors.

Yet we have seen that one of the more interesting features of the taste of the age was that the standards of even those critics and readers who remained sympathetic towards the Augustan tradition were often modified by the new currents of taste. The nature of these changes needs to be made clear, however, for it is often too readily assumed that they were effected primarily by the interest excited by the innovations of the rising generation of Romantic poets of the time. Although the Romantic poets sometimes felt that the popularity of the Augustans stood in the way of a recognition of their own work, it is less true that the revaluation of the work of the Augustan poets received its primary impulse from an appreciation of the merit of Wordsworth and his contemporaries. A much more important factor in the revaluation of the Augustan poets was the great revival of interest in pre-Restoration poetry which is a notable feature of early nineteenth-century taste. A study of the criticism of the age has shown that it was much more frequently through contrasting Pope, not with Wordsworth, but with Shakespeare and the Elizabethans, that the limitations of the Augustan poets were commonly defined at the time.

One of the more important consequences of this revaluation of Augustan poetry through comparison with the achievement of the Elizabethans, was that it resulted in a change in the *status* of the Augustans rather than a disparagement or rejection of their work. Even when it was admitted that they had been overshadowed by the greater imaginative range and depth of the Elizabethans, it was still possible to regard the Augustans as having been admirable within their own sphere. A factor which helped materially to 'place' the achievement of the Augustan age in its appropriate historical and critical perspective was the growth and development of literary history from Warton's time onwards. While the work of Shakespeare and his contemporaries was now generally regarded as the 'golden age' of English poetry (a ranking which would have been disputed in the eighteenth century), the phrase 'silver age' summed up neatly the tempered admiration now often felt for the Augustan period.

The general acknowledgement of the supremacy of the Elizabethans did not imply that the Augustan tradition ceased to exert an important influence upon poetry and criticism. A notable feature in the criticism of the age was the frequency with which the achievement of Dryden, Pope, and Johnson was used as a norm against which the poetry of the new generation of Romantic poets was judged. Here it must be freely granted that the inflexibility of response occasionally encouraged by excessive reliance upon Augustan standards sometimes blinded the more staunchly conservative critics of the time to true originality, particularly that of Wordsworth and Coleridge. Nonetheless, it would be wrong for this reason to dismiss the pro-Augustan criticism of the time as the obstinate repetition of neo-classical shibboleths. If a reliance upon Augustan standards did not always promote a sympathetic attitude towards the new generation of poets, it did foster criticism that was often vigilant and objective. On the whole, it cannot be doubted that the tendency among the conservative critics to turn back to the work of the Augustans in order to define more sharply their sense of the dangers inherent in the development of the Romantic movement in the early nineteenth century often produced criticism that was intelligent and discriminating. Numerous instances of the strength which the conservative critics derived from their association with the Augustan tradition have been mentioned, and it is a tribute to the diagnostic power which critics like Isaac D'Israeli and Peacock acquired from their close familiarity with the Augustan tradition, that their analysis of the literary situation in early nineteenth-century England anticipated some of the most acute criticisms of the period made later by Matthew Arnold.

The survival of Augustan influence may be found, not only in the criticism, but also in the poetry of the early nineteenth century. In fact, an interesting feature of the taste of the time is the diversity of poetical tendencies with which the Augustan tradition was associated during this period. Divergencies in the kind of interest evoked by the poetry of Dryden and Pope are particularly relevant here. It is generally true that the bounding vigour and negligent ease of Dryden proved more congenial to the Romantic taste of the time, while the more disciplined and complicated richness of Pope's art was more attractive to conservative interests. It is now seen, however, that the tradition was most effectively modified and adapted to suit the interests and preoccupations of the age in the work of Byron and Crabbe. But communications from the Augustans do not as a rule pass beyond them to later poets in the nineteenth century. There is good justification, therefore, for describing Byron and Crabbe as the last true descendants of the Augustan age of English poetry.

Finally, it seems worth emphasising not only that a detailed study of early nineteenth-century reactions to the Augustan tradition enhances one's sense of the diversity and richness of the literary tendencies of the age, but also that it makes one aware of much that is unexpected, ambiguous, and perplexing in the critical standards of the time. This inquiry indicates the need for caution in making easy assumptions about the nature of literary taste in this period, or indeed in any other. If the detailed study of the actual criticism of the poetry of Dryden, Pope and Johnson made during this period acts as an antidote to facile or misconceived generalisations it will have been worth while.

EDITIONS OF JOHNSON

'Dr Johnson's fame', Coleridge observed in 1817, 'now rests principally upon Boswell.'[1] Although Boswell's *Life* was undoubtedly popular reading at the time, Coleridge's evidence must not be taken to mean that a biographical interest in Johnson had replaced an interest in his critical and poetical work. Some interesting comments on the eagerness with which readers bought up editions of Johnson may be found in Alexander Chalmers's 'Advertisement' to a re-issue in 1806 of Arthur Murphy's *Works of Samuel Johnson*, which had appeared on more than one occasion in the previous century:

Besides many impressions of his (Johnson's) individual pieces, three large editions of his *Collected Works* have been bought up by the Publick, and a fourth, which has been loudly called for, is now completed. What Lord Chesterfield said of Swift, may be truly applied to this author, 'Whoever in the three kingdoms has any books at all, has Johnson'.[2]

As with Dryden and Pope, the critical standards associated with the name of Johnson were often disputed in the early nineteenth century. The popularity of his poetry during this period, too, sometimes provoked the hostile criticism of the rising generation of Romantic poets. Wordsworth, it will be remembered, severely criticised Johnson's 'poetic diction', and,

---

[1] Coleridge, *Miscellaneous Criticism*, ed. T. M. Raysor (1936), p. 423.

[2] Editorial interest in Johnson was widespread in the early nineteenth century. Murphy's 12-volume edition, re-edited by Chalmers, appeared in 1806, 1810, 1816, and 1823. Other large editions of *Johnson's Works* to appear at this time included *The Oxford English Classics* edn, 9 vols, 1825; *The Works of Johnson*, 6 vols, ed. R. Lyman, 1825; and a 2-vol. edn of *Johnson's Works*, published by Jones also in 1825. Stephen Jones's 2-vol. edn of Johnson's *Table Talk*, which had first appeared in 1798, re-appeared in 1807; and the 2-vol. edn of Johnson's *Table Talk* prepared by James Boswell (the younger) was published eleven years later in 1818. Rebecca Warner edited in 1817 a volume of *Original Letters from Dr Johnson*, and Richard Warner included some letters of Johnson in *Literary Recollections* (1830).

in conversation with Crabb Robinson, denied him 'style as well as poetry'.[1] Coleridge, also censured the great contemporary popularity of Johnson's style, and contrasted his appeal with Shakespeare's:

Everyone of tolerable education feels the *imitability* of Dr Johnson's
... style, the inimitability of Shakespeare's. Hence, I believe, arises the partiality of thousands for Johnson. They can imagine *themselves* doing the same. Vanity is at the bottom of it. The number of imitators proves this in some measure.[2]

Coleridge is perhaps not entirely fair here to the motives which impelled numerous readers to emulate the style of Johnson's verse. It is quite likely that it was not merely vanity, but a disinterested enjoyment of poetry for its own sake, which accounts for Johnson's popularity during this period.

It was an enjoyment of this kind which led Scott, as we have already noted, to choose Johnson as his favourite poet, and Scott's choice would not have been thought eccentric in his own time. Byron, too, rated Johnson very highly, and some fairly extended notes which he made in his *Diary*, dated Tuesday 9 January 1821, seem worth quoting:

Read Johnson's *Vanity of Human Wishes*—all the examples and mode of giving them sublime, as well as the latter part, with the exception of an occasional couplet. I do not so much admire the opening. I remember an observation of Sharpe's, (the *conversationist* as he was called in London, and a very clever man) that the first line of this poem was superfluous, and that Pope (the best of poets, *I* think) would have begun at once, only changing the punctuation—

Survey mankind from China to Peru.

The former line, 'Let observation', etc. is certainly heavy and useless. But 'tis a grand poem—and *so true!*—true as the 10th of Juvenal himself. The lapse of ages *changes* all things—time—language—the earth—the bounds of the sea—the stars of the sky, and every thing 'about, around, and underneath' man, *except man himself*, who has always been, and always will be, an unlucky

---

[1] *Henry Crabb Robinson on Books and their Writers*, ed. Edith J. Morley (1938), I, 103.
[2] Coleridge, *Table Talk and Omniana* (1917 edn), p. 115.

rascal. This infinite variety of lives conduct but to death, and the infinity of wishes lead but to disappointment.[1]

Johnson's concern with the central and enduring features in human experience, and his moral sublimity, qualities which appealed to Byron, appealed to other readers of the time as well.[2] Francis Jeffrey, for example, particularly admired the 'glowing and sonorous diction', the 'eloquent morality', and the 'mighty intellect' of *The Vanity of Human Wishes*, and considered Johnson's *Irene*—'a tissue of wearisome and unimpassioned declamations'—his only important failure.

F. W. Blagdon produced an edition of *The Poems of Dr Samuel Johnson* in 1805. This was received with sufficient interest to warrant the appearance of a second edition in 1820.

It is well known that Johnson's two best poems, *London* and *The Vanity of Human Wishes*, were 'Imitations' of the Third and Tenth Satires of Juvenal, and it was for his success in this special mode that he was most highly praised by his editors. Chalmers, for example, in the course of some critical observations on his poetry, noted that Johnson's

two imitations of Juvenal are not only equal to anything that writer has produced, in the happy delineation of living manners, and in elegance of versification, but are perhaps superior to any composition of the kind in our language.[3]

It is worth insisting that the term 'Imitation', which commonly refers today to an inferior copy of a genuine article, did not necessarily have this pejorative connotation in the eighteenth century. The term was widely used to describe a specific literary

[1] *Byron: Selections from Poetry, Letters and Journals*, ed. Peter Quennell (1949), p. 759. The opening of *The Vanity of Human Wishes* was criticised by Coleridge, too. Contrasting Dryden's opening of the Tenth Satire of Juvenal with Johnson's, Coleridge observed that the latter's version might be paraphrased: 'Let observation with extensive observation observe mankind.' (*Miscellaneous Criticism*, ed. Raysor, 1936, p. 439.)

[2] Byron's interest in Johnson was not excessively solemn or over-serious. Hunt, who agreed largely with Byron's high regard for Johnson, noted in his *Autobiography*: 'Lord Byron liked to imitate Johnson, and say, "Why, Sir," in a high mouthing way, rising, and looking about him. His imitation was very pleasant.' (*Autobiography*, ed. Morpurgo, 'Genoa: 1822–1823', p. 353.)

[3] The Poems of Samuel Johnson' (*The Works of the English Poets*, XVI), ed. A. Chalmers (1810), p. 570.

mode, more ambitious and difficult than translation, in which the modern poet, through a process of poetic adaptation, substituted the realities of his own social and personal experience for those of the poet upon whose work his own was based.[1] As a mode it was often preferred to translation, and Goldsmith, for example, discussing the merits of Johnson's *London*, observed that 'Imitation gives us a much truer idea of the ancients than ever translation could do'.[2] Part of the interest readers of a former time brought to a reading of Johnson's 'Imitations', was plainly related to the skill with which he maintained a continuous poetic parallel between Augustan Rome and eighteenth-century London. Both Chalmers and Blagdon, for example, in editing Johnson's *London* for their contemporaries, printed it side by side with Juvenal's Third Satire.

A critical evaluation of Johnson's poetry, however, was not among the principal interests of his editors, although Chalmers attempted a brief survey of Johnson's achievement in the various *genres* which he had used. Having praised Johnson's success in his 'Imitations', Chalmers noted that some of his translations, too, particularly of Anacreon, were 'happily executed'. Curiously enough, Chalmers found *Irene* 'remarkable for splendour of language, richness of sentiment, and harmony of numbers', though he noted that its emotional appeal as a tragedy was 'radically defective: it excites neither interest nor passion'. Of Johnson's other work connected with the theatre, Chalmers admired his Prologues which he claimed were 'perfect models of elegant and manly address'. Among Johnson's elegies, Chalmers described his poem on the death of his friend Levett as 'one of those pathetic appeals to the heart which are irresistible'. Observing that Johnson 'like Pope, preferred reason to fancy', Chalmers summed up his achievement as follows:

What he might have produced, if he had devoted himself to the

[1] According to Johnson himself, 'Imitation' meant: 'To pursue the course of a composition so as to use parallel images and examples.' (Johnson's *Dictionary* (1756): 'to imitate' (sense 3).)

[2] Goldsmith, *The Beauties of English Poesy* (1767).

Muses, it is not easy to determine. That he had not the essentials of a poet of the highest order must, I think, be allowed; but as a moral poet, his acknowledged pieces stand in a very high rank.[1]

---

[1] *The Works of the English Poets*, XVI (1810), 570.

BIBLIOGRAPHY OF THE
'POPE CONTROVERSY', 1806–26

1806–12

1806 W. L. Bowles, *The Works of Alexander Pope, with Additional Observations and a Memoir*, 10 vols.

1808 Thomas Campbell, Review of Bowles's Pope (*Edinburgh Review*, January).

1809 Lord Byron, *English Bards and Scotch Reviewers*.

1811 Leigh Hunt, 'The Feast of the Poets' (*Reflector*, No. IV).

1812 W. L. Bowles, *The Works of Alexander Pope* (Johnson's *Life* substituted for Bowles's *Memoir*, and Bowles's Notes severely reduced, probably by Nichols), 8 vols.

1819–22

1819 Thomas Campbell, *Specimens of the British Poets, with an Essay on English Poetry* (vol. I, pp. 262ff.).

Francis Jeffrey, Review of Campbell's *Specimens* (*Edinburgh Review*).

W. L. Bowles, The Invariable Principles of Poetry: in a letter to Thomas Campbell Esq., Bath.

Anon, 'Bowles's Answer to Campbell' (*Blackwood's Magazine*, July).

1820 Octavius Gilchrist, Review of Spence's *Anecdotes of Pope* (*London Magazine*, February).

Isaac D'Israeli, Spence's *Anecdotes of Pope* (*Quarterly Review*, July).

W. L. Bowles, 'A Reply to the Charges Brought by the *Quarterly* Reviewer' (*Pamphleteer*, XVII).

L. S. C., 'Mr Bowles as Editor of Pope' (*London Magazine*, July).

O. Gilchrist, 'The Character of Pope' (*London Magazine*, August).

Anon, 'Memoir of the Rev. W. L. Bowles' (*New Monthly Magazine*, November).

'Verax', 'Pope and Lady Mary Wortley Montagu' (*Gentleman's Magazine*, December).

1821 Lord Byron, Letter to (John Murray) on the Rev. W. L. Bowles's Strictures on the Life and Writings of Pope (7 February).

W. L. Bowles, 'Observations on the Poetical Character of Pope' (*Pamphleteer*, XVIII).

Lord Byron, A Second Letter on Pope (25 March; for Byron's letters, see Prothero's edn of his *Letters and Journals*, v, Appendix III, 522 ff.).

W. L. Bowles, Two Letters to the Right Hon. Lord Byron.

Anon, 'Lord Byron's Letter on Pope' (*Gentleman's Magazine*, April).

W. L. Bowles, 'A vindication of the late editor of Pope's *Works*, from some charges brought against him, by a writer in the *Quarterly Review*, for October 1820' (*Pamphleteer*).

Anon, 'Lord Byron and Pope' (*Blackwood's Magazine*, May).

William Hazlitt, 'Pope, Lord Byron, and Bowles' (*London Magazine*, June).

1822 Martin M'Dermot, Letter in Vindication of Pope (*Pamphleteer*, xx).
Thomas Campbell, 'M'Dermot's Letter on Pope' (*New Monthly Magazine*, March).
W. L. Bowles, An Address to Thomas Campbell Esq. (*Pamphleteer*, xx).

1824–6

1824 William Roscoe, *The Works of Alexander Pope, with a new Life*, 10 vols.
1825 Anon, Roscoe's edition of Pope (*Quarterly Review*, October).
W. L. Bowles, A Final Appeal to the Literary Public relative to Pope.
William Roscoe, A Letter to the Rev. W. L. Bowles (*Pamphleteer*).
W. L. Bowles, A Letter to William Roscoe, Esq. . . . In Answer to his late letter to the Rev. W. L. Bowles on the Works and Character of Pope.
1826 W. L. Bowles, Lessons in Criticism to W. Roscoe Esq.

Later discussions of the 'Pope Controversy' (1806–26) may be found in the following works:

1874 Sir Leslie Stephen, *Hours in a Library*, vol. i ('Pope as a Moralist').
1897 Ernest Rhys, *Literary Pamphlets—Poetry: Sidney to Byron* (Introduction).
1909 'George Paston' (E. M. Symonds), *Mr Pope* (vol. ii, Chapter LXIII, 'Pope Controversy').
1902 H. A. Beers, *A History of English Romanticism in the 19th Century* (Chapter II: 'Coleridge, Bowles, and the Pope Controversy'), New York.

BIBLIOGRAPHY

ABRAMS, MEYER H. *The Mirror and the Lamp* (New York, 1953).
ARNOLD, MATTHEW, *Essays in Criticism*, I (1865).
—— *Essays in Criticism*, II (1888).
ATKINS, J. W. H. *English Literary Criticism: 17th and 18th Centuries* (1951).
AUSTEN, JANE. *Jane Austen's Letters*, ed. R. W. Chapman, 2 vols (1932).
—— *The Novels of Jane Austen*, ed. R. W. Chapman, 5 vols (1923–34).
BAGEHOT, W. *Literary Studies*, ed. G. Sampson (1906).
BALL, MARGARET. *Sir Walter Scott as a Critic of Literature* (New York, 1907).
BARSTOW, MARJORIE L. *Wordsworth's Theory of Poetic Diction* (New Haven, 1917).
BATE, W. J. *The Stylistic Development of Keats* (Cambridge, Mass., 1945).
BEERS, H. A. *A History of English Romanticism in the 19th Century* (1902).
BERRY, MARY. *Journals and Correspondence from the year 1783 to 1852*, ed. Lady
 Theresa Lewis, 3 vols (1865).
Blackwood's Edinburgh Magazine (1817–30).
BLAIR, HUGH. *Lectures on Rhetoric and Belles Lettres* (1782).
BLUNDEN, E. *Leigh Hunt's 'Examiner' Examined* (1928).
BOWLES, W. L. *The Poetical Works*, ed. Gilfillan (1855).
—— *Memoir of Pope* (in Pope's Works, vol. I, 1806). (For Bowles's contributions to
 the 'Pope Controversy', see Appendix II.)
BRANDL, A. *S. T. Coleridge and the English Romantic School*, tr. Lady Eastlake (1887).
BROUGHAM, LORD HENRY. *Life and Times*, 2 vols (1871).
BROUGHAM, LORD. *Contributions to the 'Edinburgh Review'*, 3 vols (1856).
BURKE, E. *A Philosophical Inquiry into the Origin of our Ideas of the Sublime and Beautiful*
 (1757).
BURY, LADY CHARLOTTE. *Diary Illustrative of the Times of George IV* (1838).
BYRON, LORD. *The Works of Lord Byron, with his Letters and Journals, and his Life by*
 Thomas Moore, ed. J. Wright, 17 vols (1832–3).
—— *A Self-Portrait: Letters and Diaries, 1798–1824*, ed. Peter Quennell (1950).
 (For Byron's contributions to the 'Pope Controversy', see Appendix II.)
CAMPBELL, THOMAS. *Specimens of the British Poets, with an Essay on English Poetry*,
 7 vols (1819).
—— *The Poetical Works of Campbell*, ed. J. L. Robertson (1907).
—— *A History of our own Times*, 2 vols (1843–5).
CARLYLE, T. *Reminiscences*, ed. C. E. Norton (1932).
CLARK, A. F. B. *Boileau and the French Classical Critics in England, 1660–1800* (Paris,
 1925).
CLARK, R. B. *William Gifford: Tory Satirist, Critic, and Editor* (New York, 1930).
COCKBURN, LORD. *Life of Lord Jeffrey, with a Selection from his Correspondence*, 2
 vols (1852).
COLERIDGE, SARA. *Memoir and Letters of Sara Coleridge*, by her daughter, 2 vols
 (1873).
COLERIDGE, SAMUEL TAYLOR. *Biographia Literaria* (Everyman's edition) (1947).
—— *Miscellaneous Criticism*, ed. T. M. Raysor (1936).
—— *Anima Poetae: from the unpublished Notebooks of S. T. Coleridge*, ed. E. H. Cole-
 ridge (1895).
—— *Specimens of the Table Talk of the late S. T. Coleridge*, ed. H. N. Coleridge, 4
 vols (1836–9).

BIBLIOGRAPHY

COLERIDGE, SAMUEL TAYLOR. *The Complete Poetical Works of Samuel Taylor Coleridge*, ed. E. H. Coleridge, 2 vols (1912).

COLLINS, A. S. *The Profession of Letters . . . 1780–1832* (1928).

CONSTABLE, THOMAS. *Archibald Constable and his Literary Correspondents*, 3 vols (1873).

COPINGER, W. A. *On the Authorship of the First Hundred Numbers of the 'Edinburgh Review'* (1895).

COTTLE, JOSEPH. *Reminiscences of Coleridge and Southey* (1847).

COURTHORPE, W. J. *A History of English Poetry*, vols v and vi (1910).

COWPER, W. *The Life and Letters of Cowper*, by W. Hayley, 4 vols (1809).

COX, R. G. *19th Century Periodical Criticism: 1800–60* (Cambridge Ph.D. dissertation) (1939).

—— *The Great Reviews* (*Scrutiny*, vi, 2–20 and 155–75: articles later incorporated in dissertation) (1937).

CRABBE, G. *Poems by George Crabbe*, ed. A. W. Ward, 3 vols (1905–7).

—— *The Life of the Rev. George Crabbe*, by his Son (1834).

CROLY, G. *Beauties of the English Poets* (1836) (Introduction).

CRUSE, AMY. *The Englishman and his Books in the Early XIXth Century* (1930).

CUNNINGHAM, A. *Biographical and Critical History of the British Literature of the Last Fifty Years* (1834).

DE MAAR, H. G. *A History of Modern English Romanticism* (1924).

DENNIS, JOHN. *The Grounds of Criticism in Poetry* (1704).

—— *Reflections Critical and Satyrical upon a late Rhapsody, Called An Essay on Criticism* (1711).

DE QUINCEY, THOMAS. *The Collected Writings of Thomas De Quincey*, ed. David Masson, 14 vols (1889–90).

DIBDEN, T. F. *Reminiscences of a Literary Life*, 2 vols (1836).

D'ISRAELI, ISAAC. *Quarrels of Authors, or Some Memoirs of our Literary History*, 3 vols (1814).

DOBRÉE, B. (editor). *From Anne to Victoria* (1937).

DOUGLAS, SIR G. P. S. *The Blackwood Group* (John Wilson, etc.) (1897).

DRYDEN, JOHN. *The Critical and Miscellaneous Prose Works of John Dryden*, ed. Edmond Malone, 3 vols (1800).

—— *The Works of John Dryden*, ed. Walter Scott, 18 vols (1808).

—— *The Poetical Works of John Dryden* (with Notes by Joseph Warton and others), ed. H. J. Todd, 4 vols (1811).

DYCE, ALEXANDER. *Recollections of the Table Talk of Samuel Rogers*, ed. Morchard Bishop (1952).

The 'Edinburgh Review' (1802–30).

ELIOT, T. S. *Homage to John Dryden* (1924).

—— *The Use of Poetry and the Use of Criticism* (1933).

ELTON, O. *A Survey of English Literature, 1780–1830*, 2 vols (1912).

—— *The Augustan Ages* (1899).

FUESS, CLAUDE M. *Lord Byron as a Satirist in Verse* (New York, 1912).

GATES, LEWIS E. *Three Studies in Literature* (1899) (Essay on Jeffrey).

The 'Gentleman's Magazine' (1800–30).

GIFFORD, W. *The Baviad: a Paraphrastic Imitation of the first Satire of Persius* (1791).

—— *The Maeviad* (1795).

—— *Autobiography* (1827).

GILLIES, R. P. *Memoirs of a Literary Veteran, including sketches and anecdotes of distinguished Literary men: 1794–1849*, 3 vols (1851).

GORDON, MRS MARY. *Christopher North: A Memoir of John Wilson, compiled from Family Papers and other Sources* (1862).

GOSSE, E. 'Two Pioneers of Romanticism: Joseph and Thomas Warton' (*Proceedings of the British Academy*, VII) (1915).

GRAHAM, W. *Tory Criticism in the 'Quarterly Review': 1809–53* (1921).

GRAY, THOMAS. *The Letters of Thomas Gray*, ed. D. C. Tovey, 3 vols (1900–12).

GREEVER, G. *A Wiltshire Parson and his Friends: the correspondence of W. L. Bowles* (1926).

GREIG, JAMES A. *Francis Jeffrey of the 'Edinburgh Review'* (1948).

HALÉVY, E. *A History of the English People in 1815*, 3 vols (tr. E. I. Watkin) (1924).

HAZLITT, W. *The Collected Works of William Hazlitt*, ed. A. R. Waller and A. Glover, 12 vols (1902–6). (For Hazlitt's contribution to the 'Pope Controversy' see Appendix II.)

HENN, T. R. *Longinus and English Criticism* (1934).

HILDEYARD, M. C. (editor). *Lockhart's Literary Criticism* (1931).

HOOD, THOMAS. *Literary Reminiscences* (1839).

HOPKINS, G. M. *The Letters of Gerard Manley Hopkins to Robert Bridges*, ed. C. C. Abbott, 2 vols (1935).

—— *Notebooks and Papers of G. M. Hopkins*, ed. Humphrey House (1937).

HOUGH, G. G. *The Romantic Poets* (1953).

HOUSMAN, A. E. *The Name and Nature of Poetry* (1933).

HUCHON, R. *George Crabbe and his Times* (tr. Clarke) (1907).

HUNT, LEIGH. *Imagination and Fancy* (1844).

—— *Table Talk* (Including the Imaginary Conversations of Pope and Swift) (1851).

—— *The Poetical Works of Leigh Hunt*, ed. H. S. Milford (1923).

—— *Autobiography*, ed. J. E. Morpurgo (1928).

HURD, RICHARD. *Letters on Chivalry and Romance* (1762).

JAMESON, MRS ANNA BROWNELL. *Diary of an Ennuyée* (1826).

JOHNSON, SAMUEL. *Rasselas, Prince of Abyssinia* (1759).

—— *The Lives of the English Poets, and a Criticism of their Work*, 3 vols (1779–81).

—— *The Poetical Works of Samuel Johnson*, ed. F. W. Blagdon (1805).

—— *The Poems of Johnson: the Works of the English Poets*, ed. A. Chalmers, vol. XVI (1810).

KAMES, LORD. *Elements of Criticism* (1762).

KEATS, JOHN. *The Letters of Keats*, ed. H. Buxton Forman (1931).

—— *The Complete Works of John Keats*, ed. H. Buxton Forman, 5 vols (1900–1).

—— *The Life of Keats*, by Charles Armitage Brown, ed. D. H. Bodurtha and W. B. Pope (1937).

KER, W. P. '*Thomas Warton*' (*Collected Essays*, I) (1925).

LAMB, CHARLES. *The Works of Charles Lamb*, ed. E. V. Lucas, 6 vols (1912).

LANG, ANDREW. *The Life and Letters of J. G. Lockhart*, 2 vols (1897).

LANGHORNE, JOHN. *The Country Justice*, 3 parts (1774–7).

LEAVIS, F. R. *Revaluation* (1936).

—— *Mill on Bentham and Coleridge* (1950).

LEAVIS, Q. D. *Fiction and the Reading Public* (1932).

LEEDY, PAUL. 'Genre Criticism and Warton's Essay on Pope' (*Journal of English and Germanic Philology* (1946), 45.)

LLOYD, CHARLES. *Poetical Essays on the Character of Pope as a Poet and a Moralist* (1821).

LOCKHART, J. G. *Memoirs of the Life of Sir Walter Scott*, 2 vols (1837–8).

The 'London Magazine' (1820–9).

LONGAKER, J. *The Della Cruscans and William Gifford* (Philadelphia, 1924).

LOWELL, JAMES RUSSELL. *My Study Windows* (1871) (essay on Pope).

LOWES, JOHN LIVINGSTON. *The Road to Xanadu: a Study in the Ways of the Imagination* (Boston, 1927).

MACAULAY, T. B. *Critical and Historical Essays Contributed to the 'Edinburgh Review'*, 3 vols (1843).

MACBETH, G. *J. G. Lockhart: A Critical Study* (1935).

MACCLINTOCK, W. D. *Joseph Warton's Essay on Pope: a History of the Five Editions* (1933).

MADDEN, R. R. *Literary Life and Correspondence of the Countess of Blessington*, 3 vols (1855).

MARTIN, L. C. 'Thomas Warton and the Early Poems of Milton' (*Proceedings of the British Academy*) (1934).

MATHIAS, T. J. *The Pursuits of Literature: Four Dialogues* (1794–7).

—— *The Shade of Pope on the Banks of the Thames* (1796).

MILFORD, H. S. (editor). *The Oxford Book of the Romantic Verse of the Romantic Period: 1798–1837* (1928).

MILL, J. S. *Autobiography* (1908).

MITFORD, MARY RUSSELL. *Recollections of a Literary Life* (1852).

MONK, SAMUEL H. *The Sublime: a Study of Critical Theories in the 18th Century* (New York, 1935).

MOORE, THOMAS. *Memoirs, Journals, and Correspondence*, ed. Lord John Russell, 8 vols (1853–6).

MORE, HANNAH. *The Letters of Hannah More*, ed. R. Brimley Johnson (1925).

MORLEY, EDITH J. 'Joseph Warton: a Comparison of his Essay on the Genius and writings of Pope with his Edition of Pope's Works' (*Essays and Studies*, IX) (1924).

NESBITT, G. L. *Benthamite Reviewing: The First Twelve Years of the 'Westminster Review: 1824–36* (1934).

The 'New Monthly Magazine' (1821–30).

NICHOLS, JOHN. *Literary Anecdotes of the 18th Century*, 9 vols (1812–15).

NOYES, RUSSELL. *Wordsworth and Jeffrey in Controversy* (Indiana University Publications, Humanities Series 5) (1941).

OLIPHANT, MRS MARGARET. *The Literary History of England in the End of the 18th and the Beginning of the 19th Century*, 3 vols (1882).

—— *Annals of a Publishing House: William Blackwood and his Sons*, 2 vols (1897).

OSBORN, JAMES M. *John Dryden: Facts and Problems* (New York, 1942) (discusses Scott's criticism of Dryden, 72–87).

PATTISON, MARK. 'Pope and his Editors' (*Essays*, II, ed. H. Nettleship) (1889).

PEACOCK, THOMAS LOVE. *The Four Ages of Poetry* (with Shelley's *Defence* and Browning's *Essay on Shelley*), ed. H. F. Brett-Smith (1921).

—— *The Works of Peacock*, ed. Brett-Smith and C. E. Jones, 10 vols (1924–34).

POLWHELE, RICHARD. *Traditions and Recollections Domestic, Clerical and Literary*, 2 vols (1926).

POPE, ALEXANDER. *The Works of Alexander Pope*, ed. Joseph Warton, 9 vols (1797).

—— *The Works of Alexander Pope, with Additional Observations*, ed. W. L. Bowles, 10 vols (1806).

—— *The Works of Alexander Pope, with a New Life*, ed. W. Roscoe, 10 vols (1824).

PRICE, SIR UVEDALE. *An Essay on the Picturesque as compared with the Sublime and Beautiful*, 2 vols (1794–8).

The 'Quarterly Review' (1809–30).

REDDING, CYRUS. *Literary Reminiscences and Memoirs of Thomas Campbell*, 2 vols (1860).

—— *Fifty Years' Recollections, Literary and Personal*, 3 vols (1858).

BIBLIOGRAPHY

The 'Retrospective Review' (1820–8).

REYNOLDS, M. *The Treatment of Nature in English Poetry between Pope and Wordsworth* (1909).

RICHARDS, I. A. *Coleridge on Imagination* (1934).

ROBERTS, R. ELLIS. *Samuel Rogers and his Circle* (1910).

ROBINSON, HENRY CRABB. *The Life and Times of Henry Crabb Robinson*, ed. Edith J. Morley (1933).

—— *Henry Crabb Robinson on Books and their Writers*, ed. Edith J. Morley, 3 vols (1938).

ROGERS, SAMUEL. *The Poetical Works*, ed. E. Bell (1875) (Aldine edn).

SAINTSBURY, G. *A History of 19th-Century Literature (1780–1895)* (1896).

—— *The Peace of the Augustans* (1916).

SCHNEIDER, ELIZABETH. *The Aesthetics of William Hazlitt* (Philadelphia, 1933).

SCOTT, SIR WALTER. *The Letters of Sir Walter Scott*, ed. H. J. C. Grierson, D. Cook, and others, 12 vols (1932–7).

SEYMOUR, LADY. *The Pope of Holland House: the Correspondence of John Wishaw and his Friends, 1813–40* (1906).

SHELLEY, MARY. *Journal*, ed. F. L. Jones (1947) (provides lists of Shelley's reading).

SHELLEY, PERCY BYSSHE. *Shelley's Literary and Philosophical Criticism*, ed. J. Shawcross (1909).

SHINE, H. and H. C. *The 'Quarterly Review' under William Gifford: Identification of Contributors, 1809–24* (Chapel Hill, 1949).

SMILES, SAMUEL. *A Publisher and his Friends: Memoir and Correspondence of John Murray*, 2 vols (1891).

SMITH, D. NICHOL (editor). *Jeffrey's Literary Criticism* (1910).

—— *The Oxford Book of 18th Century Verse* (1926).

SMITH, JAMES and HORATIO. *Rejected Addresses* (1812).

SMITH, SIDNEY. *Essays: Reprinted from the 'Edinburgh Review'* (1874).

SOUTHEY, ROBERT. *Specimens of the Later English Poets*, 3 vols (1807) (Preface).

—— *Southey*, ed. C. C. Southey, 6 vols (1849–50).

SPENCE, JOSEPH. *Anecdotes, Observations, and Characters of Books and Men Collected from the Conversations of Mr. Pope*, ed. S. W. Singer (1820).

STEPHEN, SIR LESLIE. *Hours in a Library*, vol. I (1874) (Pope as a Moralist).

—— *Hours in a Library*, vol. II (Crabbe, The First *Edinburgh* Reviewers).

—— *Hours in a Library*, vol. III (1879) (Gray and his School).

—— *English Literature and Society in the 18th Century* (1904).

STEVENSON, S. W. *Romantic Tendencies in Dryden, Pope, and Addison* (1934).

STOCKDALE, PERCIVAL. *An Enquiry into the Nature and Genuine Laws of Poetry, including a particular Defence of the Writings and Genius of Mr. Pope* (1778).

—— *Lectures on the Truly Eminent English Poets*, 2 vols (1807).

TILLOTSON, G. *Criticism and the 19th Century* (especially Chapter III: 'Matthew Arnold and 18th Century Poetry') (1951).

TROWBRIDGE, H. 'Joseph Warton on Imagination' (*Modern Philology* (1937) XXXV).

VAN DOREN, M. *The Poetry of John Dryden* (New York, 1920).

VAN RENNES, J. J. *Bowles, Byron, and the Pope Controversy* (Amsterdam, 1927).

WAKEFIELD, GILBERT. *Observations on Pope* (1796).

WALDOCK, A. J. A. *William Lisle Bowles* (Australian English Association, Pamphlet No. 8, 1928).

WARTON, THOMAS. *A History of English Poetry*, 3 vols (1774–81).

WELLEK, R. *A History of Modern Criticism: 1750–1950*, vols I and II (New Haven, 1955).

229

BIBLIOGRAPHY

The 'Westminster Review' (1824–30).

WESTON, JOSEPH. *An Essay on the Superiority of Dryden's Versification to that of Pope and the Moderns* (1789) (In John Morfitt's *Philotoxi Ardenae*.)

(For Anna Seward's reply, see *Gentleman's Magazine*, April–August 1789.)

WHITE, NEWMAN IVEY. *The Unextinguished Heart* (Chapel Hill, 1938) (Introduction).

WILLEY, BASIL. *Coleridge on Imagination and Fancy* (Warton Lecture) (1946).

WILSON, JOHN. *Noctes Ambrosianae*, 4 vols (1864).

WINBOLT, S. E. *Coleridge, Lamb, and Leigh Hunt: The Christ's Hospital Anthology* (1920).

WORDSWORTH, WILLIAM. *The Critical Opinions of William Wordsworth*, ed. Markham L. Peacock (Baltimore, 1950).

—— *The Prose Works of William Wordsworth*, ed. A. B. Grosart, 3 vols (1876).

—— *The Early Letters of William and Dorothy Wordsworth* (1787–1805), ed. E. de Selincourt (1935).

—— *The Letters of William and Dorothy Wordsworth* (1806–20), ed. E. de Selincourt, 2 vols (1937).

—— *The Later Letters of William and Dorothy Wordsworth*, ed. E. de Selincourt, 3 vols (1938).

INDEX

Addison, Joseph,
  'coldly correct', 52n.
  critical standards, 113n.
  imitators denounced, 123
  influence on taste, 63–4
  limitations as a poet, 73–4
  prose praised, 73, 79, 191
  reading-public, 64
  reputation in 1790's, 1–2, 70
  reputation in 1811, 71
  second-class poet, 50
  works:
    Cato, 73
    Spectator, 63–4
Aeolian harp, 173–4
Akenside, Mark,
  Pleasures of Imagination, 140
Album, The, 74n, 184, 191, 194
Anderson, Dr Robert,
  Works of the British Poets, 112
anti-Augustan criticism, 3, 38, 47, 52,
  54, 73, 81–2, 103–6, 123, 137–76, 197,
  209–14
Anti-Jacobin, 93
Arnold, Matthew,
  Augustans 'classics of our prose',
    2–3, 150, 173
  'poetry of wits, not soul', 74, 123,
    153, 212–3
  responsible for revolution in taste, 3
  on Romantics, 90n., 182–3
artificiality, 45, 104, 133, 157, 211–2
Augustan poetry,
  defined, ix
  term first used, 207n.
  at height of fame in 1790's, 2, 57, 70,
    77, 140
  attacked by Warton, 26, 34, 48, 52n.
  revaluation in early nineteenth cen-
    tury, 2–5, 70–1, 74, 85–92, 96,
    154–5, 171–3, 190–1, 208–16
  conflict in nineteenth century atti-
    tudes to, 32–4, 36, 76, 101, 208–16
    (*and see* anti-Augustan, pro-Augus-
    tan)

Augustan poetry—*contd.*
  more French than English, *see*
    French
  obscenity in, *see* prudery
  an inferior order of poetry, 129,
    154–5, 157, 160
  subject-matter, 210–2
  revival of interest in (1820–5), 35,
    108–11
  as a critical norm, 57, 76–85, 95–111,
    120–6, 181–3, 214
  influence on early nineteenth century
    poetry, 5, 97–102, 150, 155–6,
    183–4, 187–91, 194–5, 198–208
  'safe and correct model', 100
  survives in Byron, Campbell and
    Rogers, 55, 183–94
  versification, *see* heroic couplet
  urbanity, 86, 181
  its critical theory, 144–5
  deficient in imagination, 146–7
  pre-Restoration poets despised, 111–3
  compared to Elizabethan, 73, 76,
    85–92, 96–7, 99–100, 111–6, 126–9,
    213–4
  a 'Silver age', 72, 180
  a 'dark age', 71
Augustan (Roman) poetry, 1, 21n., 32,
  39, 52, 70, 127–8, 180, 202
Austen, Jane, 145, 196–8
  Emma, 18
  Mansfield Park ('the Reviews'), 64
  Northanger Abbey, 197
  Sense and Sensibility, 197–8
Ayres, William, 22, 51n., 58

Ballantyne, James, 10, 19, 125
Bentham, Jeremy, 177–9
  on poetry and push-pin, 178
Bingham, Peregrine, 178
Blackmore, Sir Richard, 79
Blackwood, William, 117–9
Blackwood's Edinburgh Magazine, 74n,
  76, 85, 117–29
  founded in 1817, 66

Blackwood's Edinburgh Magazine—contd.
circulation-figures, 67, 119n.
editorial influence, 117–20
critical standards, 119–29
Romantics appear in, 119–26
attacks Cockney School, 123–4
defends Pope, 124–5
on Elizabethans, 126–9
supports Bowles, 131–2, 134
Blagdon, F. W., 219–20
Boccaccio,
Dryden's versions, 23–5, 30–1
Boileau, 45n.
model for Pope, 44, 91, 152n., 153
Boswell, James, 217
Bowdler, Reverend Thomas, 12, 210
bowdlerization, *see* prudery
Bowles, Rev. William Lisle,
pupil of the Wartons, 36n.
continues Warton's critical principles, 35–6, 47
differs from Warton's critical principles, 47–55
links eighteenth and nineteenth century Romantics, 140–2
edition of Pope (1806), 35, 47–55, 58, 82–4, 95, 130–1, 133, 185–6
edition of Pope, modified (1812), 35, 131
standards of criticism, 36, 49–55, 187
dislikes satire, 22, 50–1
dislikes ethical poetry, 51
attacks Pope's moral character, 109, 131
puts Pope in second rank, 50, 130
provokes Pope controversy, 48, 121, 124, 130–4
aggressive tone, 47–8, 83, 139
misjudges reading public, 48, 55
his poetry, 125, 141–2
Fourteen Sonnets, 141
Brontë, Charlotte, 118, 198
Brougham, Lord, 184–5
Burke, Edmund, 199
Byron, George Gordon, Lord, 18, 31, 115–6, 125, 197, 204–8
continues Augustan tradition, 55, 198–9, 204–8
defends Pope, 55, 58, 74n., 95, 109n., 121, 131–3, 143–4, 151
on Johnson, 218–9

Byron, George Gordon, Lord—*contd.*
prefers Augustans to Romantics, 95–6, 138
on Romantics, 143–4, 207
shocked by Hunt, 169
on Campbell and Rogers, 99, 183, 187–8, 206–7
likes ethical poetry, 31
versification, 168n., 205, 208
reading public, 9
works:
Age of Bronze, 208n.
Childe Harold, 205–6
Don Juan, 207
English Bards and Scotch Reviewers, 131, 167, 198, 205, 208
Hints from Horace, 205
The Vision of Judgement, 167, 207

Campbell, Thomas, 98–9, 181, 183–8, 190–2
imitates Augustans, 183–4, 190–1
defends Pope, 55, 58, 82–4, 121, 131, 144, 184–7
compares Pope and Shakespeare, 87–8
dislikes Dryden, 184–5
works:
Gertrude of Wyoming, 46n., 98–9, 206
Pleasures of Hope, 98, 184, 188
Specimens of the British Poets, 131, 184–5
Carlyle, Thomas,
on Jeffrey, 68
on *Edinburgh Review*, 68, 85
Cary, Henry Francis, 86
Chaldee MS, 119
Chalmers, Alexander, 217, 219–21
Works of the English Poets, 95, 103
Chatterton, Thomas, 147
Chaucer, 59, 89, 139, 202–4
Dryden's versions, 23–4, 30
Churchill, Charles, 167
and Dryden revival, 14n., 56, 80n.
circulation,
figures for *Blackwood's*, 67, 119n.
figures for *Edinburgh Review*, 65–8, 119n.
figures for *Quarterly Review*, 65–8, 119n.

circulation—*contd.*
figures for *The Times*, 67
of reviews greater than newspapers, 67
Cockburn, Lord, 65, 69
Coleridge, Sir J. T., 76n., 120
Coleridge, Samuel Taylor, 137–55, 177
on taste in 1790's, 70
reacts against Augustans in 1790's, 149–50
influenced by Bowles, 82, 141–2
his revolution in taste delayed, 1–2, 212
Pantisocracy, 46n.
his poetry, 72, 77, 125, 182, 183n., 214
his criticism, 18–9, 53, 165
on Metaphysicals, 128n.
on Dryden, 151–3
on Pope, 120, 144, 149–53, 193n.
attacked imitators of Augustans, 13
'Augustans a school of French poetry', 45
did not admire French poetry, 161n.
on Johnson, 217–8
on Crabbe, 146
on the great reviews, 64–5
on thought in poetry, 149, 173n.
works:
Ancient Mariner, 145
Anima Poetae, 151, 161n.
Biographia Literaria, 64–5, 106n., 118n., 133, 141–2, 149–50, 152n.
Kubla Khan, 173
Table Talk, 120
Collins, William, 140, 147, 166
Constable, Archibald, 10, 15–6
contemporary (i.e. early nineteenth century) literature,
considered of little value, 1, 70, 110
lacks intellectual strength, 20, 90, 181–3
great reviews act as a filter, 64–5
'Age of Brass', 72, 181
'St. Martin's Summer', 89
related to Elizabethan's, 89n.
compared to Augustans, 76–85, 95–111, 120–6
its problems, 181
and see Romantic
Cowley, Abraham, 112, 151n.
expurgated, 11

Cowper, William, 78–82
antipathy to Pope's versification, 79–82, 88, 158
wants 'manly rough line', 81, 158n.
and Dryden revival, 56, 80–1
influence on Romantics, 78–82
prose, 79
translation of *Homer*, 95, 105, 193
Table Talk, 79
Cox, R. G., 76, 179
Crabb Robinson, Henry, 194–6
on Bowles, 140n.
on De Quincey, 160n.
on Byron, 204–5, 207
Crabbe, George, 144–6, 198–204
continues Augustan tradition, 198–202
contrasted with Goldsmith, 98
contrasted with Wordsworth, 88
critical ideas, 122n., 202–4
works:
The Borough, 200
Inebriety, 198
The Library, 199
The Newspaper, 200
The Parish Register, 200
Tales in Verse, 67, 200, 202–3
The Village, 199–200
Croker, John Wilson, 10, 107n., 125–6, 168
Croly, Rev. George, 155–6
Darwin, Erasmus, 169
Botanic Garden, 150
Temple of Nature, 79
Universal Beauty, 79

Defoe, Daniel,
his novels 'indecent', 12n.
Denham, Sir John, 50, 128
Dennis, John, 13, 175
De Quincey, Thomas, 160–5
on didactic poetry, 163–5
on French influence, 161–2
on reviews, 68, 85
The Poetry of Pope, 160–5
Derrick, S., (editor of Dryden), 26
didactic poetry, 163–5
an inferior genre, 41

didactic poetry—*contd.*
  survives in Campbell and Rogers,
    190–1, 193n.
  and see ethical poetry
D'Israeli, Isaac,
  defender of Pope, 47n., 57–8, 131
  on Pope's critical ideas, 113
  notices revival of interest in
    Augustans (1820), 108–10
  'civil war of Popists and Drydenists',
    4, 56, 80
Donne, John, 20, 50, 78, 128, 147
Dryden, John, (Select references),
  1. GENERAL:
    amorality of, 17
    emotional poverty, 27, 29–30
    pathetic, absence of, 21, 24, 30,
      72–3, 185
    tenderness in, 90–1, 157, 185
    subject-matter, unsuitable, 17–8,
      27, 91, 128–9, 210–2
    style and versification, its 'brave
      negligence', 13–4, 17, 80–1, 91,
      151, 157, 166, 168–71, 185,
      189–90, 204
    power of intellect, 19–21, 120
    sublimity of, 21, 30–1, 72–3, 115
    range greater than Shakespeare or
      Milton, 12, 21–2
    use of language, 19, 21–2, 72, 152,
      157
    satirical poetry, 22
    lyrical poetry, 23
    narrative poetry, 23
    Prologues facetious, 43
    prose universally admired, 17
    on Elizabethans, 113
    on Donne, 20
    reputation in nineteenth century,
      13, 15–6, 23–4
    'greatest poet of his day', 72
    'a second-class poet', 50, 92
    of a 'critical school of poetry', 90
    problem of obscenity, 11–2, 17,
      31, 72
    compared to Elizabethans, 90
    compared to Pope, 13–4, 17, 21–2,
      50, 56, 80–2, 91, 151–3, 157,
      184–5, 189–90
    appealed to Romantics, 215
    'classic of our prose', 2–3, 150, 173

Dryden, John—*contd.*
  2. EDITIONS:
    Derrick's (1760), 26
    Malone's (Prose Works) (1800), 26
    Scott's (1808), 9–25, 80
    — (1821), 16
    Todd's (notes by Wartons and
      others) (1811), 11n., 25–34, 36
  3. WORKS:
    Absalom and Achitophel, 11n., 14n.,
      27, 28, 31, 189
    Alexander's Feast, 17, 23, 56n.
    Epistles, 32
    Fables, 23–4, 30, 185, 193
    Hind and the Panther, 14n.
    Killigrew Ode, 27, 32
    MacFlecknoe, 14n., 27, 32
    Oldham, Memory of John, 30
    Palamon and Arcite, 23–4, 193
    St. Cecilia's Day, 30–1
    Sigismonda and Guiscardo, 23
    Tales, 10n.
    Theodore and Honoria, 24–5, 30–1
    To Congreve, 189–90
Dryden revival,
  in late eighteenth century, (c.1789),
    14, 56, 80, 153, 169
  expected after Scott's edition, 10,
    15–6
Drydenists and Popists,
  unnatural civil war, 4, 56, 80
Dudley, Lord, 99–102
Dyce, Alexander, 189–94
Dyer, John, 147

Edinburgh, an intellectual capital, 75
Edinburgh Review, 63–92, 117–9,
  launched in 1802, 65
  its motto, 63
  circulation-figures, 65–8, 119n.
  Whig public, 69n., 93
  'indispensable to genteel families', 64
  'a Delphic Oracle', 68
  praised by Coleridge, 64–5
  Jeffrey as editor, 68–76, and *see*
    Jeffrey
  inconsistent standards, 76
  Augustans praised, Romantics under-
    valued (till 1810), 3, 76–85, 106

Edinburgh Review—contd.
  Elizabethans preferred to Augustans
    (after 1810), 85–92, 129
  turns against Pope, 76, 85, 144
  supports Bowles, 131
  dislikes Goldsmith, 97–8
  compared to *Quarterly*, 116
  opinions on Pope, Dryden, etc. *see*
  Jeffrey, and names of contributors
  elevation, 174–5
  and sublimity, 43, 197
Eliot, T. S., 22n., 40, 80n., 98, 111, 210
Elizabethans,
  neglected in days of Pope, 111–3
  made accessible by Anderson, 112
  revival of interest in, 71–2, 76, 85–92,
    96, 100–1, 139, 214
  best example of English genius, 72,
    97, 100, 111, 126
  golden, or true Augustan age, 71,
    103, 128, 180
  compared to Augustans, 73, 76,
    85–92, 96–7, 99–100, 111–6, 126–9,
    213–4
  not to be imitated, 101–2, 129
Ellis, George, 10–1, 115–6
enthusiasm, poetical, 44
ethical poetry,
  Pope the best writer of, 45
  Warton admires, 45–7, 51
  Bowles dislikes, 51
  Byron admires, 46
  and see didactic poetry

faery kind of writing, 42
fancy,
  critical term, 39, 50, 52, 84, 87, 103,
    127, 149, 165, 203–4, 220
  'sons of F.', 44–5
  'F.'s maze', 41–2, 49–50
feeling, 177, 197–8
Field, Baron, 97, 111–2
Fitzarthur, Ellen, 126
Ford, John,
  edited Weber, Jeffrey's review,
    (1811), 71–3, 88, 101, 122, 180n.
  edited by Gifford, 94
Fox, Charles James, 192–4, 199–200
Forster, Rev. Edward, 25–6

French (influence on Augustans),
  critical term of abuse, 45, 72, 103,
    105, 114–5, 126–7, 150n., 152–3
  denied, 59, 161–2, 186

Gentleman's Magazine, 131–2
Gifford, William, 93–6
  edits *Anti-Jacobin*, 93
  The Baviad, 93, 205
  The Maeviad, 93, 205
  compared to Pope, 93
  first editor of *Quarterly Review*, 93
  critical standards, 93–6
  compared to Jeffrey, 94
  Tory bias, 93, 96
  edits Jacobean dramatists, 94–5
  translates Juvenal and Persius, 94
  alters reviews, 94–5, 104
  on Wordsworth, 102–3
  defends Pope, 144
Gilchrist, Octavius, 131
Goldsmith, Oliver,
  on imitation, 220
  compared with Johnson, 97–9, 184
  influences Rogers and Campbell,
    98–100, 184, 200n.
  praised by *Quarterly*, 97–8
  works:
    The Deserted Village, 98n., 191,
      200n.
    The Traveller, 195
Gosse, Edmund, (on Wartons), 37n.,
  46–7n.
Gothick, 197
Gray, Thomas, 137n., 166
  Bard, criterion of sublimity, 30, 33,
    44
  interest in Italian poetry, 114
  precursor of Romantics, 140
  proposed *History of English Poetry*,
    139n.

Halévy, Élie,
  on reading-public (1815), 66
Hallam, Henry,
  on Dryden, 16–18, 25n.
  on Pope, 17
Hawkesworth, John,
  Adventurer, 64

Hayley, William, 2
  Life of Cowper, 80–1
Hazlitt, William, 155–60
  Augustans need 'modernising', 191n.
  on Coleridge, 150, 155
  on Dryden, 21, 157
  on Pope, 14, 95, 107–8, 132, 156–60
  on Romantic criticism, 143
  on Wordsworth, 137–8, 154–6
  Lectures on English Poets, 107–8
  Select British Poets, 157
heroic couplet, 53–4, 79–82, 87–8, 120,
  151–3, 166–71, 186, 200–1, 208
  'a pert skipping', 103–4
  'a see-saw', 167
  'a rocking-horse', 168
  Hunt overthrows Pope's dictatorship,
  170
Hogg, James, 118–9
Holland, Lord, 191–2
Hopkins, Gerard Manley,
  admires Dryden, 22, 91–2, 171
Horace, 1, 202
  'Horatian' satire, 21n., 32, 91
  Horatian idea of the poet, 172
  compared to Pope, 192, 207
Housman, A. E., 175n.
Hurd, Richard,
  on Spenser, 113n.
Hunt, Leigh, 165–71
  on Dryden, 25n., 166, 168–70
  on Johnson, 219n.
  on Pope, 95, 107, 131, 165–70, 206
  'overthrows Pope's metrical dictatorship', 200–1
  attacked by *Blackwood's* 118n., 126
  attacked by *Quarterly*, 107
  works:
    Autobiography, 165–70, 201n.
    Examiner, 63n.
    Feast of the Poets, 131, 158, 165–6
    Foliage, 107
    Story of Rimini, 88, 169
    What is Poetry?, 25n., 54, 165

imagery, 133–4
imagination,
  as critical standard, 2, 40, 89, 109,
  122, 127, 145–7, 151, 164–5, 203–4
  in Dryden, 72

imagination—*contd.*
  in Pope, 40–2, 44, 83, 109, 122, 207
imitation, 219–20
Italian, (critical term), 114, 128, 139

Jameson, Mrs., 118
Jeffrey, Francis, 18n., 68–89,
  first editor of *Edinburgh Review*, 69
  on circulation of *Edinburgh Review*,
  65, 67
  controls taste, 69, 75, 85
  'middleman of ideas', 69n.
  his reputation, 69, 75
  reputation highest in 1816, 68, 70
  on exhilaration of reviewing, 67–8
  critical standards, 70–89, 180n.
  praises Elizabethan age, 71–3, 76,
  85, 88
  on Jeremy Taylor, 88
  on Augustan poetry, 1–2, 70–4
  dislikes French influence, 45, 72, 115
  on Dryden, 21, 72–3
  dislikes obscenity, 72
  on Addison, 1–2, 70–4
  prefers late to early Augustans, 73
  changing attitude to Pope, 73–4, 76,
  85, 122, 131
  on Johnson, 219
  on Cowper, 78–82
  on literary taste in 1790's, 1–2, 70
  on Longinian raptures, 46, 101
  on contemporary literature, 70, 72,
  101
  and Wordsworth, 69n., 72, 77, 89,
  102n.
  on Southey, 77–8
  on Crabbe, 98n.; 200
  compared to Gifford, 94
Johnson, Samuel, (Select references),
  217–21
  on Pope, 13, 148
  Life of Pope (1779), 58, 131, 150
  on Dryden, 13, 21, 27–30, 32
  on heroic couplet, 171
  on blank verse, 152
  cyclical theory of poetry, 162
  disagrees with Warton, 27–35, 37,
  50n., 204
  'his ear deficient' (Bowles), 53–4

Johnson, Samuel—*contd.*
  reputation in nineteenth century, 70,
    217
  reputation in 1808, 3, 83
  compared to Goldsmith, 97–9, 184
  Scott's favourite poet, 10, 18–9, 138
  and Crabbe, 199
  editions of, 217–21
  Works:
    Elegy on Levett, 220
    Idler, 63
    Irene, 219–20
    Lives of the Poets, 112
    (*Life of Pope, see* above)
    London, 114n., 219–20
    Prologues, 220
    Rambler, 63–4
    Rambler, Scott's edition, 10
    Rasselas, 162n.
    Tour To The Hebrides, Croker's
      edition, 10
    Vanity of Human Wishes, 184, 188,
      191, 218–9
Juvenal, 94
  compared to Dryden, 21n., 91
  Johnson's Imitations, 218–9

Keats, John, 167–71, 177
  influenced by Dryden, 14, 138, 168–
    71
  dismisses Augustans, 107, 123, 138,
    167–8
  compares heroic couplet to rocking-
    horse, 103, 168
  relegated to 'minor current' in
    literature, 183
  works:
    Endymion, 107
    Hyperion, 168n., 171
    Lamia, 170–1
    Sleep and Poetry, 79, 107, 123, 138,
      158, 167–8

Lamb, Charles, 77, 94, 102, 141, 165
Langhorne, John, 201n.
'Lauerwinkel, Baron von'
  see Lockhart
Lawrence, D. H., 174–6
Leavis, F. R., 29n., 80n., 201
  on Scott's *Dryden*, 10
Liberal, The, 167

literary history, growth of, 89, 139–40,
    214
Lloyd, Charles, 138
Lockhart, J. G.,
  contributes to *Blackwood's*, 118–20
  editor of *Quarterly Review*, 76n., 120
  'Baron von Lauerwinkel', pseudo-
    nym, 76
  on Augustans, 76–7, 85, 88, 120
  on Scott's *Dryden*, 10, 14–6, 56n.
  on revival of Elizabethans, 85–8
  on Jeffrey, 69
  on changes in taste (1810), 85–8
  admires Wordsworth and Coleridge,
    120
  Life of Burns, 120
  Life of Scott, 10, 14–6, 18–9, 56n.,
    194
London Magazine, 117, 131–2
Longinus, 45–6, 174–5
Lowes, John Livingston, 173
lyrical poetry,
  nineteenth century revival of interest,
    23, 40–1
  proper function of, 40
  Pope deficient in, 40
  and new conception of verbal style,
    52–3

Macaulay, Thomas Babington, Lord,
  on Dryden, 89–92
  on four ages of poetry, 89, 115,
    180n.
  praises Jeffrey, 75
  historical essays, 69n.
  Life of Addison, 91
Mackenzie, Henry, 197–8
magazines defined, 117
Malone, Edmond,
  edition of Dryden's *Prose Works*, 26
  praise of Johnson's *Life of Dryden*, 27
Marvell, Andrew, 72n.
Mason, William, 2, 97, 106, 140
  Life and Writings of Gray, 114
Massinger, (edited by Gifford), 94–5
Mathias, Thomas, 93
Maturin, Charles, 115
Metaphysicals, 103, 128
  lack of appreciation of, 128n., 147
Methodist Magazine, 106

Mill, James, 177n., 178–9
Mill, John Stuart, 177–9, 194n.
Milton, John,
  a first-class poet, 50
  his 'noble Diapason', 53
  versification, 54, 158
  formed himself on Greeks and Italians, 44–5, 114
  'no man master of himself while he reads M.', 44
  compared to Pope, 86–7, 127, 166
  early poems rediscovered, 33–4, 44
  early poems preferred, 195
  Il Pensoroso, influence on *Eloisa to Abelard*, 43
  L'Allegro, 52n.
  Lycidas, 54
  Paradise Lost, 113
mimesis, 144–5
mock-epic, praised by Warton, 41–2
Moore, Thomas, 181, 207
moral fable, 200–2
More, Hannah, 8on.
Morehead, 86
Morley, Edith J.,
  her study of Warton, 37–8
Murray, John, 95, 117
  publisher of *Quarterly Review*, 66

nature,
  (critical term), 39, 78, 83, 133, 147, 157, 212
  poetry inherent in, 53
  Pope did not describe, 54, 104–5, 186
New Monthly Magazine, 132
Noctes Ambrosianae, 124–5
Northcote, James, 143n., 156

Pamphleteer, 131–2
passion,
  (critical term), 39, 109, 115, 120, 127
  in Pope, 84, 109, 151, 207
pathetic, the,
  (critical term), 17n., 36, 40, 50, 78n., 100, 115, 154–5, 190, 197–8
  Dryden's lack of, 21, 24, 30, 72–3, 185

pathetic, the—*contd.*
  Pope's lack of, 36, 38–9, 155
  present in Pope, 42–4, 49, 54, 84, 158, 186
  see also Dryden, tenderness
Pattison, Mark,
  his account of revolution in taste incorrect, 2–3
Peacock, Thomas Love, 138, 179–83
  The Four Ages of Poetry, 20, 71–2, 89, 115, 171, 172n., 179–83
  Elizabethans, 'the golden age', 71, 180
  Augustans, 'the silver age', 72, 180
  Romantics, 'the age of brass', 72, 181
  on lack of intellect in Romantic poetry, 20, 71, 182
  Crotchet Castle, 180
  Gryll Grange, 179n., 182n.
periodicals, critical, 63–134
  eighteenth century tradition, 63
  early nineteenth century, 63
  their function (Coleridge), 64–5
  their circulation, 65–8
  competition between, 66
  wider read than newspapers, 67
  influence of editor's personality, 68
  anonymous reviewing, 68
  magazines different from reviews, 117
  minor, 130–4
  and see by name, Edinburgh, Quarterly, etc.
Philips, Ambrose, 78
Poe, Edgar Allan, 174–6
poetry,
  classes of, 50, 133
  four ages of, 89, 115, 162, 180–3
  inherent in nature, 52–3
  style in, 127–9
  produced by unconscious mind, 172–6
  a 'sophisticated game', 150
  'like push-pin', 178
political bias, in reviews and criticism, 65, 69n., 78, 93, 96, 101, 168n.
Pope, Alexander, (Select references)
  1. GENERAL:
    moral sensibility, 17, 41, 46, 84, 91, 110, 148, 163–5
    moral character, 55n., 91, 108–9, 133

Pope, Alexander—*contd.*
pathetic, lack of the, 36, 38–9, 155
pathetic, presence of, 42–4, 49, 54, 84, 158, 186
imagination in, 40–2, 83, 109, 122, 207
pre-occupation with contemporary life, 41–2, 44, 52, 86–7, 127, 148, 163n.
does not describe nature, 104–5, 186
sublimity, lack of, 36, 38–9, 54, 155, 158
sublimity, presence of, 42–4, 84
style and verification, 13–4, 53, 79–81, 87–8, 127, 137n., 151, 158, 163, 165–70, 186, 189, 204
'Poet of Reason', 45, 122, 177, 190
poetical enthusiasm, suppressed his, 44
best ethical poet, 45–7
satires compared to epic, 41
early satires and poems preferred, ('Fancy's maze'), 41–2, 49–50
'Horatian satire', 21n.
satirist rather than poet, 73–4
deficient in lyrical poetry, 40, 84
deficient in sensibility, 49
wit disliked, 17, 39, 40, 74, 147–50, 186
formed on French models, 44–5, 152–3, 161–2, 186
wasted his talent, 44, 147
'Romantic passages' preferred, 39, 42–4, 49
reputation, in late eighteenth century, 12—4
reputation, in 1790's, 1, 70
reputation, in 1808, 3, 83, 87
reputation, in early nineteenth century, 13, 39, 130–4, 156
not 'dethroned' in early nineteenth century, 2–3
revival of interest in, (1820–25), 108–11, 166–7
fading of personal references in, 39–40
model in schools, 194–5
appealed to conservative interests, 215
relegated to second rank, 37–8, 49, 121–3, 126–7, 162–3

Pope, Alexander—*contd.*
'classic of our prose', 2–3, 150, 173
defended against Romantics, 106–10, 143–4
on Pre-Restoration poets, 113
compared to Spenser, 86–7
compared to Shakespeare, 86–7, 127
compared to Milton, 86–7, 127
compared to Dryden, 13–4, 17, 21–2, 50, 56, 80–2, 91, 151–3, 157, 184–5, 189–90
compared to Wordsworth, 126
imitators of, 13–4, 79, 98–102, 155–6, 185–6, 194–5, 205

2. EDITIONS
Joseph Warton's, (1797), 26, 35, 37–55, 58, 95, 133
Joseph Warton's, (1803), 35
Joseph Warton's, (1822), 35
Bowles' (1806), 35, 47–55, 58, 82–4, 95, 130–1, 133, 185–6
Bowles', modified, (1812), 35, 131
Roscoe's, (1824), 13n., 35–6, 55–9, 110–1, 132–3
Roscoe's, (1847), 35
Croly's, (1836), 156
interrelation of these, 35, 47–55, 58
and 'Pope controversy', 37, 55, 130–4

3. WORKS:
Dunciad, 28–9, 32, 40–2, 56n., 58–9, 84, 114n., 158, 196, 204, 205n.
Elegy on Unfortunate Lady, 43, 124, 158, 186
Eloisa To Abelard, 17n., 39, 43–4, 46n., 49, 56n., 84, 124, 158, 185–7, 191
Epistles, 124, 195
Epistle to Dr Arbuthnot, 43, 158
Epistle to Augustus, 205
Epistle to Lord Oxford, 17n., 84, 187, 192
Epitaphs, 147–9
Epitaph on Mrs. Corbet, 148
Essay on Criticism, 46, 161n.
Essay on Man, 56n., 124, 149, 186, 191, 195

Pope, Alexander—*contd.*
Homer, 95, 104–5, 107, 124, 149, 166, 193, 206–7
Imitations of Horace, 42, 192, 204
Moral Essays, 201
Ode for Music, 56n.
Prologue To Cato, 43, 187, 189
Rape of the Lock, 39, 41–2, 51–2, 56n., 84, 87, 124, 149, 158, 166–7, 187, 195
Satires, 158, 161n., 196, 204
Windsor Forest, 39, 158, 186
'Pope Controversy', 36–7, 55, 57, 95, 104n., 121, 124, 130–4, 213
originated in mid-eighteenth century, 4
provoked by Bowles, 48
history of, 130–4
bibliography of, 222–3
Popists and Drydenists, *see* Drydenists
Porson, Richard, 192–4
pro-Augustan criticism, 3, 57, 108–11, 124–5, 129, 177–208, 214
prudery, early nineteenth century, 210
disapproval of Augustans, 12, 72, 106
and Dryden, 11–2, 17, 31, 72
and Byron, 31
and Shakespeare, 12, 210
and the Bible, 210n.
puns, Warton objects to, 42n.

Quarles, Francis, 72n., 78
Quarterly Review, 63–8, 85n., 93–120
founded in 1809, 65, 93
circulation-figures, 65–8, 119n.
draws level with *Edinburgh*, (1818), 66
Tory bias, 16, 93, 96
'literary conscience of the world', 68
Gifford as editor, 93–6
edited by Sir J. T. Coleridge, 120
edited by Lockhart, 119–20
critical standards, 96–116, 157, 165
defends Pope, 47n., 57, 106–8, 131, 133, 168
Elizabethans superior to Augustans, 99, 111–6, 129
on revival of Augustans, (1820–5), 35, 57, 108–11
praises Campbell and Rogers, 98–102, 183–4, 187–8

Quarterly Review—*contd.*
Romantics appear in, 102–8
see also Gifford, and names of contributors

reading public,
mid-eighteenth century and Addison, 63–4
late-eighteenth century and Augustans, 12–3, 28
ignores Warton strictures on Augustans, 26, 35, 37–8
early-nineteenth century, sources for information, 5
total estimated, 67
wide and middle-class, 64
guided by great reviews, 63–8, 85
lags behind Romantic criticism, 57, 142–3
and Augustans, 13, 27, 35–7, 48, 106, 108–11, 191–8
prefers Dryden's *Fables*, 23–4
and Pope's satire, 40
likes Pope's *Imitations of Horace*, 42
dislikes Bowles' *Pope*, 48–9
and *Dunciad*, 28
and Johnson, 217
and booksellers, 16
for Erasmus Darwin, 150
of Scott, 9
for Scott's *Dryden*, 11, 15–6, 56n.
for Warton's *Dryden*, 25–7
for Warton's *Pope*, 37–8
criticised by Warton, 38
for Roscoe's *Pope*, 55–7
(1825), for Pope, 35, 55–7, 108–11
for Wordsworth, 1–2
of Byron, 9, 206
of *Edinburgh Review*, 69n.
for magazines, 117–8
realism, 203–4, 206
reason
(critical term), 19–20, 45, 147, 151, 177–9, 220
Dryden's, 19–20
Pope the 'Poet of Reason', 45, 122, 190
Reflector, 131
Retrospective Review, 126
reviews, *see* periodicals, *Edinburgh*, *Quarterly*, etc.

Reynolds, Sir Joshua, 199
Rogers, Samuel, 98–102, 183–4, 187–93
    imitates Augustans, 183–4, 187–91
    and Pope, 144, 189–90, 192
    on Dryden, 189–90
    works:
        Human Life, 189
        Jacqueline, 188
        Pleasures of Memory, 183n., 188
        Poems, 99
        Voyage of Columbus, 100, 188
'Romantic',
    not a fair description of Scott, 9, 18,
        25
    vocabulary in Milton, 44
    affinities sought for in Middle Ages,
        181
    affinities sought for in Elizabethans, 87
    affinities sought for in Shakespeare,
        52n., 87
    affinities sought for in Pope, 39, 42–4,
        49
Romantic movement,
    not the contemporary name for
        early nineteenth century, 1
    origins, 140–1
    influence of Wartons, 106, 115,
        139–40
    'a pouring out of the spirit', 106,
        172–6
    preference for song in poetry, 53–4
    criticism of Augustans, 137–77
    attitude to didactic, 163–5
    dislike of wit and satire, 187, 211
    finds reception in *Blackwood's*, 119–23
    adverse criticism in *Edinburgh*, 76–85,
        89–90
    dangers of, 57, 78, 129, 181–3
    negligent versification, 81–2
    age of Brass, 72, 181
    revolution in taste delayed till
        Arnold, 2–3
    see also contemporary
Roscoe, William,
    edition of Pope, (1824), 13n., 35–6,
        55–9, 110–1, 132–3
        (1847), 35
    critical standards, 57–9, 183
    defends Pope, 58–9
    prefers Pope to Dryden, 56
    praises Johnson, 58

Saintsbury, George, 15
    on Jeffrey, 75–6
Satire,
    Horatian, 21n., 32
    Juvenalian, 21n.
    mock-epic, 41–2
    moderns excel ancients in, 41
    '*MacFlecknoe* best in any language'
        (Warton), 32
    '*Rape of the Lock* best in any language'
        (Warton), 42
    in epitaphs, 148
    not approved of in nineteenth cen-
        tury, 22, 41, 186–7, 191
    Warton objects to, 28, 39
    'transitory and perishable', 39–40
    Bowles objects to, 22, 50–1
    'thorns and briars', 50
Scott, Sir Walter,
    not 'Romantic', 9
    critical standards, 18–25
    edition of Shakespeare, 10
    edition of Swift, 10
    proposed edition of Pope, 10
    edition of Dryden (1808), 9–25, 80
        (1821), 16
    'unduly partial to Dryden' (Roscoe),
        56n.
    places Dryden above Shakespeare
        and Milton, 12
    his poetry influenced by Dryden, 14,
        120
    his poetry influenced by Pope, 194
    'Monarch of Parnassus', 187
    valued Augustan poetry above his
        own, 9
    admires Johnson's poetry, 10, 18–9,
        138, 218
    edition of *Rambler*, 10
    admires Jane Austen, 18
    admires Byron, 18
    on Campbell, 98–9
    on *Edinburgh Review*, 64
    dismissed by Arnold, 183

sensibility,
    (critical term), 44
    moral, 17, 41, 46, 84, 91, 110, 148,
        163–5
    excessive, 46n., 110, 197–8
    Pope deficient in, 49

Seward, Anna, 9, 14n., 56, 80n.
  defends Pope, 56n.
  Memoirs of Dr Darwin, 79
Shakespeare, William,
  first-class poet, 50
  Dryden's range greater than, 12
  compared to Pope, 86–7, 127
  Augustans under-rate, 111–3
  revival in late eighteenth century,
    52n.
  romantic passages in, 52n.
  'warblings wild', 52n.
  Scott's edition, 10
  bowdlerised, 12, 210
  Midsummer Night's Dream, compared
    to *Rape of the Lock*, 42, 51–2
  source of 'faery' writing, 42
  Theseus on poetry, 122, 203
Shenstone, William,
  on 'Pope's dotage', 42
Sheil, Richard,
  The Apostate, 115
Shelley, Percy Bysshe, 163–4, 171–7,
  179
  Defence of Poetry, 138–9, 171–6
Sheridan, Richard Brinsley, 193–4
Shiels, Robert, 22, 51n.
simplicity,
  (critical term), 78, 86, 128
  in Wordsworth, 103
Southern, Henry, 126
Southey, Robert, 152–5
  considered leader of Romantics, 77
  on origin of Romanticism, 106, 140
  on Augustans, 97, 103–4, 152–5
  Augustan 'the dark age', 71, 154
  dislikes French influence, 103–4,
    152–3
  on Pope, 104–6, 144, 152–4, 206
  on Dryden, 153–4
  on Elizabethans, 112–3
  and Gifford, 94–6
  on 'Judge Jeffrey', 75
  generous to Wordsworth, 96, 102
  on circulation of *Quarterly*, 66–7
  poetry, 72, 81–2, 125, 181, 182n.
  imitated Augustans, 194n.
  imitates Bowles, 141–2
  works:
    Madoc, 82
    Thalaba, 77–8

Southey, Robert—*contd.*
  Specimens of Later British Poets,
    127n., 153
Spectator, 63–4
Spence, Joseph,
  Anecdotes of Pope, 74, 80, 108–9, 113,
    131
  Quelques Remarques Historiques, 207n.
Spenser, Edmund, 112, 113n., 114,
    128, 166
  compared to Pope, 86–7
Steele, Richard,
  Tatler, 63
Stephen, Sir Leslie, 213
  'eighteenth century lasted till 1832',
    3, 15, 191
Stockdale, Percival, 87–8
style,
  conversational s. of Augustans, 73
  new verbal s. of nineteenth century,
    53–4
sublime, the,
  (critical term), 17n., 24, 30–1, 36,
    40, 50, 78, 100, 154–5, 189, 197
  in Chaucer, 24
  Dryden's mastery of, 21, 115
  few s. lines, 72–3
  in *Fables*, 31
  in *Ode on St. Cecilia's Day*, 30
  presence in Pope, 42–4, 84
  absence in Pope, 36, 38–9, 54, 155,
    158
  Gray's *Bard* an example, 44
Swift, Jonathan, 1, 12, 50, 70, 191n.,
    192
  reputation in 1808, 3, 83
  Scott's edition, 10
  on editors, 58n.
  Tale of a Tub, 192

taste, literary, 208–16
  Augustan, limitations of, 32–4
  late eighteenth century revival of
    Milton, 33–4
  in 1790's, 1–2, 70
  no revolution in early nineteenth
    century, 2–5, 191–6
  and song-like style, 52–3
  Elizabethan revival, 71–2, 76, 85–92,
    101, 126
  change in 1810, 85–88

taste, literary—*contd.*
  influence of, prudery, 11–12, 210
  'deterioration' in hands of Romantics, (1813), 101–2
  influence of Warton's *History*, 139–40
  Italian influence, 114
  Regency, for sensational extravagance, 116
  and satire, 22, 28–9
  influence of periodicals on, 63–8, 69n., 117
  reviewers rejoice to influence, 67–8
  controlled by Jeffrey for 25 years, 69
  Carlyle on, 68
  and Metaphysicals, 128n., 147
  and Dryden, 92
  and *Alexander's Feast*, 23
  and *Fables*, 23–4
  and Pope, 35–7, 39, 48, 55–6, 73–4, 76, 83, 108–11, 130–4, 159, 191–8
  changing attitude to Warton, 26–7
  Scott's, 18–9
  Wordsworth and, 1, 69n., 195
  in late nineteenth century, 2–3
Taylor, Jeremy, 88
Tennyson, Alfred, Lord, 41
Thackeray, William Makepeace, 196n.
Thomson, James, 104–5, 147, 166
  Castle of Indolence, 195
Thomson, Thomas, 79
Times, The,
  circulation in 1816, 67
Todd, H. J.,
  edition of Dryden, notes by Warton, (1811), 11n., 25–34, 36
transport,
  (Longinian critical term), 45, 101, 175

use of language,
  Dryden's, 19, 21–2, 72, 152, 157
  Pope's, 52, 164
  Wordsworth's, 164–5
  Utilitarians, 177–80

Van Doren, M.,
  The Poetry of John Dryden, 15n., 23n.
Van Rennes, J. J., 130
Virgil, 52
Voltaire,
  on Pope, 161

Waller, Edmund, 50, 128, 139
Warton, Joseph,
  classical training, 51
  headmaster of Winchester, 36n., 106n.
  anticipates early nineteenth century taste, 22, 39, 48, 73–4, 106, 140, 163, 210
  outcry against (1756), 26, 35–6, 48
  belated recognition of, 26–7, 35, 39, 48
  critical standards, 27–35, 38–55, 114–5, 175, 210
  disagrees with Johnson, 27–35, 37, 50n., 204
  influence on Bowles, 35–6, 47–55
  on qualities of a true poet, 40
  fourfold classification of English poets, 50–1
  objects to wit in lyrics, 40
  likes ethical poetry, 45–7, 51
  likes Milton, 33, 50
  on Addison, 52n., 50
  notes to Todd's edition of Dryden, (1811), 25–34
  objects to Dryden, 27–30
  puts Pope above Dryden, 50
  Essay on Pope (1756), 24n., 30, 35–41, 47, 49n., 50–2, 123, 146, 150–1
  history of later editions, 38n.
  edition of Pope, (1797), 26, 35, 37–55, 58, 95, 133
  (1803), 35
  (1822), 35
  objections to Pope, 36–40, 147
  objects to *Dunciad*, 28–9, 42, 58
  change in views on Pope, 37
  finds good qualities in Pope, 41–47, 104n.
  likes *Rape of the Lock*, 41–2, 51
  Enthusiast, (1744), 52n.
Warton, Thomas,
  Master of Trinity College, Oxford, 36n.
  Professor of Poetry at Oxford, 36n., 139
  influence on Bowles, 36n., 142
  History of English Poetry, 139–40
  To the River Lodon, 142
  Preface to edition of Milton, 33–4
Wellek, Professor, R., 133n.

West, Gilbert, 106, 140
Westminster Review. 178–9, 182
Weston, Joseph, 14n, 56, 80n., 93n.
  calls Pope 'a jealous tyrant', 56n.
Whigs,
  and *Edinburgh Review*, 69n.
Whitaker, Thomas Dunham, 114
White, Newman Ivey,
  The Unextinguished Hearth, 1, 101
wild, (critical term), 52n., 115
Wilson, John, 67, 118–9
Wilson, Mrs. John, 75
Winchilsea, Anne, Countess of, 105
wit,
  (critical term), 200
  disliked, 39, 147–50, 153–4, 177,
    186–7, 212–3
  should be absent in lyrical poetry, 40
  characteristic of third-class poets, 50
  'logic of w.', 149–50
Wordsworth, William, 137–55, 212–4
  early nineteenth century not the Age
    of W., 1
  critical ideas, 18–9, 164, 177
  on Dryden, 17, 21, 137–8, 152–4
  influences Scott's Dryden, 10n., 23n.
  likes *Fables*, 23
  on Pope, 137–8, 144, 146–9, 154–5,
    163n., 206
  on Pope's *Homer*, 104–5, 206

Wordsworth, William—*contd.*
  imitated Pope, 195
  criticised Pope's imitators, 13
  condemned French writers, 161n.
  and Akenside, 140
  on Johnson, 217–8
  and Bowles, 141–2
  and Crabbe, 145–6, 201n., 203–4
  and Jane Austen, 145, 197–8
  on the tyranny of reviews, 69n.
  reactions to Jeffrey's criticism, 69n.
    (*see* Jeffrey)
  reputation, contemporary opinions
    of, 1–2, 18, 72, 77, 82n., 89, 95–6,
    102–3, 118, 120, 125–6, 156, 165,
    174, 181–3
  influence on Mill, 178
  tranquillity in, 147–9
  'language thought's incarnation', 152
  works:
    A Slumber Did My Spirit Seal, 148–9
    Essay on Epitaphs, 147–9
    Essay Supplementary to Preface, 105,
      112n., 206
    Excursion, 125, 149n.
    Lyrical Ballads, 1–2, 77, 82n., 102,
      195–6
    Michael, 149n.
    On Westminster Bridge, 142
    River Duddon, 142
    White Doe of Rylstone, 102